This and That

This and That

A Book of Essays

David A. Zohn

VANTAGE PRESS
New York

Published by Vantage Press, Inc.
516 West 34th Street, New York, New York 10001

Manufactured in the United States of America
ISBN: 0-533-13989-9

Library of Congress Catalog Card No.: 01-130636

0 9 8 7 6 5 4 3 2 1

Contents

Acknowledgments

I owe a great debt to Norman Weiss and Curt Sandler. They not only repeatedly nursed my sick computer back to health, but they patiently tried to teach me the intricacies of computer usage, the techniques of which seem to constantly confound me. I confess to having, at times, nostalgia for a typewriter, a dictating machine, and a good secretary, but I realize that those days are gone forever.

Introduction

I knew from the beginning that the ideas I held were different
from most of those around me. I didn't know then, and I do not
know to this day, why they were different and have continued to
be different, but they were. I was raised in a very liberal section
of a very liberal New York City. FDR was worshipped as a god,
and it was far from rare to have friends and neighbors who
were socialists and even communists. Many more were at least
sympathetic to such ideas. There was no such creature as a
Republican around. It must not be forgotten that the country
was recently convulsed by the Great Depression, times were
very, very hard, and wealth and power were held in the hands
of a very, very few. Things were stacked against the poor working man. To many it seemed unjust.

As I moved into high school, World War II had already
begun. (I should mention that in spite of their views, the people
I knew were extremely patriotic and supportive of the war,
largely because of a fear and loathing of the Nazis and, of
course, the unprovoked attack on Pearl Attack.) Around this
time the news of the terrible things happening in the Soviet
Union had begun trickling out. The Soviet/Nazi pact of 1939
was the last straw for some, but there still remained an underlying sympathy for socialism as a solution to economic problems
for many other people. And, of course, the Soviets were our
wartime ally; therefore, doubts about them were held in
abeyance.

What shocked me as a young high school student and ever
since was the underlying hostility to the United States by so

many. Given the above-mentioned about American society, there was much to criticize about the country, but the unremitting hostility was incomprehensible to me. After all, many of the parents of those who felt that hostility were immigrants. Had they stayed where they came from in Europe, it is not likely that they would have survived the war. Whatever the injustices that existed in this country, there was still opportunity and freedom, perhaps not perfect, but certainly far more than where their immigrant parents came from. I still recall a teacher in my third or fourth year of high school who taught us American history. He spent the entire year telling us how terrible the United States was and what awful things the country did. They were not necessarily untrue, but they were never told in context, in context of all the good things about America. I cannot recall a single positive thing he said about the country during the entire year, the country that had given shelter to his parents and undoubtedly saved their (and his) life.

As times passed, I repeatedly heard and saw the same attitude expressed. A constant drumbeat of criticism of this country was heard. It seemed that to some we could do nothing right. If bad things happened in the world, they were always because of what we (the U.S.) did or didn't do. Nobody else in the world was responsible for anything bad, only the U.S. This attitude was present throughout the entire Cold War and certainly was exacerbated during the Vietnam War (actually a battle in the Cold War rather than a separate war) and the Civil Rights movement. With the end of the Cold War, when it was proved beyond the shadow of a doubt that our overall policy, with all its mistakes, false moves, stupidities, etcetera, was correct, there was no recognition on the part of some, that freedom and democracy triumphed and that there was hope for a better future for millions of people. Indeed, they went on as before, deeply involved in criticism, not of themselves for being so wrong, but of the United States.

During the past few decades, indeed, starting with the sixties and picking up steam in the nineties, there has been a disconcerting disconnect between, on the one hand, never-before-seen wealth on such a broad scale and never-before-seen personal freedoms and, on the other hand, a clear breakdown in civil society. Never-before-seen widespread violence, violence so brutal and often so casual as to turn the stomach. Rage and violence throughout all of our social activities: driving, jobs, schools, professional sports, even children's games. Lack of concern for the good of the community seemed common place.

An example of this was the repeated loss of any self-control and concern for danger to others when on the road: speeding, weaving, tailgating, running of red lights, etcetera. Widespread illicit drug usage and widespread alcohol use and abuse have been present. Group oral sex amongst teenagers, often very young teenagers. With parents apparently on Mars, not knowing or not caring what was happening, or both. The huge breakdown in marriages. More and more children raised by single parents. Teenage pregnancy in alarming number. The widespread presence of sexually transmitted diseases. Total lack of respect for authority in whatever form it takes. Behavior governed to a large extent by fear of lawsuits rather than what was felt to be right. Political correctness run rampant. Free speech (at least, politically incorrect free speech) mercilessly squelched on one college campus after another, the very places where the free trade of differing ideas should be most tolerated and welcomed. How could all this be happening? Surely everyone can see that something is terribly wrong with our civil society, but apparently that is not true.

I knew in my heart that the things mentioned above were wrong and that they were the result of wrong policies and wrong attitudes, with a resultant weakening of our country. And yet there was no time to put down my thoughts on paper. Now, with retirement, there has been time, and this book of essays is the result. I must admit that there has been a certain cathartic effect in getting on paper what had been on my mind for many, many years. I have striven to be concise, even brief, in putting down my thoughts, because I strongly believe that verbosity is not the same as profundity.

Certain themes run through the book, themes that repeat themselves in different ways. I believe they go to the heart of what kind of society we are and what kind of society we should be. What is wrong and what is right. We clearly have a culture clash about that. We have always had it, but the difference is that in many ways we see the breakdown in civil society to an extent that, to my knowledge, has not been present before; that is very dangerous. Thankfully, we have no major foreign threat facing us; therefore, we should be able to focus our energies on resolving the social problems before us, if we have the will.

These problems involve the balancing of the rights of the individual against the needs of the community; the overall permissiveness of our society with some declaring that there are no rights and no wrongs, just differences; the growing separation of groups, one from the other, rather than the coming together; the presence or lack of presence of defining values under which we can all unite and which we can call American; the emphasis on the positives of America while not neglecting the negatives; the rejection of our past as if irrelevant to our present and to our future; the rejection of many of those who produced our past; the proper role of the various levels of governing and their involvement in our lives; the necessity for doing good, even if it is painful, rather than just feeling good.

I consider myself to be a conservative, in what I hope is the best sense of that word. I am proud to be a part of what I consider to be the greatest nation on earth. I am not in the least bit ashamed of being openly patriotic, and I cannot understand the attitude of those who consider themselves too sophisticated or too superior to be openly patriotic. Never before in history has any nation provided its citizens (and the world) with so much in the way of personal liberties, opportunities, and protection from what is always the worst instincts of governments to control the lives of its citizens. Never before has any nation offered its citizens such opportunities to rise to their full potential as humans, provided they are willing to make the requisite sacrifices. It would be foolish in the extreme to deny the flaws in this country, flaws that at times loom large indeed. But it is the glory of this country that it is self-correcting, gradually evolving to a better nation of its citizens.

It does not require revolution here to make changes, as it does elsewhere. It does require patience, persistence, education, and, eventually, new laws and new attitudes. Because it has such a glorious history in the annals of nations, I wish to conserve all that is good from the past. Change is necessary. Indeed, change is life. But it should be slow and evolutionary. Changes always bring about unintended consequences, and these should be minimized by careful thought and careful crafting of new laws and openness to new approaches to problems. I am always amused by people who claim that this or that Congress is a "do nothing" one, as if the passing of laws is an end in itself. Far better to have fewer and better laws, with maximum thought as to what the consequences of these new laws might mean to society down the road.

I am uncomfortable with both political parties. The Democrats, among other things, are far too eager to have the federal government solve difficult social problems, primarily by means of ever-larger government programs. Failure to solve the problem simply means, in their mind, that more money, much more money is needed to be spent if the problem is to be solved. And that of course means more taxes and more supervision. There is little openness to new approaches to problems other than the requesting of more funds. There is also a smug sense of moral superiority in their approach to problems. Either one agrees with them or one is hopelessly, morally inferior.

The Republicans also exude a certain smugness. In their case, smugness with the status quo, and a lack of a sense of the necessity to continue grappling with, and solving, the myriad social problems that plague us, a lack that makes me feel quite uncomfortable. I also believe that, by and large, they are not open to all the minority groups, which in toto are slowly becoming the majority of Americans. Unless they do, they are doomed to be the perpetual minority party. I am encouraged by Republican presidential candidate George W. Bush's attempt to bring about a greater diversity in the party but only time will tell whether he is successful. I therefore find myself a conservative in my viewpoint, but politically, I am independent, a position that is not an isolated quirk but one that is taken by one-quarter to one-third of the electorate—in effect, a pox on both your houses.

This and That

I

Brief Random Thoughts

Aphorisms

Over the years I have collected some aphorisms that highlight how I view the world. I wish I could say that they were all mine, but they are not. Here are some of them.

Aging

- Inside every older person is a younger person wondering what happened.
- Getting old is not for sissies.
- As you get older, you play ball hurt or you don't play at all.
- For retirees, Monday is just like Sunday, with less mid-day traffic.

Social Commentary

- Self-help is the best of all kinds of assistance.
- It's easy to be a cheerful winner.
- When facts clash with beliefs, facts must go.
- If reality does not bend to preconceived ideas, then rather than bend ideas, you bend reality.

- Life is a series of chores. Finish one list of chores, and the next one magically appears.
- Flattery will get you everywhere.
- One cannot help those who cannot (or will not) help themselves.
- Some people are unable to differentiate between their wants and their needs.
- Beards when neat and trimmed are a fashion statement. When shaggy and unkempt, they probably represent hiding.

Politics

- People mix up their politics and their principles.
- Democrats and Republicans make it their life's work to spend money; they only differ on the recipients.
- Strength of opinion is all too often inversely proportional to knowledge of the subject.

Finances

- Rich or poor, it is good to have money.
- Unearned money is unappreciated money.
- Money may not buy happiness, but it certainly buys lots of other things.

Miscellaneous

- Feeling good is not the same as doing good.
- Conventional wisdom is oftentimes conventional stupidity.

- First things first.
- The best batters fail seven out of ten times and therefore, try, accept failure, and learn from it.
- There are good reasons, and then there are real reasons.
- Why use a proper word when a euphemism will do.
- Don't listen to their words, watch their feet.
- Everything takes longer.
- If it appears to be too good to be true, it probably is.
- Eternal vigilance is the price of liberty.
- Everyone is wise in hindsight.
- Liberty is not the same thing as license.
- Some people demand sensitivity to their needs. That doesn't mean that they have to be sensitive to the needs of others.
- Never buy a chair you have not sat in.
- To the fathers of the brides—you will get through the experience if you keep your mouth closed and your checkbook open.
- Good news appears to make some people terribly unhappy.
- No good deed goes unpunished.
- It takes no great amount of courage to denounce those who strongly disagree with you. It does take a great deal of courage to denounce those who strongly agree with you.
- In a restaurant that provides table service, I differentiate between a real restaurant with a real wait service and a "Here you go."
- Luck beats skill every time.
- There are those who mistake verbosity for profundity.

Bankruptcy–Then and Now

Bankruptcy is an all-too-frequent solution to financial problems these days. This is portrayed by supporters of this economic solution as "stiffing" the greedy gouging banks and credit card lenders, but unfortunately, it is much more. The banks and credit card companies may be hurt by these bankruptcies, but they simply add it to the cost of doing business, passing on the costs to the solvent customers and hurting everyone in the process. Therefore, we all pay the costs of bankruptcy.

However, it is not just these large banks and credit card companies that suffer from bankruptcies. Small merchants, vendors, providers—far more marginal business people—all get hurt by bankruptcy. Then they too pass on the costs to society in the form of higher charges to their customers, if they can. If not, they take it on the chin, financially, since many of these businesses are on the cusp and may be forced to go under if there are too many defaults on debt. Strange that their fate is not mentioned by the supporters of the use of bankruptcy as a means of getting out of debt.

Therefore, other innocent people are hurt by what is all too often irresponsible behavior on the part of some. It is certainly true that unfortunate circumstances force otherwise reliable people to get into financial difficulty with no apparent way out, but it is clearly not the case for all. If it does happen, there are available organizations dedicated to helping people with financial difficulties to reorganize their debts and their finances. If one wishes to avail oneself of such agencies, one can readily do so.

What is striking to me is that there appears to be no personal sense of responsibility on the part of the debtor. Financial troubles leading to bankruptcy just happen, somehow passively. After all, the banks and credit card companies did not force

4

anyone to use their services. The various vendors and providers did not force the debtors to use their services. That they, the debtors, acted irresponsibly is somehow forgotten. It was not always so. Further, and perhaps even more significant, there is little or no societal shame at being a debtor and declaring bankruptcy. It is seen as just another financial option. It was not always so.

I am not suggesting that we reinstitute debtors' prison. Hardly. I am suggesting that societal disapproval of bankruptcies return some element of guilt and shame and that there be some punishment for bankruptcy in addition to restrictions on borrowing for some period of time. Also, there should be some partial restitution to the creditors. These conditions seem reasonable to me.

Below the Line

For many reasons, there are clearly three groups who are below the line. The first is lawyers. I do not wish to impugn the behavior of what is undoubtedly a majority of practicing attorneys (or indeed in the other groups to be described), but there is a significant minority whose behavior is so bad that all are tarred with the same brush (see Lawyers). Greed can be channeled to good uses, but greed masquerading as helping the little guy is hard to take. Charging private clients and corporations outrageous fees and stirring up the waters for personal gain rather than compromising and settling matters is another unlovely attribute of attorneys.

The second group is politicians. What we are seeing in our current congress is pols, from both sides of the aisle, who are petty, partisan, and unprincipled. They run campaigns that are negative, mean spirited, and personal. They let their politics interfere with their principles on a regular basis. They appear to stand for nothing but their reelection. I am amazed when they are amazed when voting drops to frighteningly low levels and when the public tunes them out completely, feeling that they, the pols, are not relevant to their lives. How terribly sad.

The third group is the media people. They have come up with the idea that they are somehow above the law. Any attempt to bring justice to an injustice perpetrated by a media person is said to have a "chilling effect" on their pursuit of the news. Apparently they can do nothing for which a remedy exists. Who can take seriously their cry about the people's right to know when everyone realizes that the real right at stake is self-promotion. The overkill of the media is legendary when fortune or, more commonly, misfortune, occurs to a previously unknown individual or family. The same holds even true for the paparazzi in their stalking of the famous, the infamous, and the previously unknown. The descent of the print media into tabloid-style news is embarrassing. All of the above seems to be accompanied by a mixture of smugness and arrogance.

The strange part about all of this is that all these groups are quite affluent. There are many who have celebrity status. They are recognized and feted wherever they go. They can take advantage of their affluence to get the best of everything. Yet, their low status is recognized by most of the general public.

By the way, what is the line that they are below? Why, used car salesmen.

Blame America First

It is interesting to watch some people's response to political problems in other countries. Almost by reflex, these people blame America for the problems. If it is not an act of commission by us that brought about a situation, then it is an act of omission. What we did was wrong, and, conversely, what we failed to do was wrong. All the time.

Now of course we do do wrong things—of both commission and omission. We are not a nation of noblemen. We have our share of knaves and fools, as well as well-meaning people who just make mistakes. It is of course always a lot easier to look at a situation from hindsight rather than from a proactive point of view. But leaving that aside, there is no question that we make mistakes, sometimes bad mistakes. But all the time?

Do the critics ever ask themselves whether their criticism is balanced? Do they ever take time and effort to praise the good as well as criticize the bad? Are they aware that others do bad things and that we are at times powerless to stop them? Is their criticism reasonable in that the United States is truly responsible for a given situation? Aren't some situations murky with no definite right or wrong, just choices? Aren't there legitimate differences about an approach to a problem? Aren't there often countervailing pressures for one course of action versus another? Does their constant criticism help us as a nation or hurt us?

If the answer to all of the above questions is no, then why do they continually criticize us? Are they being noble and making an effort to improve the country, or are they simply acting out their frustrations, whatever they may be? Why do they make themselves so miserable in what must be, judging from their drumbeat of criticism, a terrible country? Perhaps they just enjoy being miserable.

Communism, Chicago Style

Many years ago I knew a young woman who came from Chicago. She told me about her parents, who were Communists, and how they lived. They and their friends, who were also

Communists, all lived in the comfortable middle-class suburbs of Chicago. During the week they drove their comfortable middle-class cars to their comfortable middle-class jobs. Their children went to nice middle-class schools, and the families took nice middle-class vacations. As American citizens, they enjoyed all the rights and privileges of American citizenship.

On Saturday nights, however, things were different. They gathered in each other's living room, sang the "Internationale" and told each other how wonderful Communism was and how wonderful America would be when there would be a Communist state here. Poverty would be abolished. Equality would reign. Injustice would be just a memory. Brotherhood would preside. A benign government would direct things. Wonderful.

Then they would return to their comfortable middle-class homes in their comfortable middle-class cars and begin their weekly cycle all over again.

Conspiracy Theories

I have no doubt that conspiracies exist, but most are simply figments of the imagination. It usually takes many people to plot the assassination of a high public figure, although a number have been performed by the hand of a lone gunman. Many people, perhaps the majority of people, believe that a conspiracy to kill President Kennedy existed, and that there was no way a lone gunman could have done it. Various groups considered to have entered the conspiracy were the CIA, the FBI, the military, the Mob, the Soviets, the Cubans, and many, many shady individuals.

As pointed out (see Psych 101), a sudden stressful situation brings out descriptions of the events and the people responsible that are often at great odds with each other. It is these differences that are seized upon by "experts" or conspiracy theorists to "prove" that we do not yet know the full extent of the plot, for example, to kill President John Kennedy.

But think for a minute. Thirty-eight years have passed since the assassination, and no individual or organization has come forward to claim credit. There have been no claims to what surely would be fame and fortunate if one could prove to have actually taken part in the assassination or even known about it. There have been no deathbed confessions. The United States and Russia are now allies, and their files (Russian) have been opened on their dirty tricks. Not even a hint of involvement in a conspiracy. Think how much the destitute Russians could make from a provable case of conspiracy to assassinate a very popular president. Think also who profits from roiling the waters of conspiracy. Book writers, lecturers, film makers, all have profited mightily.

I put in the same category of conspiracists those who believe aliens from outer space are among us, but for some reason, there is a conspiracy of silence. The same holds true for UFO sightings. Imagine, creatures as wise and advanced as these aliens, able to transport themselves through the universe to us, are unable to make their presence known in a fashion that all of us could readily understand and acknowledge. People with this outlook also believe in field markings and such, even though most have been proven to be complete hoaxes.

When looked at clearly, most of these claims of conspiracists, aliens, and UFO sightings are ridiculous on the face of it, for the reasons enumerated above. Yet they persist. Why? I believe it is because people need to explain what to them appears to be inexplicable.

Core Beliefs

Some stunning revelations have taken place in the last quarter of the twentieth century. The Soviet Union was indeed seen to be an evil empire, held in place by brute force and barely able to feed its own people, let alone compete with the Western world. Its fall came with no regret to most people on either side of the Iron Curtain. The economics of socialism, in its myriad forms throughout the world, has been shown to be a disaster, leading to economic stagnation, lack of entrepreneurship, high unemployment, and an ever-growing and ever more autocratic bureaucracy.

Yet the suddenness of the collapse of the entire system, its demonstrated corruption and evil ways, and the wish of its subjects to adopt the norms of the West appear to have brought about no recognition of the mistaken ideas that many held for nearly a half-century. More recently, the inability of the left, both in Israel and in this country to recognize the mistaken ideas of appeasement towards the Palestinians, where every concession to them in the name of peace is seen as a weakness, to be further exploited by means of violence and hostility, is quite remarkable.

In our own country, social programs, such as welfare programs, were considered sacrosanct. And yet, with welfare reform, there appears to be some progress in freeing an enormous number of people from the numbing role of dependency. I have no doubt that reform would benefit recipients of other social programs as well. Yet there has been no willingness on the part of many to recognize that, by and large, the instituted changes have been beneficial to the recipients. Instead, they have persisted in the very same beliefs that held before these social changes were put in place.

Given the above, one might ask how bright, thoughtful people can persist in ideations which have been clearly shown to be false. Perhaps it is because opinions held about the above make up one's core beliefs and, therefore, are not easily subject to change, no matter what the reality. They are the underpinnings of that individual's world view. Other beliefs can readily be shed without accompanying loss of self-esteem, but not core beliefs.

We all make mistakes, from the superficial (picking the winner of the World Series, the Super Bowl) to the more profound (investment choices, business decisions), without feeling any sense of challenge to ourselves. On the other hand, changing our core beliefs leads to decreased feelings of self-worth. They force people to admit, to themselves as well as to others, that if these core beliefs are false, other core beliefs might likewise be false. Other people, those who held opposite beliefs may have been right after all. What a horrible thought.

Doctrine of Unequal Equals

When something bad is done, either by an individual or by a nation, the reaction of apologists for such action is all too often to say, in effect, that you too are doing it, so you should not be criticizing us. As if two wrongs make a right.

Oftentimes, however, it is not at all the same thing. There are differences in magnitude, differences in kind, which make the two events only superficially the same, yet the differences are so great that they are really very different. For example, driving thirty-five miles per hour in a thirty-mile-per-hour zone is a moving traffic violation, and so is driving seventy miles per hour in the city, tailgating and weaving in and out of traffic. Although generically the same, they are in actuality very, very different in their consequences. Equating them would be nothing but foolishness.

So too would be the corporal punishment of a child. It can be done for disciplinary reasons but in the context of love, which, in this context, truly hurts the parent more than the child. No lasting damage is done to the child. Compare this to the beating of a child by one in a drunken rage, where lasting

11

physical damage is done. The two are superficially similar but they are really quite different.

Therefore, things may superficially appear to be equal, but further examination reveals that, in reality, they are quite different. There really are unequal equals.

Entitlements

We live in an age of entitlements. Everyone is aggrieved and everyone wants redress—from the federal treasury of course. Democrats and Republicans differ on the recipients, but both want the same thing—entitlements. The Democrats prefer social entitlements, and the Republicans prefer entitlements for farmers and businessmen, but they both want the same thing—preferred treatment for their constituencies. There are no bad causes. Every single entitlement is explained as something that is not only proper and necessary but which will benefit all of America, although that of course is not true.

Two recent episodes point out that everyone wants to get on the entitlement train. Minorities have been clamoring that they are entitled to go to the best, most prestigious colleges and universities in the land. Never mind that their SATs as a group are much lower than their white cohorts. Never mind that they struggle mightily in school and usually end up in the bottom half of their class. Never mind that they would be much better off in a less strenuous and competitive academic environment. When some schools were forced by law to accept applicants solely on their merit, minority acceptance dropped markedly. This was somehow seen as a prejudicial act, when the true feelings and political beliefs of the admissions people, administrators, and faculty members are well known. They would gladly discriminate if it were not against the law.

It is not terrible to go to a less competitive school, with the next generation better prepared to compete for the best academic schools, and indeed, that is the way it has been throughout the past century. By new groups, I mean not only new immigrants but also those groups where higher education was rare. Specifically for blacks, higher education, other than the all black schools, was rare indeed. The commonplace for new immigrant groups was that the first to go to college went to a local community school, two- or four-year school, but the next generation, or the one after that, assuming they had the ability, would be a recipient of better schooling and would move up the ladder of school excellence. But not now. Entitlement is the watchword, and one starts at the top, not the bottom.

Another type of entitlement, and one far more humorous, is the right to use ATMs (automatic teller machines), not only from the withdrawaler's bank but from any bank. Without extra charges. They (the ATMs) provide convenience including twenty-four-hour service, which is of value to some. For that convenience they are willing to pay a surcharge. Those who do not bank at the ATM's parent bank also get the convenience, but are charged an additional surcharge because they bank elsewhere. It seems fair to me. After all, banks are not charitable organizations. But those who bank elsewhere feel they are entitled to the same service as the bank's customers, but at no extra fee.

It is not as if they are without choices. They can use their own bank's ATMs. They can visit their own bank, either going inside or via drive-through windows. They can take advantage of the extended hours virtually all banks provide. I grew up in an era when you banked 10 A.M. to 3 P.M. Monday through Friday or you didn't bank at all. What a bewildering range of choices there are now. Yet some still feel that they are entitled, for their own convenience, to go to the nearest ATM, even if not of their own bank, and yet pay no more for it than regular banking customers. How bizarre.

To me, our society appears to be developing some strange and unwholesome ideas. Victimhood is not something to be avoided but rather something to revel in, while everyone appears to need entitlements.

Finding the Destination

Women often have a good laugh at the reluctance of men to ask for directions when they are driving to a new destination, preferring to try and find the destination by themselves. They do not understand what drives men. In prehistoric times, the male was the hunter, and finding game and tracking it was essential. If successful, he provided food for the family. If unsuccessful, he brought starvation. The game being pursued was often bigger than the hunter, making it extremely dangerous work; injury was common.

Over millennia, only the cleverest and the strongest survived. It is foolish to think that over a few thousand years of history (a nanosecond of time) that these traits have been lost. There are, however, few ways to express this trait, and exploration is one of them. This has led to exploration of the entire landmass of the world, the highest mountains, the deepest oceans and of course outer space. In a far more prosaic sense, the gratification of having tracked and found the destination (prey) without outside help is still with us.

It is beyond stupid not to ask for help if there is a deadline for reaching the destination. Otherwise, men are just following their genetically preprogrammed nature.

Hackers

Although computer hacking has been with us since the beginning of the mass use of computers and the Internet, the problem was recently elevated to a new level with the deliberate shutdowns of several companies by flooding them with information overload via multiple preprogrammed computer information. Fortunately, content was not touched, but who knows how long it will be before mass erasures or changes of information take place. That is indeed a rather scary thought. Motives vary. Some wish the Internet to be free and not commercialized. Others wish to do harm, perhaps because of some grievance. I suspect, however, that for most, it is simply the thrill of displaying their technological expertise by showing they are able to hack into secure systems.

To me stealing of intellectual property is theft. Damaging someone else's business is industrial espionage. The resultant blocking of commerce is burglary. Higher levels of protection can be put into place, with the certain result of more intensive efforts by hackers to overcome the new protection. This protection has costs however, which certainly will be passed on to the consumer.

I suspect that to many people, the hackers are just fun-loving kids who love their computers. To many hackers, they are not doing anything wrong, just demonstrating their expertise. The damage they can create, however, is considerable, and they should be punished appropriately. Repeat offenders deserve jail time. Just as a convicted felon cannot legally obtain a gun, a convicted hacker ought to have no rights to a computer. Of course, there are ways to obtain a computer, but it would be illegal and punishment for that would be appropriate. For those very few who are in the employ of companies, those companies should guarantee any losses suffered by another company at the hands of their employed hacker. Having the potential to produce a nationwide crisis, these hackers should be punished appropriately.

"He Was Such a Nice, Quiet Man"

Over and over again, after a serial killer or a war criminal is captured, the neighbors say, "He was such a nice, quiet man" or "He was so polite" or "He was very helpful with little chores" or "He kept to himself and was not a busybody." After this, they express doubt that he could have done the things he is accused of doing. After all, they personally observed him, didn't they?

After a busy day at the concentration camp of beating and tossing people into the ovens, the Nazi guards would relax at home with their families and friends—tender birthday parties, listening to Beethoven, and cakes and Schnapps were all enjoyed. Very touching. Hitler was tender with his dogs and gentle with his women. Eichmann in Argentina was soft and quiet to the point of mousiness. Stalin loved his daughter and had long friendly bonding sessions (read drinking) with his comrades. Serial killers were as described above when they were not busy butchering their victims.

How to explain the comments of neighbors? First, we all have different persona, whether at work or school or home or with different friends. Fortunately for most of us, there is not a great deal of variation of persona, just different emphases. Second, we believe, at least subconsciously, that an evil person should look and feel evil. Perhaps not Mr. Hyde or Dr. Frankenstein's monster, but there is a conceit that one would instinctively know that evil is present. And yet the truth is the opposite—evil lives amongst us and is undetected.

Hate Crimes

A recent spate of terrible, brutal crimes has raised the cry to apply more frequently and, if necessary, for even tougher hate crime legislation. The theory is that hate crimes deserve a special treatment and a special punishment. There are, however, problems with this type of thinking.

First, it pretends to look into the heart and mind of the assailant, something very, very difficult to do. For some, the problem seems apparent, whereas for others, it is less apparent. Second, it seems to apply only to certain approved victims; only they can be the "beneficiaries" of hate crime punishments. Third, we can have the option of applying the full extent of the law, wherever it takes us, up to and including the ultimate sanction—the death penalty. Brutal crimes deserve brutal punishment, for the sake of society and for the sake of the relatives of the victims. Properly applied, that should be enough.

"I'll Get Back to You" and Other Tall Tales

Has anyone ever said to you, "I'll get back to you" or "Let me think it over" or "This is a bad time"? It is entirely possible that they will indeed get back to you or they will think it over and then contact you, but I wouldn't hold my breath waiting for it to happen. Plain and simple, they are giving you the old shoveroo. There are always white lies, which are helpful in greasing the skids of social interaction, but I am talking about a deliberate attempt to avoid.

I understand that requests are made that one does not want to face. I also understand that it is difficult for some people to say no directly. Nevertheless, using old dodgeroos, as mentioned above, show a certain lack of spine and a certain lack of honesty. The speaker knows he is prevaricating. The recipient knows he is prevaricating. Yet the charade goes on. Far better for the speaker to summon his courage and say no. It should not be left at that however, but a brief and plausible explanation of the course taken might be given. If said graciously enough, both parties might be left with their dignity intact.

JFK, Jr.

How terribly sad to see his young life snuffed out so quickly (as well as that of his wife and sister-in-law). How dreadful for the parents (the Bessettes) to lose in an instant two of their three daughters and to be around to bury their children. The promise of JFK, Jr. was great, which he never got the chance to demonstrate. All of it terribly, terribly sad.

In addition to the fame of the father (and mother) and the shame of the public at what happened to him (the assassination), America has grown up with JFK, Jr. His birth was celebrated and publicized, his very early years were captured in various locales, including the Oval Office. His salute to his father's coffin, whether staged or not, was extremely moving and will be in our national archives forever. His young manhood, demonstrating vigor, his incredible good looks, his reportedly decent behavior in the face of continuous stalking by the press, all explain why the country mourns him.

However, there is something else, something that seems to be a Kennedy trait, and that is recklessness, the sheer courting of danger just for the thrill of beating it. JFK's behavior in the White House was reckless; discreet trysts outside the White House could have been easily arranged, but the thrill, the thrill of nearly being caught would not have been there. Ted Kennedy's driving at night after heavy partying and drinking was not the judgment of a prudent man. One of JFK, Jr.'s cousins had sexual relations with an early teenaged babysitter and, of course, was found out. Another cousin was playing football while skiing and struck a tree—the tree survived but he didn't. Other examples of such behavior by family members are present.

What about the behavior of JFK, Jr. himself? He preceded his fatal airplane flight with a series of high-risk activities, all of which he succeeded in conquering. The piloting was another thing. Nobody, understandably, wishes to say a bad word, but it is clear that he was undertrained and underexperienced for the type of flying conditions that existed. A more prudent person, given the existing conditions of flying over water and under hazy conditions would have avoided taking off at night, putting it off until the next morning. Indeed, others at the same airport did so. But he was what he was, a person with a need for excitement bordering on recklessness—therefore, on to his death. He had two other lives for which he was responsible, that of his wife and his sister-in-law, which makes his actions seem all the more strange.

One hears a lot of talk about "living on the edge" or "living life to the fullest" as excuses for the Kennedy family behavior from generation to generation, but that seems to be less than the full truth. People who live on the edge may be admired from afar but seldom emulated. Do we really want people in political power (it was generally assumed that in time JFK, Jr. would enter politics) who exhibited reckless behavior? Why did Gary Hart challenge the media to find out about his indiscretions? The thrill of the chase? Why not just keep it secret and discreet? However one feels about the governance of President Clinton, the impeachment and the trials, virtually all are united in the belief that his behavior, in addition to being boorish and stupid, was reckless to the extreme.

There is another idea at play, one that implies that those who are prudent in their behavior, do their job day in and day out, raise their families, etcetera, are somehow inferior to the recklessness exhibited by some of the Kennedy family and others, that somehow they live stunted lives because they do not routinely engage in reckless or near-reckless behavior.

It is a terrible tragedy to see young lives, so filled with promise, extinguished in a single moment. The other side, however, is that it need not have occurred had there been more prudence and less recklessness in JFK Jr.'s makeup.

Linear vs. Nonlinear Thinking

My experience over many years of involvement with all types of organizations, business and charitable, has made me realize that there are two primary kinds of thinking, linear and nonlinear. Linear thought is perhaps more common. In many cases, it is the proper way to get tasks done. A goal is identified and then single-minded attention is given to the achieving of the goal. The more pressure to achieve the goal, the more focused the individual becomes. Other thoughts are considered an outside distraction and are either shrugged off or discarded.

Nonlinear thought, however, looks for different ways to accomplish the same goals. Not only the same goals but also other beneficial goals that are a fallout from the effort. Another difference is that linear thinking tends to look at past experience as a guide to the future while nonlinear thought tends to look more to the future and is willing to take more risks for potentially greater rewards.

Furthermore, it is more eclectic, drawing on a wide variety of sources and experience to create new ways to the goal, with the hope of developing unexpected beneficial effects as a by-product of the different approach. Linear thinkers have a solitary goal on which they focus as a laser (sometimes not as a laser but as tunnel vision). Nonlinear thinkers often have multiple goals. Linear thinkers see mistakes (correctable ones at not too high a price) as unmitigated disasters. Nonlinear thinkers see the mistakes as a learning experience and possibly an opportunity for a new approach.

I suspect that the two types of thinking form a rough bell-shaped curve. At the extremes, those with only linear thought tend towards rigidity, using one way and one way only to solve a problem. On the other hand, solely nonlinear thought may produce chaos if not goal-oriented and without differentiation of the important, the relevant, and the practical from the unimportant, the irrelevant, and the impractical.

Fortunately, most people seem to share, to a greater or lesser extent, the ability to think in two fashions, linear and nonlinear.

Morality of Governments

It is often said that governments should act in a moral fashion. It is hard to dispute that idea. The problem is: whose morality? In foreign affairs is it the morality of the pacifist or the hawk? In domestic affairs, is it the morality of those who wish larger government programs or those who wish problems to be solved by smaller units of government or by private enterprise? Who judges which course is more moral?

There are clearly religious and political beliefs that guide behavior. Former president Jimmy Carter, during his presidency and afterward championed the idea that the government should act morally. But what are the moral principles governing political acts? Morally we should have nothing to do with China, should not interfere in the internal affairs of Serbia/Kosovo, should interfere throughout Africa. What about our wartime alliance with the Soviet Union? Everyone who cared to know, knew about the mass executions, the man-made starvations, and the show trials. Should we have aligned ourselves with such a country?

The truth is, our country acts, as do all countries, in what it consider its own best interests, not on an abstract concept of morality. We may find that we miscalculated, that the long-term consequences of our actions were not favorable to us, but vital interests are a preferred reason for action rather than what one individual or group interprets as morality. Needless to say, there would be some things so egregious that there could be absolutely no justification at all for, for instance a U.S. alliance with Hitler.

There is a role for morality, however, which occurs in the relationship of government to its citizens. Lying to the citizens (except in the case of national security) by government officials, cover-up of misdeeds, misdeeds themselves, corruption, personal aggrandizement at the cost of the truth are all examples of immoral behavior that should be strongly condemned. Individual morality rather than the morality of public policy is what we should expect, no, demand, of our government officials. It's hard to believe that, looking at Washington today.

Museums and Governments

There has been a recent heavy flap over an art exhibit held at the Brooklyn (N.Y.) Museum of Art over a painting of the Virgin Mary splattered with animal dung. Dudgeon is high amongst those who cherish "freedom" from anything and everything. Dudgeon became higher when New York City Mayor Rudolph Giuliani threatened to withhold municipal funding (about five million dollars) from the museum.

It should be clearly understood that the city is not and should not be in any way saying the museum cannot exhibit what it wishes, although the exhibit seems to be primarily an attempt to shock, combined with incredibly bad taste and a lack of sensitivity on the part of the museum directors. Those people deeply offended by the work, including a large number of Catholics, are apparently not on the list of those with approved sensitivities, so their feelings are not taken into account. Granted, if everyone who had a gripe could cancel a museum exhibition, then museums would be able to do little, but we are not talking about some tiny minority gumming up the works. Rather, we are talking about a significant percentage of the population of New York City, perhaps even a majority.

In this case, the city (and also the federal government via the NEA) is acting as a patron. It used to be that patrons of the arts were kings and other royal personages, prominent and wealthy citizens and the like. It was clearly understood by all that offence to patrons resulted in loss of patronage. Therefore, it is not surprising that the city did not in any way wish to censor the show, but only to stop its patronage of a show that deeply offended a large number of its citizens, to deny the museum its patronage by withholding its subsidy.

However, some argue, the people in government are just a bunch of Philistines, without the requisite knowledge and culture to evaluate art. Keep the money coming though.

Open Spaces

America is a vast land, stretching 3,000 miles from ocean to ocean, with still enormous open spaces, particularly in the west. However, things are changing dramatically, as suburban sprawl has devoured large areas of the country, leaving environmental problems (as well as a general unsightliness) to be worsened as constant pressure for more and more transportation and shopping centers eats up ever more of the previously rural land. On top of that, people are rediscovering previously undeveloped open spaces and subjecting the spaces to gentrification, bringing along its own set of problems.

One would think that this appalling sprawl would lead people to try and limit immigration, but one would be wrong. The very people who decry the use of open spaces for development often see no limits on immigration. The folly of that type of thinking happened to me when I was showing my suburban area to a gentleman from India. Although an enormous amount of building has taken place since I moved into the area, there were still open spaces, including small plots of land that were still being farmed, although only a shadow of their former selves.

It was springtime, it was dusk, and there were few cars and few people about. The gentleman turned to me and said, "Do you know what I like about America?" I assumed he was going to say "democracy" or "opportunity" or "a classless society" or something like that. Instead, he said, "I like not being constantly surrounded by people." To me that said it all. We must at the same time protect our ecology and our economy, doing it in such a fashion as to preserve the beauty and bounty of our country for generations to come.

Psych 101

I remember it distinctly although it was a long time ago. It was Psych 101, Introductory Psychology, taken as a freshman in college. The professor, a school icon, described an experiment he had performed. In the middle of a class, a group of people rushed into the room, wearing garish clothing, shouting some comments, and then suddenly leaving. Immediately after, a questionnaire was handed out and questions regarding the event were asked. In a nutshell, the students got everything wrong: the number of intruders, the color of their clothes, the nature of their hats, what they said and what they didn't say. Since that time I have never expressed surprise at variations in descriptions of events that took place during a period of unexpected high stress.

Reasonable Vs. Unreasonable

World leaders all have the same conceit—if only they could sit down face to face with their opponent, major benefits would accrue. A measure of the man across the table would be taken, he (the opponent) would see the reasonableness of the leader's position, and some compromise could be worked out.

The above is premised on the fact that both parties are reasonable people and that their goals are basically the same, although the emphasis may be different. There is, however, a difference in the thought processes of reasonable and unreasonable people. Reasonable people recognize that to have a successful negotiation, one cannot get everything—one must make compromises. Further, once a reasonable person has entered negotiations, the object becomes an agreement that one can live with for a long period of time.

For unreasonable people, talk and negotiations are merely tactics towards one's goals of complete victory. If saying one thing (and subsequently doing another) is necessary to get what one wants, then it is fine for one to do so.

All too often, reasonable people project their own thought processes on their unreasonable negotiating partners, not understanding that a whole different set of imperatives are at work. In truth, one can negotiate with totalitarians, terrorists and the like, but only from a position of strength and only for limited goals for a limited period of time. That is why we were able to work out disarmament agreements with the Soviets. After all, a nuclear holocaust would be of benefit to no one.

What happens, however, if one party is reasonable, and reasonably flexible, and the other is inflexible and completely unreasonable. If the parties negotiate between themselves, stalemate is certain, unless the reasonable party makes concessions. The unreasonable party then interprets any concession as a sign of weakness and pushes harder, hoping for more concessions, and then still more concessions, while still withholding any concessions of significance on his part. If a third-party negotiator is present, he would like to show results (movement) and would therefore call upon the more reasonable party to make even further concessions. When these are not reciprocated, still more concessions are asked of the reasonable party.

Underlying this tactic is the assumption that both sides are basically reasonable and concessions from one side are bound to produce concessions from the other. Unfortunately, in most cases of negotiating with unreasonable people, unilateral concessions are more harmful than helpful.

Reparations

Every now and then an article surfaces from someone in the black community that reparations should be made to the community by this country for the awful episode of slavery. It is obviously a topic of continuing discussion within that community. To me, it is extraordinarily wrongheaded. Here is why.

No treatment to any other group compares to the phenomenon of slavery. However, at the same time, no group has completely avoided the lash of discrimination, brutal treatment, and worse. They are bound to say that yes, blacks were treated horribly, but if reparations are to be made, then we were not treated so well either and we deserve reparations as well. This would of course be particularly true if monetary reparations were involved. One would then have to figure out that if blacks are at one hundred percent of whatever reparations are given, what percentage would be appropriate for other groups who have felt badly treated?

For blacks themselves, what percentage would go to those who were not of one hundred percent black ancestry? How much black blood would be necessary to get on the reparations bandwagon? What about blacks who migrated here from the Caribbean or from Africa after slavery was abolished? Are they entitled to reparations too? We have seen that problem with Native Americans who claim to be part of a tribe (although they have had nothing to do with it in the past and many of whom are not full-blooded) and the tribe came into a great deal of money from gambling casinos or from extraction of oil or minerals. It would be inevitable that a new kind of law—reparations law—would come into being.

But suppose reparations do not involve money but merely an apology? That seems harmless enough, but shouldn't an apology be made to others who were mistreated? The problem would be to work out an apology that would not be as profound as the one for blacks. One could see a whole cottage industry developing here—how exactly to apologize to each group. The whole problem could be finessed by apologizing to everyone for everything, but that would hardly assuage the feelings of those who feel that reparations are necessary.

Additional problems would arise. Blacks would have to give up on group preferences, since presumably reparations would wipe the slate clean. They could no longer cry racism since the country would have demonstrated that it is not racist by agreeing to reparations. The Equal Employment Opportunity Commission (EEOC) and other governmental agencies will have to be abolished or markedly diminished. Are they willing to do that? Further, would the next generation be entitled to reparations as well? Would it go on forever, as long as society is not perfect?

Getting beyond the practical problems, which would consume an enormous amount of time and effort, probably to no one's complete satisfaction, the whole purpose of the exercise would be to mend fences and to move forward. Reparations would do exactly the opposite. It would encourage bitterness and resentment. Many would say, with justification, that they and their ancestors were not even in this country when slavery was in force. Why should they be forced to use their tax money to pay for something about which they had absolutely nothing to do? And if it is to be an apology, they would want something too, since their forbears were not treated so well either. The truth is, it is a backward-looking, rather than a forward-looking idea and, for that reason, is likely to produce nothing but divisiveness and dislike, exactly the opposite of what it would be expected to accomplish.

Selective Violence

The intelligentsia of our country have a conceit; that is, even if an individual is terribly violent, and has even committed murder, he should not be punished at all or, at the most, only minimally if he has any artistic or literary talent. Further, although the facts and jury may show otherwise, the intelligentsia always believe the protests of innocence and berate the police, justice system, and politicos for not seeing what they, the intelligentsia, see so clearly: a bright, sensitive man who, because of his underlying talent, could not possibly do what he did. Whereas virtually all, either publicly or privately, were perfectly willing to give the extreme sanction to Timothy McVeigh and others for the Oklahoma City bombing, they wish freedom for the Philadelphian Mumia al Jamar who killed a police officer and was convicted in court, both because of his race and because he does seem to have some literary talent. They also believe that it is racism in action, with the white police as villains. Why the police would want some other man who killed a police officer to go free so they could get this one is yet to be explained, and all in spite of the evidence against him being overwhelming. Oh, well, another example of our not-so-intelligentsia in action.

Sensitivity

There are certain groups in this country, along with their supporters, who ask (demand) that others be sensitive to their needs and situation. What's wrong with that? Absolutely nothing. The problem arises when they are asked to be sensitive to others, particularly to those whose views are different from theirs. This thought came to mind when Southerners flew Confederate battle flags and wished to place a mural of Robert E. Lee along a walk in Richmond, along with other distinguished Virginians. A howl came up from the black community that whites, by doing these things were celebrating slavery.

It is a strange argument to make, for a number of reasons. In this era of multiculturalism, when every group wishes to have others recognize their unique contribution, why should it not include those with white southern ancestors who were involved in the Civil War. Were they wrong about slavery? Of course, they were—clearly a blot on our national history, but it should be remembered that only about five percent were slaveholders. So why did the rest fight? Because of the issue of state's rights versus the federal government, a debate that began with the very beginning of this country and continues to the present day. There even seems to be a recent movement, at least within the Supreme Court, towards devolution of power not enumerated in the Constitution, to the states. Most of the people wish simply to honor their ancestors and show that they fought bravely in a cause that was bound to fail (at least the slavery portion).

Here was a wonderful chance for the black community and their supporters to exhibit the kind of sensitivity that they ask of others. Indeed, in giving and getting, they had an opportunity to present to the white Southern community what their real current day concerns are—access to jobs, educational opportunities, housing, etcetera—and to have them answered. A bit of discomfort for the larger good. It was not to be. More pleasure was obtained from confrontation than from accommodation.

Taunting and Flaunting

I freely admit to being an old fogey, and so, there are many things about American society today that I do not understand or do not like. Two of the things that I particularly dislike are what I call taunting and flaunting.

Taunting occurs at sporting events, most particularly at the professional level, but by example, it filters down to lower and lower levels of competition. It is manifested by verbal abuse (trash-talking), gestures, and even dances as if over a fallen enemy during war. Whatever happened to the idea that you were competing against an opponent, not an enemy? Whatever happened to the idea that one should be magnanimous in victory, gracious in defeat? Whatever happened to the idea that one should behave as a gentleman? Whatever happened to the idea that tomorrow would be another day and the tables could be turned? Whatever happened to the entire idea of sportsmanship?

Flaunting occurs with wealth, and with our new economy there is plenty of that around. In the past, wealth was to be enjoyed but understated. Those who were ostentatious about it were considered to be *"nouveau riche"* and were roundly denounced. It was a term of shame. Now there is no shame with displaying wealth as ostentatiously as possible. The very idea of a program about the lifestyles of the rich and famous could not have been possible in the past. Now it is not only possible but very successful. As are magazine spreads, TV programs, etcetera.

My dislike of both the taunting and flaunting is personal. However, I do believe it contributes to a coarsening of our society, and that is definitely not personal.

Term Limits

From time to time, the concept of term limits for Congress is brought up, only to be denounced with horror by its opponents as being positively undemocratic. The only way a Congressman (representative or senator) should be retired, they say, is by the ballot box, that is, defeated in an election. This is something I have never understood.

The idea of term limits is not exactly something foreign to the American electorate. The president of the United States may serve only two four-year terms and many state governors are limited to two or, even, one term. The argument put forth against limits is that they, the legislators, could not possibly learn their job if they are given term limits. However, it is difficult for me to see how a president or governor could learn his job in eight, let alone, four years. But a legislator, one of 435 in the House and 100 in the Senate, could not possibly learn his or hers in say, ten years in the House or twelve years in the Senate. Indeed many legislators have played skilled roles and accomplished much within those time frames.

Another argument put forth is that the legislators, so confused by lack of knowledge and experience would simply be putty in the hands of their legislative assistants. That could be readily overcome by passing fewer laws and having them more skillfully crafted so that the legislators would be thoroughly familiar with their content. Imagine that—fewer and better laws. Difficult to see how that would be a step backwards.

There is a definite advantage to having citizen legislators. Some would come up through the state legislative ranks. Others would have real other lives, lives of accomplishment, and would be willing to give some years to public service. They would be much less likely to develop Potomac fever, a highly contagious disease developed by all too many of our legislators. Since incumbency grants major advantages, once elected, an individual stands an excellent chance of being in Washington for a long, long time.

As time goes by, they put down roots; they buy a home, belong to clubs, have their children in local schools, and live less and less of their lives in their home district. They begin to see themselves as Washingtonians, very privileged ones at that. It is then in their interest to continue that lifestyle, and reelection becomes paramount. Self-interest and public service are not mutually exclusive, but self-interest for them becomes first.

One can expect that those who have term limits and who are more likely to return to their home district when their term is over would see public interest predominating. A life outside of Washington and an election defeat would not be the end of the world to them. After all, when presidential terms are over, they leave the confines of Washington and lead their own lives, don't they?

A drawback to that idea is the loss of seniority for the home districts, with a resultant decrease in the opportunities for home hands to be in the cookie jar. Not a tragedy, one might be tempted to say. Nevertheless, as a trial over a period of time, those districts or states that elect to try term limits could be given some compensation for their loss of seniority. If after a period of time, the districts or states do not feel that they are well represented by this system, then it could be stopped. To me, it is worth a try.

War Criminals

The Nuremberg trials after the conclusion of WWII established the idea that individuals could be held accountable for crimes against humanity, generally accepted to mean crimes against civilian populations. Many were convicted and several were put to death, while others served long prison terms. In the half-century since, we have, unfortunately, seen a large number of others who clearly deserve to have been brought before a tribunal for their horrific acts. Again unfortunately, for a variety of reasons, they have not been.

All of the above were considered war criminals because of acts of commission, but what about those who by acts of omission unleashed a torrent of death and destruction. I refer specifically to Neville Chamberlain and Edouarde Daladier, respectively the prime ministers of England and France, who, by failing to act early and decisively against Hitler permitted the greatest destruction the world has ever seen. England and France, even with their depleted military (due to a combination of reasons), were still much stronger than Hitler and his forces. When Hitler marched his troops into the demilitarized Rhineland in 1936, his military was so weak that he marched in the same troops over and over again to make it look like a force larger than it really was.

He could easily have been defeated by determination and the employment of several divisions of troops. Instead, he had his first great triumph, consolidated his power and went on to step after step (the Anschluss with Austria, the defeat of Czechoslovakia by political and not military means, the nonaggression pact with Soviet Russia to divide Poland) and finally the invasion of Poland in 1939, which set off WWII. Thus started the greatest destruction the world has ever seen. The complete destruction of a continent, tens of millions (estimated at up to seventy million) of people killed, many tens of millions more wounded or used as slave laborers, the Holocaust, the war in the Pacific with its own terrible destruction of life and property, and the prostration of the Western democracies at the end of the war.

It is perfectly true that one cannot prove a negative. If something did not happen, it cannot be proved that it would have happened, but to me, it is extremely likely that an early and decisive defeat of Hitler would have brought about his overthrow. He was cordially detested by the Prussian military and the industrialists, who only tolerated him as a bulwark against Communism. The Nazis were low-class street brawlers and bullies and were also disliked on this account. They did appeal to the German's sense of pride at reversing the humiliation of the Versailles treaty at the conclusion of WWI, as well to the general population disgusted with the ineffective Weimar republic and the ravages of the Great Depression. Even so, a decisive defeat would probably have brought the regime to an end.

If England and the United States were not distracted by the necessity of defeating the Nazis, it would probably have been unlikely that the Japanese would have launched their war of expansion. If they did, the full force of the United States and England would have been brought to bear against them, and they would have been defeated in much shorter order. Finally, there would be no excuse for Stalin to conquer all of Eastern and much of Central Europe, and the Cold War could have been fought at a much lower intensity and in a limited, not global, fashion.

In short, the world would have been a much different place if Chamberlain and Daladier had recognized the menace early and acted accordingly. Is such an overwhelming act of omission a war crime? You tell me.

What to Do With Navy Fighter Pilots?

What Navy carrier pilots do is simply beyond comprehension to most of us. Being catapulted off the deck in a multiton fighter aircraft at several hundred knots is scary enough. Engaging in bombing runs or dogfights while dodging missile or triple-A artillery is another, but landing on a carrier deck, to my mind, takes the cake. A tiny speck of solid ground in a pitching, rolling sea, often at night. A tiny mistake may lead to instant death. There are characteristics that are not possessed by most of us that permit them to do just that. We, of course, owe an enormous debt to them for doing things that are necessary for our defense and yet could not conceivably be done by most of us.

It is these very characteristics—incredible bravery, daring, machismo, fearlessness, courage—that gets them into trouble when they are not on the deck of a carrier but on dry land. Hence the repeated problems of Tail Hook. So what to do with them when they are between assignments at sea? My solution is that the younger, single, lower ranks be given very large, very comfortable, and very well-furnished cages until they ship out again.

Why Boys Kill

It has been pointed out that there are pronounced gender differences in violence resulting in homicide between males and females. There is also a marked age difference among males regarding violence, with the teens and early twenties being the rage years and then tapering off. Women want to do what men do, so there seems to be a rising incidence of violent crimes among females, but it is still small potatoes compared to what men do. An interesting sidelight is the racial differences, as well as gender differences, among serial killers. Females, blacks, Asians, and Hispanics (there was recently a case in the west involving a Hispanic male) rarely become serial killers. I wonder how the antiprofilers would think if a killer were on the loose and the police were unable to concentrate their energies on the likely group identity of the killer.

What has been forgotten in the attempt to homogenize boys and girls is that there are fundamental, genetic differences, not just nurturing, between boys and girls. Young boys are restless, aggressive, constantly checking their role in the pack. Boys are constantly running around shooting guns or objects made to look like guns. A mother told me that if her boy were given a doll, he would use it as a gun. Their childhood games center about tracking, hunting, and killing. When older, they play football, which is modified warfare. Girls are more passive (hence, the oft-heard cry that they do not volunteer in the classroom) and are more concerned about harmony and achieving consensus. These differences are neither good nor bad—they are simply there.

The above does not completely answer why boys kill, but it does seem to follow a genetic impulse, which is moderated but not completely stifled by community control. The less community control, the greater the violence. Feminists have tried to remake society in their own image, one in which gender plays no role in anything, including male and female behavior. That erroneous concept stifles thought on how we could better control violence in our society.

WWII Vets—Larger Than Life

There has been a spate of documentaries, books, TV programs, movies, etcetera that have glorified WWII vets and the role they played in saving the United States and the West from Germany and Japan. They are portrayed as larger than life, braver by far than, it is clear by inference, the current generation.

I don't believe that that is so. I knew many of them. Indeed, many were relatives, and like everyone else at the time, I read about them constantly. They were ordinary people called upon to do extraordinary work. Most were poor (we were just coming out of the Great Depression). Many were the children of immigrants. They were far less educated than today's youth. There were, however, two traits that separated them from what we see in the current generation. First, they were intensely patriotic and openly so. They felt a love of country without embarrassment or shame. Second, they understood that the needs of the community at times surpassed the needs of the individual and, therefore, at times sacrifice—even the ultimate sacrifice—was necessary. I recall seeing in the newspapers and newsreels of the time the long lines of young men trying to enlist, not waiting for their selective service number to be called. Can one even conceive of something like that happening today?

There is yet another difference between then and now and not often mentioned; that is, the involvement of the entire community in the war effort. My father, as did many physicians, volunteered to examine inductees. It was considered to be a badge of disgrace, not pride, to be labeled 4F (not fit for military duty). Women volunteered (for example, the Red Cross), and for the first time went into manufacturing jobs previously held solely by men (the famous "Rosie the Riveter"). Older men and women volunteered at many jobs, including air raid wardens. Even we children played our role. We collected old newspapers, balls of twine, old rubber, scrap metal, etcetera. In school we bought twenty-five cent stamps to eventually become a War Bond. We followed the progress of the war closely with maps and discussions.

We did not consider ourselves heroes, nor were we. We were all ordinary people who deeply loved our country and were willing to sacrifice for it and for the greater good. This apparently seems astonishing to younger generations.

Zero Sum vs. Win/Win

I have been in a fair number of negotiations myself and have closely followed national and international negotiations. All too often, these negotiations have been performed as a zero sum game—if I win you lose and vice versa. The negotiations are oftentimes extremely bitter and often leave an aftereffect, a residue of bitterness at having given up more than the negotiating partner. This leads to a desire for revenge—not a very healthy or productive state of mind.

A far better way, albeit more difficult, is to try to make the negotiation a win/win situation. For that to happen, both sides have to give; one cannot have a negotiation of this sort without flexibility and compromise. Going in to the negotiation, each side must understand the aforementioned, as well as that there will be losses on both sides. The other side of the coin is that both sides have to win something. It is hoped that the wins and losses will be reasonably symmetrical. For obvious reasons this is a difficult negotiating posture, with each party having to slip into the shoes of the other, picturing how they see the situation. A successful outcome, however, is wonderful to behold, since both sides give something, both sides get something, and the future is not filled with rancor and bitterness.

II

Miscellaneous

CEO Salaries

President Clinton likes to imply that he is somehow responsible for the unprecedented economic boom that we have been enjoying during the past decade. This claim conveniently omits the role of Congress, the Federal Reserve, and the benefit of cheap energy for most of that period. More important, it ignores the real architects and the heroes of our robust economy—the nation's CEOs and their boards of directors.

Bloated, complacent, poorly managed—that characterized U.S. companies in the seventies and early eighties. It was so bad that there were those who felt that the U.S. economy was in a permanent decline; they felt that we should instead model ourselves after the Japanese—Japan Inc.—where there was a close relationship between supplier and producer, where wages were kept low in return for hard work and permanent employment, and where fundamental decisions about which industries were and were not to be given support, and preferences were made by an all-powerful governmental agency—the Ministry for Industry, Trade and Investment (MITI). How very prescient were these prognosticators. Within a short period of time, the Japanese economy went into the tank, and it has yet to fully emerge. The very rigidities of the system and the again-proven lack of ability of government bureaucrats, any bureaucrats in any country, rather than market forces to pick winners and losers in an industrial society, was shown to the world.

Instead, spurred on by a more favorable business climate in the late 1980s and 1990s, a spate of new technologies, as well as the lure of large personal profits via stock options, American industry revolutionized itself. Layoffs took place, with certainly a lot of pain absorbed by those laid off. However, the redundant ten percent of the work force made the companies more efficient and guaranteed employment for the remaining ninety percent. In addition to greater efficiency by decreasing the redundant portion of the work force, CEOs spun off or sold assets that were not as productive of profit or were not related to the core business, and acquired the size necessary to compete in the global marketplace via mergers and acquisitions, use of new technology and emphasis on globalization of the business.

Further, a remarkable group of CEO/entrepreneurs founded not just whole new companies but whole new industries, leading us into the twenty-first century equivalent of the industrial revolution of the twentieth century, namely the information revolution. This has created hundreds of thousands of well-paying jobs and, in turn, given us the lead on a worldwide basis in such industries as computer technology and biotechnology. The truth is, our economic prosperity does not depend in large part on how well or how poorly a particular government agency performs but how well or how poorly the people who produce our goods and services perform.

Whose well being are CEOs responsible for? Obviously the company's employees and their families. Also their suppliers, who also have employees with families. The same holds true for distributors with their employees and families. And for outsourcing work, such as advertising, security, legal, accounting, etcetera, all of these firms having employees with families.

The CEO of the company must also be mindful of the communities in which it works and the effect of company action upon them. Finally, the CEO is responsible to the stockholders, who risk their capital (frequently pension capital) and who expect to see a reasonable return on that capital. In medium- and larged-sized companies, all this could amount to hundreds of thousands of families dependent in whole or in part on the well being of the company. For a CEO, this is hardly a simple task. It should be contrasted with people, such as professional athletes or entertainers, who make large sums of money but who are responsible only to themselves.

So what are we to make of the claim that salaries and options are too high. In some cases, of course, both are. To my mind, it is pernicious to grant a CEO new stock options at a lower price if he failed to cause the stock to go to the agreed price at which time the previous options would have kicked in. This painlessness does not benefit the company's operating efficiency. Then there are some CEOs who make what appear to be outrageous money in the form of salary, bonuses, and options. First, it should be pointed out that there are very few of these. Second, it is difficult to begrudge a CEO his reward (as high as it is) if he provides incredible returns for his investors. Bill Gates of Microsoft and Michael Eisner of Disney come to mind as CEOs who generated enormous returns for their investors (stockholders) and have earned their rewards. There are, however, plenty of just bad CEOs, such as "Chainsaw Al" Dunlap, who practice slash-and-burn tactics and appear indifferent to the fate of the employees and the community, and then make a handsome profit from the sale of the company. Because some such as he exists is no reason to condemn an entire group of people. It is difficult for some people to give credit where credit is due for our prosperity—the nation's CEOs.

Christendom vs. Islam

It is bizarre to think of the seemingly perpetual troubles in southeast Europe, the Middle East, Africa, and beyond as having anything to do with centuries-old religious rivalries, but I believe it is so, at least in part. Two waves of Islam struck Europe, the first being the original Arab invaders who conquered North Africa and then went on to conquer the Iberian Peninsula. It took hundreds of years to evict them. When the Franks (Christian) defeated the Moors (Muslims) the Muslims retreated to North Africa from whence they had come. The second invasion was by the Muslim Turks, who invaded southeastern and central Europe and were not stopped until the battle that took place at the gates of Budapest.

The tide slowly receded, but millions of Muslims were left behind. Between these invasions, the Christians invaded the Middle East via the Crusades. Over time, they were defeated and retreated to Europe from whence they came. They came back as colonialists during the nineteenth and twentieth centuries and again were displaced over a period of time. Virtually all of the European/Asian/African conflicts of modern times occur at the interface of Christendom and Islam.

This is not to say that there are not other factors present, which are universal—land, economics, mineral rights, etcetera—but there is still a strong religious element present. It is also not to say that sides are chosen strictly according to religious belief. For example, the Christian nations of Europe sided with the predominantly Muslim populations of Bosnia and Kosovo rather than with Christian Serbia, but these are exceptions. Here are some of the conflicts that have occurred between Christians and Muslims in modern times.

Yugoslavia is as good a place to start as any. Held together by the iron grip of Marshall Tito, the country fractured into many pieces with the demise of Tito and the end of the Cold

42

War. There was no fighting over the breakaway Slovenia and relatively little fighting over Croatia (it appeared to be primarily a struggle over land). The really brutal struggle took place in Bosnia and Kosovo, where the Eastern Orthodox Christian Serbia tried to subdue both lands, each with predominantly Muslim populations. As bad as the behavior of the Serbs was, the Albanian Kosovars (Muslims) were and are just as intent on doing to the Christian Serbs what was done to them.

Although there are some glimmers of hope, Christian Greece and Muslim Turkey have been in a state of hostility for centuries. This is mimicked in Cyprus, where the Christian Greek sector of the island is in a cold war situation with the Turkish Muslim portion of the island. Further north in the Caucuses, Christian Armenia is in a constant struggle with Muslim Azerbaijan. There is a long-term hostility between the Muslim Turks and Christian Armenians as well. Slightly further north, the struggle between Muslim Chechnya and Dagestan on the one hand and Christian Russia on the other is currently in a hot war phase. On the other end of Eurasia, Christian East Timor is involved in a bloody struggle for independence from Muslim Indonesia. On the African continent, the northern, Muslim portion of Sudan is in a constant state of civil war with the southern, largely Christian portion of the country. Open warfare between Christian and Muslim tribes in Nigeria and elsewhere in western and central Africa have repeatedly taken place.

Turkey is a long-term member of NATO and contributed troops to the Allied effort during the Korean and Vietnamese wars. It had been on the forefront of the Cold War struggle with the Soviet Union because of its geographic location. It had every right to expect, with of course necessary changes in its economic and political system, to be admitted to the European Union. It was not. Although many reasons were put forth, the most telling one to me was the comment by one of the EU officials that it was not a Christian nation. The struggle between Christianity and Islam is not dead and buried in the past. The conflict between Turkey and Greece, as well as between Turkish and Greek Cypriots has been in part a struggle between Eastern Orthodox Christians and Muslims. The same can be said for the struggle in Bosnia and Kosovo between Eastern Orthodox Christians (Serbia) and Muslims.

What about the Middle East, and Israel in particular? Other than Africa, which appears to have sunk into the worst excesses of tribalism, totalitarianism, and despair, no region has embraced Western systems, values, techniques, technology, etcetera less than the Arab states of the Middle East. There are undoubtedly many reasons, but surely part of the problem is the reluctance to embrace contemporary Western values developed in Christian countries, including democracy, a constitution, free speech, free elections, as well as the technological advances that have revolutionized the modern world. It is true that starting with the Crusades, Christians have attempted to conquer and, later, to colonize the Middle East. The earlier Crusades were, in addition to adventure and plunder, a religious undertaking blessed by the Popes. The more recent conquest and colonization in the nineteenth and twentieth centuries was driven by a desire to secure oil and, for the British, a lifeline to India, then the jewel in the crown. Hence the efforts to drive out Christian invaders (harking back to the campaigns to drive out the Crusaders).

The Arabs have not, however, recognized the difference between the Western Christian colonists and the ideas that they espouse—ideas that have become the foundation of modern democratic societies. This failure has resulted in a combination of totalitarianism and grinding poverty. Those with natural resources (oil) are holding their heads above water, but most of the rest are falling further into the arms of backwardness and despair.

This brings us to Israel. The basic rejection of Israel by the Arab masses (and to a lesser extent the Muslim non-Arab masses) has many causes, including the ascension of previously second-class citizens in the Muslim world to an independent and viable state, the battle over holy places, and anti-Semitism (yes, Semites can exhibit anti-Semitism). Perhaps the most important, however, is the view of the Arabs that Israel represents an outpost of the hated Christian colonialists and exhibits the above-mentioned Christian values. It is their conceit that the Jews are no different from the Crusaders and will in a short time disappear from the Arab (and Muslim) world. Time only will tell.

It is far-fetched to believe that ancient struggles based on religion are still present, but in case after case it seems to be true. Other than in Africa where bloody tribal struggles continually take place, most of the world's conflicts are still based in large part on religion and mostly Islam versus Christianity.

The Defining Values of America

We in America are living in a time of great paradoxes. On the one hand we have witnessed in this century the triumph of democracy over the two "isms", fascism and communism, largely based on our leadership. The third "ism", Muslim fundamentalism, is still lurking out there, but whether it will prove to be a major adversary as the other two or merely an annoyance is unclear at this time. We are clearly the dominant power in the world, with nobody even a close second. Although Germany and Japan are powerful economic forces (they have recently suffered setbacks but in all likelihood will come back in the economic sphere), they neither approach us economically nor are they competition for us in the political arena.

America is still the destination for most of the economically and politically afflicted, and no other country is seen as a comparable land of opportunity. We have seen a universalization of our values and customs from the superficial (clothing, movies, sports, food, music) to the profound (our political and economic systems and our belief in the rights of the individual). Yet at the same time, we can feel ourselves careening apart. We are discovering major flaws in our political, economic, social, and cultural institutions. We are disturbed by more than bickering; we are seeing major clashes about our fundamental values and how we define ourselves as Americans. This has led to paralysis, in terms of solving our problems, as competing and often diametrically opposed views of the nature of our problems have paralyzed our institutions.

The increase in single interest and special interest groups, coupled with increased sophistication in the use of the media and the manipulation of the political process has further led away from compromise and problem solving. Vocal and articulate groups and individuals have questioned the very idea of America as a beacon of light and a goal to be reached by other nations. Their hostility poisons the atmosphere and leads yet again to a feeling of malaise.

Before the process gets out of hand, we have to ask ourselves whether there are defining values that make America unique and on which the majority of us can agree. If so, can they be stated in terms simple enough for all Americans to recognize and incorporate into their being, starting at the grade school level and carried through for a lifetime.

Language

It would appear to be a truism that a country functions best with a single national language—in our case, American

English. There are, of course, many countries that function with more than one language. Even more have small groups of people who use a different tongue in family and social circumstances. One can of course make a theoretic case for employment of more than one language, but the sad and unhappy experiences of Canada point to the fact that more problems are created than are solved with more than one language. Besides, in a multicultural society such as ours, who will pick what are the second, third, and fourth languages? Will we force New Englanders to learn Spanish if that is the second national language and Southerners to learn an East Asian language if one or more is also chosen as a "national language?" Our American language has been enriched beyond measure by the words and expressions of each group as it becomes part of the American mosaic, but the first defining value of America is to have a single language—American English.

Political Governance

It doesn't seem so remarkable now that our system of governance is that of a democratic republic bolstered with a Constitution and a Bill of Rights to clarify and to define further some basic principles, but at the time of our founding, we were the first democracy and the first republic. We had truly embarked on uncharted waters, and after two centuries, we are clearly running into rough seas. Issues of electoral reform such as financing our political campaigns and legislative term limits, division of the executive and legislative branches between different parties, federal versus state responsibilities, all create turmoil and uncertainty. Despite all these problems, however, we clearly have the best of all existing systems and clearly would be loath to change it. Improve or modify it—yes, but change it—no.

Economic System

Our economic system is that of capitalism with a free-market economy. Everything is relative of course, because we have neither completely unfettered capitalism nor a completely free economy. Tax laws, inheritance laws, regulatory laws, tariff and trade laws modify behavior in the economic sphere. Whether there should be more or less in the way of government intervention in the process is obviously a matter of intense and continuing debate, depending upon the individual's political philosophy. Only few individuals at either extreme believe in absolutely no regulation or in complete government control. It should be recognized, however, that this system most closely approximates the needs, desires, and behaviors of the majority of citizens in this country, let alone the world.

This has been clearly demonstrated by the rise of Japan and the East Asian "tigers," the collapse of Communism and the complete failure of their economic system, as well as the behavior of the mainland Chinese when presented with the opportunity to use the capitalist system for their own benefit. It therefore behooves our government officials to harness the energies, needs, and desires of the citizens for the maximum benefit to our economy. Each new law, rule, and regulation should not be looked upon merely as an issue of fairness but how it will impact upon the behaviors of people. Will it cause them to work harder and more productively, save more, invest more, or will it do the opposite?

Using fairness as our sole guide to controlling behaviors is tricky at best and dangerous at worst. First, to state the obvious, life itself is not fair. Further, everyone differs on what is considered to be creating more fairness, and finally, the creation of fairness for one group may create unfairness for another group. A more helpful concept would be that of a just society, one that feels an obligation to assist those temporarily or permanently in need. A corollary would be to attempt in every way to help those able and willing to help themselves to become independent, productive citizens, leaving the safety net only for those who are truly incapable of helping themselves—a very small minority. The best system would be a cooperative effort between public and private agencies—not rivalry, not competition, but cooperation.

Cultural Values

This is an area of fierce fighting as multiculturalism comes in conflict with what has been the dominant culture. It is difficult to define culture, since so many elements make it up. But clearly, until recently, the dominant public culture was WASP (white Anglo-Saxon Protestant), although in the home and in the local community, each ethnic group sought with varying degrees of intensity and success to maintain their original culture. It was the overwhelming desire of all new immigrants to become, as fast as possible, Americans, meaning adopting in public WASP values and outlooks. And indeed this dualism has served us well. Furthermore, it has by no means been a one-way street, as each ethnic group has contributed something—language, music, food, art, literature, clothing style, etcetera—to the dominant culture, constantly shaping and reshaping it so that it bears little resemblance to what it was, say fifty years ago, let alone at the beginning of the republic. Nevertheless, we all owe a great deal to the dominant culture. We must never forget our immigrant ancestors (black slaves being the sole exception) were drawn to these shores primarily because of the values and culture of the WASPs. They in turn were influenced by their ancestors who came from England and who, in turn, were influenced by British and French philosophers and by a strong adherence to Judeo-Christian values. By all means, let new values and culture enter the mainstream. Let the dominant culture grow and expand and take on new hues. But let us recognize that there is a dominant culture and where it came from. Those who gave original shape to our country were, with the exception of a few male Catholics, all male WASPs. There is nothing we can do to change it, so why not recognize it and study it as the origin of our distinctive political and social culture.

It is more than slightly ironic that as the fighting gets fiercer within America as to what constitutes American culture in all its various guises, our dominant culture has been universalized. This includes not only our pop culture but our deeper political and social culture as well. We must be doing something right!

Individual Rights

Our rights as individuals are guaranteed in the Bill of Rights and are certainly precious to us, but they cannot exist in a vacuum. As we hear ever-shriller cries for expansion of individual rights, we hear no comparable cries for communal responsibilities. Yet how can we have an ever-expanding list of rights with an ever-expanding list of people who lose their rights? Don't the rights of criminals come in conflict with the rights of law-abiding citizens to be free in their home and to move about the community without fear of harm to their person? If we fail to recognize that we have a responsibility to each other, of what value are individual rights? It is difficult to answer the call by some for more and more individual rights with a similar call for more and more government programs. However benign, greater control by government means a reduction of individual rights.

Individual Opportunity

It is one of the glories of America that an individual has the opportunity, wherever he starts in life, to rise to the level of his abilities. We tend to forget how stratified other societies were and how one stayed in the station to which one was born. To be sure, life is not pure and simple, and the principle is often honored in the breach, but it is a goal towards which we can as a society strive. Therefore, however well meaning we are when we decide on certain groups of individuals to be selected out for treatment different from those of the majority, it is a condition that clearly leads to conflict and results in more hostility between groups.

Conclusion

If we are to define America and what it means to be an American, it seems to me, we should state simply that we require a common language and an approved system of political governance and economy. We have a common adherence to a dominant culture but a recognition of the wide diversity of a multiethnic system. Our adherence to the rights of the individual is bedrock but cannot be held in isolation from responsibilities to the community. Finally, we believe in the opportunity for each individual to rise to the level of his ability regardless of race, creed, or color. These are the defining values of America.

Lawyers

Seeking remedies through the courts is as old as our republic and an important, even vital, part of our rights and our civil liberties. However, in the past, the exercising of those rights were relatively rare, whereas today we are overwhelmed by them, so much so that much of our behavior is predicated upon the likelihood of a suit being filed. Lawyers have changed too, from serving as counselors to being sharks, ever on the lookout for prey.

Why has all this come about? I believe it is as much the changing attitudes of the public as the new behavior of the lawyers. If anything goes wrong, somebody must be responsible and somebody must pay. There is not even a hint of individual responsibility, whether through carelessness, negligence, or just plain bad luck. I have known for decades that smoking is a filthy, dangerous habit with terrible health consequences to the individual. I have further known that the tobacco companies have been despicable in their behavior, lying and stonewalling for decades as their profits piled up. Of course they should be punished, but doesn't the individual who smokes bear any responsibility for his or her behavior? How do we teach individual responsibility if irresponsible behavior is rewarded? How can we explain the tens of thousands of new smokers (and that includes cigar smokers as well) each year, mostly young people. They would have to be from another planet not to know the hazards of smoking, and yet they proceed anyway. Then, when they get into tobacco-related health problems, they immediately cast about for others to take the blame and to shower them with money.

Another problem with the public: when they serve as jurors they tend to have a Robin Hood mentality, taking money from the large and the wealthy and transferring it to the "poor" plaintiffs. It is "sending a message" and "they can afford it" all rolled up in one. Where there is clear-cut negligence or clear obstruction of justice, of course the offending party should be punished—severely. But where there is merely an untoward reaction? Where, as in the breast implant controversy, there is no scientific evidence that the silicone implant causes systemic (yes, it does cause local inflammation) disease? Should a company be brought to bankruptcy and others have their profits melt away when there is no evidence that they did anything wrong? Raising the cost of doing business raises the cost for all, something jurors don't seem to understand. One cannot but feel, aside from the obvious financial benefit that accrues from either a successful suit or the threat of one, that there is a political dimension to these actions.

Rage and greed are also problems of the public. We recognize road rage and the rage fueling the terrible shootings we have witnessed in schools and at the workplace; isn't it rage that makes people insist on a lawsuit when compromise, in the form of arbitration or mediation, would accomplish the same thing? Greed, in the form of the application of the green poultice, also fuels the desire for more and more.

What of the lawyers? They are hardly an innocent party in this societal problem. They stimulate demand. They were called "ambulance chasers" in an earlier time, and that concept is still true today. Let any tragedy occur, anywhere, and they are right there. I find that deeply distasteful, as do many others. That is relatively passive behavior compared to class action suits, which are organized and run by lawyers, with the targets being anyone with deep pockets. Trial lawyers, like any other group, have the right to petition the government (in the form of campaign contributions), but the extent of their influence peddling should be made more noticeable to the general public. All of the above explains why lawyers, like pols and media people, are "below the line" (see "Below the Line").

There are remedies of course. The first would be to adopt the rules that are found around the globe—loser pays court costs. This would go far to decrease the public appetite for law suits. Frivolous suits filed to see if someone could be bought off should decrease. Adequate and rapid binding arbitration as well as mediation enables plaintiffs with a complaint that does not appear airtight to have a prompt "day in court." When this is considered to be a violation of federal law, the plaintiff is in heaven; the initial investigation is undertaken at the expense of the government. After that, frequently the defendants will settle out of court to avoid the nuisance and expense of protecting themselves. It would be a great benefit if the entire society looked upon the actual going to court as a failure of the system to resolve the problem by other means and upon the litigants with disapproval.

The contingent fee is a curse. Ostensibly it is to permit people without means to be able to mount a legal action. Typical contingent fees range from one-third to forty percent of the reward. Add to that all of the expenses in bringing the case to trial, and the plaintiff ends up with less than half of the judgment. On top of that, the recent killer judgments in class action suits has netted plaintiff attorneys not merely adequate compensation for the time and effort put in. I am talking about hundreds of millions, even billions, of dollars for attorneys. If that doesn't cause solicitation among lawyers, what will? If a company or business gets into some perceived trouble, the Internet screen immediately lights up with law firms who will represent you in a class action suit. Their basic point is valid, however, and something has to be done to have representation, good representation, of those who cannot afford it. I propose that a multiple of their hourly fee be used. That at least is comprehensible. It would be set by a judge or master. Let us say that five or ten times the firm's usual fees plus all costs would still be an incentive to take a case and still have reasonable compensation.

The public, therefore the juries, have to understand that their verdicts are not risk-free. The cost of doing business rises and is passed on to the consumer. The costs of these actions lower profits and, therefore, lessen stockholder's return on their money (most Americans are now stockholders). New products are slower to come to market. Manufacturers of riskier but necessary and helpful products have the government indemnify them before producing the product, vaccines, for example.

The law schools could do their part as well. Law schools are nothing but classrooms, offices, and a library. Compared to a science building in a medical school, they are relatively cheap to build and maintain. Further, the addition of more students simply means more chairs and more income with little or no additional expense. Yet there are far too many lawyers being turned out. There are far too many poor to mediocre law schools as well. An effort to either upgrade or eliminate the weakest of these schools would benefit everyone but the prospective students and the faculty.

To compensate the law schools for decreased income due to decreased class size, I would propose that they admit students who wish an education in the law but do not wish to practice law. They would be given a different degree, as are foreign lawyers who attend our law schools. For example, they could be given a degree as an adjunct in law. They would be treated exactly the same as other students but would not be permitted to take the bar exam or practice law.

There is no doubt that a good legal education can be invaluable in many fields of endeavor. We do not need a flood of new graduates each year, each struggling to make a living from the practice of the law. This would be a solution; it would maintain the law school's income, educate many individuals in the thinking process of the law but not in the practice of the law, and decrease the number of practicing lawyers turned out. After all, we have more attorneys than the rest of the world put together; there must be something wrong with that. Finally, the law schools and the bar associations could tighten ethics, with appropriate sanctions for violating them.

These problems do not apply to all lawyers. I believe that at least some of them are appropriately embarrassed by what is happening. Some recognize that they are being tarred by the same brush. It is also true that some industries, some companies, and some individuals behave badly and need to be taken to the whipping shed via the courts. The pendulum has swung too far and, to my way of thinking, is out of control. Some changes can be made by changes in public perception, but changes in legislation—the heart of the matter—are not doable for two reasons: the power of the trial attorneys' lobby and their campaign contributions, and the fact that most legislators are lawyers themselves.

Microsoft vs. Government

I freely admit that I do not know all the facts or all the legal ramifications of Microsoft v. U.S. I also admit that as an investor I own Microsoft and other tech stocks and have profited from their growth. It is to be assumed that Microsoft engaged in some sharp business practices. If more than that, if for example, Microsoft broke the law, it should be punished. The punishment should be in the usual form for businesses—fines, the amount to be determined by the court. Nobody, and certainly no corporate entity is above the law. Appropriate punishment for corporations that break the law is usually a stiff fine, not the breakup of a company, which is one of the choices that the Justice Department is considering.

First of all, we as a society owe a tremendous debt of gratitude to Wintel (Microsoft and Intel), IBM, Hewlett Packard, AOL, etcetera, for creating essentially out of nothing an entire industry, an industry that has changed the way we communicate with each other, look at the world, and do business. It has had as profound an effect on the United States and world economy as did the Industrial Revolution at the start of the twentieth century. Fortunately for us, as a country, due to a combination of entrepreneurship, creativity, persistence, and guts, we have taken a leading role in what will be a leading industry in the twenty-first century. It has created an enormous number of high-paying jobs and has produced an enormous amount of wealth never before seen in this country on such a wide scale. I am not talking about a few executives who made a killing in their stock, but millions upon millions of investors who can look forward to better retirements because of the appreciation of their equity holdings, in large part fueled by the tech stocks.

It didn't happen anywhere else in the world, at least not to the same degree it happened primarily here. Thanks goodness, because imagine what would happen to our country if the industry was not born and bred here and we had to import it all. The fuel that caused this colossus to move forward was entrepreneurial skills, creativity, and rewards. Primarily financial of course, but also large doses of self-satisfaction.

Now let's look at the government. Governments do not create anything (except ever-larger bureaucracies) or build anything (except very large construction projects). They certainly don't create wealth. They only say no, a necessary "no" at times, but one that should be used only very sparingly. If Microsoft is such a terrible monopoly, why are there thousands and thousands of new companies in related fields springing up? Not all related to Microsoft, of course, but a result of the technological revolution led in large part by Microsoft. Government talk is of the monopolies that developed in the latter part of the nineteenth and early part of the twentieth centuries, such as Standard Oil, U.S. Steel, and the railroads.

The analogy does not completely hold, however, since the earlier monopolies did not help create complementary companies as did Microsoft. Eventually, the monopolies did break down, with the government's intervention of course, and alternatives arose. For example, railroads no longer dominate transportation, and can put a stranglehold on only a few industries, particularly those that need to ship in bulk. What if technology evolves (we should remember that monopolies change at lightning speed in these times) and Microsoft technology is no longer necessary. What if new software codes such as Linux become the standard? What if PCs are no longer necessary to access the Internet and they become nothing more than sophisticated typewriters? Will the government turn around and subsidize Microsoft? Hardly.

Much has been made by the government that Microsoft could have made a profit at forty-nine dollars for new Windows and, instead, charged eighty-nine. Such *chutzpa*. The government, not the marketplace, will decide what is a fair profit? Are we to have a regulated utility, with a government agency deciding what a fair price for services is? Furthermore, people do not have to buy upgrades but can keep the original technology. Their access to a computer is not denied. They willingly do so because the new product is better, has far more features for example. Computers as a whole are constantly improving while dropping markedly in price—now, that's the kind of monopoly I like to see.

Further, there is no groundswell of opposition to Microsoft (competitors in the industry of course object) among purchasers. They know what they are getting. They also know that the money Microsoft earns is funneled back into research, more creativity and more products, from which we all benefit. It is also passed on, not to just a few company officers but to millions and millions of investors, who in turn help to fuel this remarkable economy.

I have a funny feeling about the Department of Justice actions, based on my many years of government service. It is the revenge of the little guys, the bureaucrats, on the big guys, Bill Gates and company. They have the power to stick it to the big guys, and they enjoy doing it, while talking about the good of the country of course. To some, bigness and success are evils in themselves.

Much has been made of memos where Microsoft executives, including Bill Gates, talk about crushing the opposition. Such trash talking, unfortunately, is now common in sports and business, particularly among entrepreneurs. I suppose it is a form of psyching themselves up. Not a very desirable form, I admit, but I am willing to make a small wager that similar talk takes place in most new entrepreneurial businesses amongst very aggressive businessmen.

Not very smart to commit such talk to memos, I admit. There is also the personality of Gates to deal with. He is both plain speaking and impolitic, and one can see where he rubs people the wrong way. To my way of thinking, Intel in chips, AOL in net access, and other such companies are similar "monopolies" (in quotes because what is a monopoly today could be a has-been tomorrow due to technology change) but their chiefs are much more politic.

What will happen if Microsoft is deemed a monopoly? Punishment can be anything from a fine to a breakup of the company. The fine will be a setback for the company but only a temporary one. If forced to break up, there will in all likelihood be two or more successful companies put into play. Even now, the trial lawyers are contemplating class action suits against Microsoft. Microsoft will spend its time, money, and creative energy defending itself instead of building new technologies to put to work for the benefit of all of us. How sad.

My Investment Philosophy

It is difficult to believe that I have been involved in investments in the stock market for nearly fifty years, starting with an inchoate idea of investment and dependent upon the mercies of a series of brokers—a few good, far too many bad. Through a series of hard knocks, I gradually developed a philosophy of investing that suits me, although I readily admit that it does not suit everyone. I do not claim that my way is the right way and another the wrong way. There is no right or wrong way, because there is a very pure, unmuddled end point—how much money has been made. Whatever the intermediate steps, it is the end point that counts.

The spectacular rise in the market during the 1990s has made winners of virtually everybody—whatever their investment philosophy—provided that they do indeed invest. It never hurts, however, to have a coherent philosophy and then sticking to it. My first principle is that I am not smarter than the professionals. I am probably dumber. I do have access to an enormous fund of information, more than could be dreamed of in an earlier age, and yet, separating the wheat from the chaff is not always easy. That is why I use a knowledgeable broker and am willing to pay his commissions. Professional advice does not come free, and to me, it (the commissions) is a small price to pay for good advice. Sometimes I accept the advice and sometimes not, but I do have a profesional who is concerned about my money. If he is not, he will no longer be my broker. I have also found that there are many services that a brokerage house offers that could probably be done by myself but only at enormous sacrifice of time and energy. Some examples are tax disputes, stock donations to charitable organizations, settlement of estates, location of old trades that cannot be found, a backup record system in case something happens to mine, and many more.

Even with the enormous reams of information about bonds and equities on the Internet, I make the assumption that the news is old hat to investing professionals and, therefore, my acquisition of such news is late. I also like to sleep at night. That can be done by investing in bonds and certificates of deposit, but I would gladly trade a small loss of sleep for what hopefully might be capital gains. To my mind, bonds and CDs are a poor choice except in bad economic times or when they are part of a larger portfolio, representing safety and yield rather than capital gains. Why I sleep soundly will be discussed below. Depending on luck in the market is a fool's game; I never had it and I never will.

I try to keep my ego out of my decisions. I am an investor, pure and simple. I have no desire to have bragging rights about how much money I made by cashing in. I have no desire to load up with speculative stocks, hoping that one of these will hit the jackpot. I have no need for excitement, and my ego is not dependent upon gains and losses, although it would be inhuman not to have a lift from rising value and a downer from falling value. In short, in my belief, investing and gambling have no relation to each other. If one needs excitement, go to Las Vegas; if not, be an investor.

I am interested in quality companies, and for the long haul, which may mean decades. I understand that all companies, including quality companies, have down periods. To hold or sell should be determined by the judgment as to whether it is a temporary glitch or a more fundamental problem. I usually give quality companies the benefit of the doubt because most overcome their problems and come roaring back. Although I am geared for the long run, I realize that no garden will flourish without judicious weeding, and so I do indeed unload stocks when I consider it appropriate.

I believe in the miracle of compounding. Unfortunately, the magical results only come later, much later; in the beginning, it seems as if one is progressing at a snail's pace. This requires the incredible discipline of saving all of the principal and reinvesting the dividends. In other words, one needs to live one's life without access to the accumulating portfolio. Dipping in for current needs will markedly lessen future benefits.

My effort is to obtain quality companies in preferred areas of investment. I have favored areas of investment of course, but other industries are needed for purpose of balance. With the recent market downturn, it has become apparent that one cannot be totally dependent on only one or two industries. The stock market bears a relationship to a symphony; first one instrument or group of instruments carry the melody, then it passes to another, and another. Therefore, some diversity in other industries is necessary. I also am old fashioned enough to look at earning's growth. Admittedly there are some companies that do not demonstrate this, perhaps because of a down period, new acquisition, employment of new technology, etcetera. In general, however, I like to see quality companies with rising earnings. I like to see adaptability to new times and new technologies. I also like to see skilled management. The difference between Jack Welch (GE) and Al Dunlap (Sunbeam) is simply enormous. Intelligent growth versus slash and burn; long-term goals versus short-term goals; business decisions mixed with sensitivity versus total unconcern for the welfare of workers and stakeholders.

What about bonds? To me they are an integral part of the portfolio. They provide diversity, safety, and increased yield. If the money is to be reinvested, then a steady income stream greater than for equities is necessary. In tax-free accounts, corporate bonds are desirable, since they pay a higher yield, while in a taxable account municipal bonds, because they are tax-free, are preferred. I regard preferred stock as essentially a fixed investment. The percentage of the portfolio in fixed income securities should vary with the nature and goals of the portfolio.

Virtually everyone who invests regularly has at least two accounts, an IRA or 401k and a personal account. For tax-exempt accounts, a higher percentage should be in fixed equities, since the income received is tax free; in a more aggressive personal account, the percentage of fixed incomes should be less. Balance is a key word to me, both within various types of equities and between equities and fixed investment modalities.

What about mutual funds? There is no doubt that some people have done very well with them, and they require little effort after the particular fund has been chosen. There is a great deal of security in turning over the management of the money to professionals. I prefer in large part to make my own investments, to decide whether or when particular investments should be sold or held, but I understand that there are other thoughts about that. I do try to make use of mutual funds to participate in areas where I have little or no knowledge: for example, overseas funds, small cap stocks, etcetera. I also participate in index funds to access companies that I would not invest in on an individual basis, since I would have little or no knowledge of these companies.

It is helpful not to look back; shoulda, coulda, woulda is not the way to spend your time. Look back only to try and learn from the inevitable mistakes we all make. After that, spend your time looking ahead. Jealousy is also a poor substitute for sensible decisions. One cannot but have a twinge of jealousy when one hears about people who have made an extraordinary amount of money, sometimes due to shrewdness and other times to luck. The same reaction occurs when someone wins the lottery. After that fleeting thought, however, one needs to get on with one's own life and not worry about others. I am fully cognizant that there are many ways to invest and that the only way that counts is how much money is being made, but I am comfortable with my investment philosophy and plan to stick to it.

Socialism

Socialism is essentially a twentieth-century phenomenon, as most modern countries during that period of time experienced a wrenching change: the movement of rural populations to the cities, changing from an agrarian to industrial existence (to the postindustrial high technology we see today). The inevitable inequities and burdens produced by such deep shifts of population led many to postulate that the national government should become more involved in economic matters. In many countries the state had ownership of basic industries (transportation, fuel, electricity, telephone, etcetera). In a few cases, the state controlled all industries. In others, powerful government agencies dictated which industries should be promoted and protected and which not. This promotion included access to capital, protectionism for industries when they were in their infancy, and dumping techniques to gain a foothold on foreign shores.

We have, therefore, seen in this century a worldwide flirtation with socialism, albeit in many different forms. The National Socialism of WWII Germany permitted private industry to exist, but their needs were subject to the needs of the state. Communist socialism had the state owning all economic activity, with centralized government agencies dictating which projects should be undertaken and setting production standards, wages, and output. Indeed everything related to economic activity was controlled by a centralized bureaucracy. It is not difficult to see how, over time, such a system would stifle initiative and be completely unresponsive to local needs and conditions.

Western socialism (including Israel) differed greatly, but in most cases the basic industries were in the hands of the government, and this in turn affected all economic activity. Trade unions were extraordinarily powerful and were certainly not a force for change; the status quo and the perpetuation of their perks were their main driving force. East Asian socialism (particularly Japan) and also others put the power of decision making not in the marketplace but in an all-powerful government ministry, which eventually foundered badly as government bureaucrats tried to outguess the marketplace and failed.

All have failed. The how and why can be illustrated in the hundred years of Israeli (a version of Western) socialism. At the beginning of Israeli settlement, a century ago, there was nothing, a tiny untrained population in a barren and desolate land. It is difficult to understand the problems faced by the early settlers, since no infrastructure for a modern industrial state existed. Transportation (railroads, roads, harbors, airports) was primitive or nonexistent. Public utilities to provide power and lighting were also primitive, as were communications. Access to capital was limited by the absence of a banking system. Other than small family enterprises, there was no manufacturing and very few individuals indeed with the knowledge and ability to run large business enterprises in place. All this in the face of extremely harsh and difficult conditions—both of the land and the relentless hatred of the Arabs.

Socialism was the only way to go. After the establishment of the state, the Labor party ruled uninterruptedly for the next twenty-nine years, and the weakness of the socialist system began to become apparent. In basic industries, powerful labor unions fought tooth and nail to maintain the status quo—bloated work forces with inefficient management and an ever-larger government bureaucracy to oversee the industry. Stifling of competition was endemic. Nepotism was rampant. Noncompetitive industries, which needed the state to bail them out, as well as those organizations that got into trouble through their own ineptitude and mismanagement were present in all fields of business and industry. It was more important to have proteksia (contacts in the government) than business smarts.

Satisfying all of these various groups' needs meant ever-higher taxes with resultant inflation. In short, a socialism that started from necessity and commitment deteriorated over time to a dangerous situation in which the country became noncompetitive within the world economy. The efforts of the last decade or two have been to reverse the process and make Israel a competitor in the world economy—with resistance from those who benefited from the old system all of the way.

If socialism on a worldwide basis is such an abysmal failure, why do so many people continue to believe in it? Feeling good is a common ideal of adherents to socialism. But feeling good is not the same as doing good. It is perfectly true that capitalism, in the hands of some people, can be heartless, and some people are left behind. Efforts should be directed towards reducing to a minimum the number of people in such straits, with those who are found to be unable to compete and even function within the system taken care of as wards of the state. Those who condemn capitalism forget that there is a trade-off—the concept of fairness and equality (with all the problems that those concepts eventually bring about as shown above) versus the release of an enormous amount of energy and self-interest, which transforms nations and their inhabitants. Our current economic boom (and indeed the boom around the world) clearly demonstrates this transformation made possible by capitalism—enlightened capitalism. I believe the fundamental problem with those who tout socialism is a misinterpretation of what socialism is. They fantasize a kind, wise, genteel bureaucracy objectively and fairly dispensing aid for the overall good of the state. People like themselves.

We Won

They call each other guys. They wear shirts and ties and suspenders to go along with their suits. They wear tuxedos. They smoke cigars. They have their own single-sex clubs. They attend strip shows and raucously cheer on their favorites. And, not least, they work extremely hard in high stress jobs, with consequent damage to physical and mental health.

It looks like we males won. After all, imitation is the sincerest form of flattery. However, I believe we lost, badly. What an individual or a family does is absolutely none of my business. They will choose whatever is best for themselves. However, looking at the problem from the point of view of society and its needs rather than from the point of view of each individual and family unit, we have lost a great deal.

The recent disclosure that more than half of the applicants for a teacher's certificate, coming from various teachers' education facilities, were unable to pass a standardized examination is nothing short of shameful. The breakdown in school discipline, the generalized lack of teaching ability and the poor results obtained by students on standardized testing, and the push for vouchers and charter schools all suggest that we are in an education crisis. Wouldn't it be better for society to have the best and the brightest educating our next generation? Do we really need more lawyers? Do we need more ad executives, business people, etcetera? Remember, I am looking at this from the point of view of society, not of the individual.

Well, you might say, why does it have to be females? Why can't men do the teaching? Of course they can and they should and they do. There is an interesting gradient of male teachers from preschool to postgraduate school. Although there are virtually no males teaching preschool, kindergarten, and the first few grades, by the time one reaches graduate school, there is a preponderance of males, and most particularly in the hard sciences and math. Perhaps the predominance of females in the lower grades is related to the need for nurturing in the very young, and females do that better than males. But whatever it is, the bulk of teaching in the lower grades has been the province of females, and we as a society need the very best there is. This is unlikely to happen for a wide variety of reasons, but included among them is the apparent glamour of other jobs compared to the perceived humdrum of teaching.

More important perhaps than having females participating to the full in such occupations that are most important to society is the role of females in the home. Feminists disparage the role of the homemaker. In my view they are completely wrong. For whatever reason, females are the ones who socialize and domesticate males. The males' natural tendency, as is true in most mammalian species, is to roam far and wide and spread their seed as widely as possible for the propagation of the species. It is the female of the species, by a combination of techniques, who trains the male to become reasonably monogamous and to become a part of the family unit, participating in the rearing of the young. It is of course with the young, whose growth and development is necessary for the survival of the species, where the female role is so critical.

Children are born wild (in a state of nature) and must be civilized, a process that has been refined and perfected over tens of thousands of years. An interesting experiment (albeit not planned) has taken place in our inner cities. With children having children (and not having the foggiest notion about child rearing) and with the disappearance of the male from the home and the disappearance of community organizations to show what is permissible and what is not, we have unleashed a large number of males as predators and females as breeders. What a tragic waste of human resources. What a waste of money on such nonproductive enterprises such as welfare, a greatly enlarged judicial and police system, as well as a vastly enlarged system of incarceration (prisons).

I firmly believe that everyone should have the opportunity to reach his or her maximum potential. But by no means should this be carte blanche to do anything (legal) that one wants. There are needs of the larger society, which must be met if one is to sustain such a society. This implies sacrifice, denial of the present for the future, financial costs, and many others. This idea of rights of the self versus the needs of society was firmly enshrined within each citizen. Now the scale has tipped so far to individual self-fulfillment that the larger needs of society are neglected. This is a loss for all of us.

III

Politics—Domestic

Bard College and What It Teaches Us

It was a typical William Buckley "Firing Line" TV program. There was a moderator, a conservative panel, and a liberal panel, as well as a live audience on the campus of Bard College. Of note, on the liberal panel was the president of the host Bard College (Dr. Leon Botstein) as well as the president of the ACLU. Each side would make its points, in the usual debate minuet, accompanied by a few bon mots, quips, and zingers, designed to emphasize their point and to show how very, very clever they all were. All according to form, when noises were heard emanating from the back of the auditorium. These noises became louder and louder until it was impossible for the panel to continue.

The cameras swung around. Approximately four or five young people were standing in the rear and chanting something unintelligible, at least to me, at least in the beginning. The chanting died down, and the program resumed, only to be interrupted again by even louder chanting. The group requested (demanded would be more accurate) to come to the podium to present their demands. The spokesman of the panel announced to the audience that they had a series of demands relating to multicultural studies and multicultural faculty hiring and that they wanted their demands met in full, right then and there.

The president of the college was completely flustered. He mumbled almost incoherently about working out problems together, but eventually he told them he would meet with them at a later time. Somehow they were persuaded to stop, and what remained of the program continued.

The cameras periodically turned to the conservative panel. All kept a straight face but their body language showed enormous enjoyment. The moderator was completely nonplussed and appeared to be in over his head. The moderator certainly received no guidance from anyone, including the president of the college as to how to proceed. A call for a five-minute break and a request from the panelists as to how to proceed would have been appropriate. The faces on the liberal panel showed dismay, surprise, confusion, and extreme embarrassment, and clearly wished it would all go away.

When they rose to speak, however, their words were of conciliation, the importance of free speech, the necessity of listening to each other, the correctness of the protesters' cause, etcetera. Not a word of outrage. What a lost opportunity. They (the panel) could have thoroughly denounced the students for the inappropriateness of their timing. They could have emphasized that the panelists, the attending audience, and the TV audience also had civil rights, and these were being impinged upon by the protesters. They could have emphasized that in a democracy, people have responsibilities in addition to rights.

One panelist finally mentioned that this was not the forum for a protest, but it appeared to me to be a weak and mealy response. Dr. Botstein also responded and gave the most flaccid, vacuous response possible—long on working out their problems together and short of anything decisive. He could have said very firmly that the persistent violation of the rights of others would lead to physical removal from the hall. He and the other panelists did none of those things. Instead they mumbled platitudes, caved in, and, in effect, agreed to the terms of the protesters.

Several interesting lessons were learned from that night. It was easy to see how liberal administrations on various campuses had caved in so easily to protesters (in at least one case, armed protesters) during the Vietnam War and Civil Rights movement protests. It was easy to see the difference in behavior when abstract, philosophic, scholarly academic discussions were taking place and when the presence of unpleasant reality forced its way upon the scene. One would certainly not want these liberals beside oneself in foxholes. The question arises: how would people with this mind-set behave when faced with far more dangerous situations on a national and international level? The answer is not very encouraging.

Cinq a Sept

It is now more than a year since the Clinton scandals resulted in an impeachment trial by the Senate, with resultant acquittal. But the arguments and the discussions continue. The waters are continually muddied by the claim that the problem was strictly about sex, when the real charges were lying under oath and suborning perjury. Further, there is a segment of the population that says it is okay to lie under oath about sexual matters. What these people do not say is what other civil matters it is okay to lie about—divorce proceedings, child custody, etcetera? Why bother to take an oath to tell the truth, the whole truth, and nothing but the truth when, at the same time, it is felt okay to tell lies when it is convenient?

Another segment of the population compares the sexual behavior of President Clinton with others in public life, such as the putative Republican candidate for the U.S. Senate from New York, mayor of New York City, Rudolph Giuliani. These people cannot say that it is all right for Clinton but not all right for their political opponent, without being a laughingstock, but they do say that they can see no difference between the behavior of the two men.

Yet there are fundamental differences between their behavior, with the admitted unifying theme that both were having extramarital affairs. Clinton had his affair in the White House. Giuliani had his outside the mayor's residence, Gracie Mansion. Clinton had his affairs while at least some of the time conducting government business. Giuliani had his on his own private time. Clinton had his with an individual who only technically was an adult. Giuliani had his with a real adult. Clinton had his with an individual whom as a White House intern was under his supervision. Giuliani had his with a woman over whom he had no supervisory relationship. Finally, and most important, Clinton lied under oath about his relationship, and Giuliani did not.

The underlying question is how we, the public, and the media, deal with marital infidelity by public figures, assuming it is done discreetly and without the circumstances outlined above. None of us wish to see the White House up for sale to the highest bidders, neither do we wish to see it turned into a brothel, but what about discreet liaisons outside the White House? Is it our business, or is it something to which we should turn a blind eye, leaving it to the family to sort it out? It is interesting to see the public claiming that it is none of their business and yet clamoring for every bit of gossip and more from every possible source.

In the past, the media had an unwritten agreement not to report on the dalliances that were going on by the occupants in the White House and without. That is no longer possible because of the sheer number of media people, the levels of bribery available to White House personnel by the media (directly and indirectly via book publication, etcetera), and most important a changing code of honor and of discretion in our society. I therefore think a new paradigm is necessary. Such behavior within the White House cannot and should not be tolerated, and they should be exposed as soon as they are known. We cannot accept misbehavior of any kind within the White House if we are to place our trust in that individual and that institution, the executive branch of our government. However, the president is an individual who is entitled to some privacy, and what he or she does on his or her own time really shouldn't be our concern; it should only be the concern of the family.

The French have done it that way for years with the hallowed tradition of the *cinq a sept,* where from the hours of 5:00 P.M. to 7:00 P.M. the businessman or public official would discreetly spend the time with his mistress before returning to the bosom of his family for dinner and quality time. Ideally the media should turn a blind eye to such behavior and truly be the sophisticates they claim to be. On the other hand, the president should know that if he indulges in such behavior, there is a high risk of being found out. Once the tabloids, web sites, etcetera have such information, it will be open season for all the media, and the clamoring of the public for more will be insatiable. It is up to him.

Clinton: Impeach or Not

As this is being written, the House Judiciary Committee is in the process of voting our Articles of Impeachment against President Clinton. Two of the four articles have been passed. Therefore, it is clear that there will be a debate and vote on the floor of the House as to whether or not to impeach, setting up a trial by the Senate. I do not deny the rightness of the position of the majority in wishing to impeach the president.

Surely subversion of the judiciary system, by itself as powerful a charge as any against President Nixon, deserves punishment by impeachment. The question on my mind, however, is not whether it is right to impeach this president but whether it is wise.

Serious constitutional questions regarding this impeachment have been raised. That of course does not make them right. (I am deeply suspicious that these very same historians, lawyers, etcetera would have a very different take on the situation if it were a Republican president involved and they were appearing before a Democratic majority Congress.) Nevertheless, the questions raised are serious, not frivolous, and for the sake of history, one should have general agreement on the constitutionality of the actions of Congress. Second, it is nowhere near a bipartisan action and will clearly be labeled partisan no matter what the outcome. I find it difficult to credit the argument that impeachment is thwarting the will of the people who elected the president. I never once heard that argument during the entire, long, dismal Watergate affair, but you can be sure it will be made. Also it is clearly the duty of Congress to consider impeachment of the president, but it is under no obligation to do so. Finally, there are the legal (and illegal) actions on the part of the president that play a role in limiting his maneuvering ability.

Well, what about censure. Whatever the language, it will come out as "Mr. President, you were a very, very naughty boy, and we don't approve of your actions. Please don't do it again." It will not take twenty-four hours after passage of such a censure resolution for the president and his supporters in Congress to proclaim that it was nothing more than a partisan witch-hunt by his enemies that brought this about; the act itself was nothing more than a private peccadillo, which he would work out with his family. And so on.

Clearly something more than censure and perhaps less

than impeachment is needed. I would suggest censure plus humiliation. Here's how it would work. The president should be relieved of legal liability so that aspect of his problem does not cloud his judgment as to whether or not to accept his punishment. Then, on State of the Union night, the drama would unfold. Instead of the backslapping, hand-shaking, cheering, and clapping going on, the president would enter the Chamber to utter silence, preceded only by the sergeant at arms, walking at a funereal pace. Undoubtedly some of the Republicans would turn their back on his slow progression down the aisle to the well of the chamber. There he would receive the treatment suggested by President Ford. I would suggest two members of the House and two members of the Senate, two Democrats and two Republicans, who would deliver strong rebukes to the president for his action. None would speak longer than five minutes, twenty minutes in all. The president would then hand to clerk his State of the Union address, no longer than thirty minutes. He would then be escorted out of the chamber in the same fashion as he entered, slowly following the sergeant at arms. Then the clerk would read the address, in a monotone, again to complete silence. In one hour, it would all be over and perfectly obvious to the entire country and, indeed, the world that the president sinned grievously and received the one treatment he likes the least, public humiliation.

Some other details are necessary. It should be made known that his presence for the State of the Union message in the year 2000 was not welcome either. He would voluntarily pay a token fine for the expense and trouble he put the country through, and he would commit to a certain amount of community work after he retired from the presidency. The White House and the congressional democrats would have to agree with the process and sign a letter to that agreement so that they could not later claim that they did not approve of the treatment of the president. Those who do not sign should be banished to the outermost reaches of the House chamber, so that they could not disrupt the proceedings.

It would be difficult (although certainly not impossible) for anyone to complain that the president was treated too harshly, since virtually everyone will admit in private that he is clearly guilty and he (and we) was spared the nightmare of impeachment and trial. The Republicans would be seen as taking the moral high ground, carefully pointing out to the public the damage he has done to the Constitution, the presidency, and the country and, yet, sparing him not for his own sake but for the good of the country.

More likely the Republicans will travel a self-destructive path in trying to be right, but not too wise.

Clinton

It is now a year since the nation was in turmoil over the president's impeachment and trial. There was intense partisanship on both sides. Democrats insisted that it was "only sexual," a personal failing having nothing to do with the running of the country. Republicans acted as they did because many did not simply differ with him on political issues but truly despised him, for a variety of reasons. One reason is simply that he clearly outmaneuvered them politically, something clearly mortifying to these old Washington hands. Another reason is that he appears to be a man of no fixed beliefs, governing by polls and changing beliefs to fit the polls. For example, if he proclaimed "the end of big government as we know it," why is he now proposing more and more social programs?

Perhaps more important, people are truly upset not only about his moral laxity (probably a nearly universal feeling) but also by the multiple abuses of his office. The selling of the White House and its perks (sleeping in the Lincoln bedroom, rides on Air Force One, coffee and tea with the president, etcetera) were hardly unique to this president but were done on a massive scale, far more massive and far more organized than anyone previously.

There has been a general atmosphere of tawdriness that has accompanied the current occupants of the White House. If things were not specifically illegal, the sheer number of unpleasant events had made many people distinctly uncomfortable. It smells more of corrupt local politics than the high mindedness one should expect from the nation's chief executive officer. Finally, there is a disconnect between the high moral tone and the low behavior, which makes for even more discomfort.

In my opinion, the Democrats have a great deal to answer for. Their argument that this was a personal foible is patently false and may come back to haunt everyone. If sexual relationships are purely personal and therefore permit lying under oath, what would happen in the future if a sitting president were involved in, say a divorce proceeding or a child custody case. These are personal, too. Indeed, how much lying is permissible (national security issues aside)? Should we have a list of subjects where lying is permissible? The president of course was not impeached because of personal foibles but for lying under oath to a grand jury and for obstruction of justice. In these areas, whatever the outcome of the trial, damage to the presidency has taken place.

Here are some of the damages. For the first time, it was determined that the secret service must testify under oath, presidential aides must testify under oath, and the president himself must testify before a federal grand jury. Although perhaps implied, the above was never put to the test, and probably should not have been. One can debate who was responsible for this, but it would never have come up if the president had behaved differently. I find it nothing short of incredible that the chief law enforcement officer of the land lied under oath to a federal grand jury. How can that have positive effects in the future?

I do not believe, in general, that it is any of my business what a person's extramarital life is like. It is between the individual and the spouse. But I do have a big problem with the use of the Oval Office as the site of trysts. It is clear that he is an attractive and desirable male. Had he wished to indulge, he could have found a discreet nest or multiple nests somewhere in the Washington area where he could do what he wished, and only a very few people would have known about it. He did not do that but rather had sexual relations (his contesting of this to the contrary), often while having political discussions, that is, carrying out the business of the country. There must be a reason for it. I believe he did it there because, as he always had, he felt he could get away with it. He was figuratively thumbing his nose at the American people.

One can claim that the actions of the independent counsel and the congressional Republicans were motivated by animus alone and had no other basis for their actions. There, of course, may be some element of truth to that, although, as I outlined above, there is more than enough damage caused by Clinton to make their actions seem reasonable. That is something that I think will be seen in the future, as current passions wind down and people start looking more objectively at the situation. It is the Democrats who should be blushing, since their position, I believe, is untenable. I have noted the adverse effects on the office of the presidency, which are quite real and can only be revealed in the future.

There are at least two examples of double standards employed by the Democrats. The first is Watergate. I never heard anyone state that Nixon was responsible for only a burglary, and a third-rate one at that. When Reagan's attorney general was apparently involved in a shady deal, the hatchets were out.

When he had a trial and was acquitted, they (the Democrats) said that he (Edwin Meese) breached the appearance of propriety to be expected of an attorney general, and he should therefore resign. One decade later that idea was turned on its head. The president committed improprieties, but he should not be impeached and he should not resign. Could the Democrats be substituting partisan politics for underlying principle? Of course they are. They are saying that economic times are good and they agree with his politics, so that makes it right.

The attitude of the public is difficult to understand. In spite of everything, he still gets high approval ratings. The vast majority of the public knows, in the nonlegal sense, that he lied under oath and was involved in a cover-up to hide it. They also know, again in the nonlegal sense, that a rape took place in Arkansas, with Juanita Broadderick as the victim. There were also multiple episodes where he was involved with less than willing partners, where he used his powers of office to obtain sexual favors. Yet they continue to support him. Why? Is it that economic times are so good that people are willing to overlook what they consider to be personal peccadilloes? Is it that moral relativism is the current feeling in the land?

It cannot be denied that he is not only the president of the United States, an office of incredible power, as well as a skilled politician, but also an attractive man, young, energetic, charming. He claims to feel everyone's pain. He has diversified his presidential appointments, bringing many people into the government who might not be there under other administrations, particularly Republicans. To my mind, however, they cannot overcome the damage that has been caused. It is clear to me that politics have been masquerading as principles. I believe that the phenomenon known as Clinton fatigue, which is a weariness with regard to all things related to the Clinton travails, is not just weariness. Rather, it is a secret recognition that he did things that were terribly wrong, and in a way, by supporting him, the public was compliant.

The behavior of Hillary is also difficult to explain. She claims that she is a strong individual in her own right and not a victim. Yet she appears to benefit from victimhood. The dynamics of their marriage are simply too difficult to figure out, so I will pass on that.

We as a country have had a gut-wrenching experience. For most, partisan politics (on both sides) have dominated the supposedly high-minded principles. I believe that lasting damage has been done to the office of the presidency. Already, in interviews, Clinton is on the attack, claiming that he was a victim, and by not resigning he was a defender of the Constitution. These will probably become more frequent in months to come as he struggles to have a lasting and positive legacy. My own feeling is that for the preservation of the presidency, the avoidance of the impeachment and the trial by the Senate, with the resultant paralysis of the government and the country, for the abysmal judgment exhibited and, yes, for honor's sake, he should have resigned the presidency.

Elia Kazan

The recent reinstallation of Elia Kazan into the good graces of Hollywood predictably raised old questions that had lain dormant for decades: was there a real Communmist threat coming from Hollywood? Was it proper for Kazan to "give up" friends? What would have been the consequences to him and to his country if he did not do so? Many people who write about those times in a disparaging fashion have no real idea of what the world was like after WWII (1945 to, say, the early sixties).

Western Europe was prostrate. We dismantled our huge army in Europe and brought it home in extraordinary haste.

Some were bound for the Pacific and the assault on Japan, but most were destined to be demobilized. I think it can be safely said that it was not our remaining army but the presence of nuclear weapons that held the Soviets at bay until NATO could be organized and equipped as a shield against Soviet expansion. The brutal takeover of the Central European states with suppression of all opposition was followed by the Berlin blockade, revolutionary "wars of national liberation," assistance to the North Koreans in their invasion of the South, and enormous spying and propaganda wars against the West. As I have noted, I believe the only thing that held them in check until a defensive alliance could be formed was the atomic bomb.

One can understand the attachment by some to a socialistic (communistic) society. In the 1930s we were in the midst of the Great Depression. There was significant disparity in income with a very small and wealthy upper class, a relatively modest middle class, and a large underclass, with the pain and disparity made much worse by the Depression. A society in which everyone was equal and was treated equally was certainly appealing.

However, feeling good was not the same as doing good. By the mid thirties the nightmare that was Communism started to be known. Show trials, murder of small land owners (Kulaks), communist-induced starvation with millions of deaths, the establishment of the gulag, and the reign of internal terror was surely known, at least in general outline, by those involved in the Communist party, USA, as well as related and similar thinking organizations.

It is difficult to know why they did not leave the Party en masse after such knowledge became generally known. Denial was clearly one factor. A second was the difficulty in admitting that closely held beliefs were totally wrong. It was also difficult to know, as they observed at close hand the workings of the Commmintern (Communist international), with constant internal propaganda, endless group think and group speak, hatred of the U.S., intolerance of diversity, and forgiveness of anything and everything by the USSR, that something was not right.

Given the above facts, it is difficult to understand the continued acceptance by the left of a system that in every way proved to be bankrupt. Although that is difficult to understand, I find it impossible to understand how well-meaning people could countenance the Nazi/Soviet pact of 1939. It was anti-Fascism more than anything else that was the glue that held them in the party and let them avert their eyes to the reality of what was happening in the Soviet Union in the thirties. How could anyone remain a loyal Communist or, to use the phrase then current, a fellow traveler, not realize what they were dealing with. To their credit, many did leave, but we are talking here about those who did remain in that orbit.

The threat posed by the Communists (China included) in the post-WWII era was quite real, revisionist historians to the contrary. The Communists had extraordinary luck in having as opponents charlatans and fools like Joseph McCarthy, Martin Dies, Karl Mundt, and others. However, foolishness and malignancy on the part of the above political class did not mean that there was not a real threat. To the contrary, it was a very real threat.

It is perfectly true that Hollywood people did not work in sensitive industries where they could spy or commit sabotage. They did not work in basic industries where strikes could cripple the economy, although others did and the unions had a knock-down drag-out war to rid themselves of Communist influence. Many in Hollywood were members of the Screen Actors Guild, the Screen Writers Guild, and the Screen Director's Guild, and all were the site of wars similar to those in other unions. They were, however, involved in communication—mass communication—and that did make a difference as to how we viewed the starting struggle that became the Cold War. After all, the work of Josef Goebbels and his propaganda machine on the part of the Nazis was recent and well known for its powerful effects. Why not in other causes as well?

Given the above, was Kazan right or wrong in informing on others? It should be understood that the blacklist of the people who were named was put in place by the studio heads, not Kazan. They were for the most part super patriots, but they also saw the potential damage to the industry if known Communists held positions of influence in what was at the time the only national means of visual communication (radio did not have the same impact on people's imagination as movies and, later, television) for the general public. Television was in its infancy. It is also true that everyone hates an informant (a snitch), although they do not hate the information provided. Crime fighting would be far less effective if every cop on the beat did not have a snitch who would keep him informed of pending trouble. The mob would be far more potent today if the FBI and the district attorneys did not have informants. Defeating the Nazis and subsequently the Soviets would have been difficult if the CIA and other government agencies did not carry informants. The current war on drugs would be a complete sham without the aid of informants. And so on. So we have a dilemma. Informants play a central role in the struggle of the good guys against the bad guys, and yet they are looked down upon as a lower form of human being.

All those under suspicion could have confessed and recognized their errors. Some did, but others remained defiant. Those who remained defiant claimed that they were victims and martyrs, but were they? The overwhelming evidence was that they were mistaken and were following a false God. Facts were never permitted to intrude on their thought processes. They must therefore still have felt kinship for CPUSA, which was part of the Commintern, and it, in turn, was under the control of the USSR, with whom we were in a Cold War. They deserved to be outed.

Enigmas

As this is being written, the Senate is still hearing testimony and asking questions in the impeachment trial of President Clinton. The outcome at this time is uncertain although one could certainly make an educated guess about the result. Throughout this yearlong ordeal, there have been for me three enigmas.

Enigma #1: What could have motivated the president to do it? Remember, he came with a great deal of baggage from Arkansas, where he was known by the sobriquet of Slick Willie, in part because of his ability to shade the truth. In 1992, he and his wife did "Checkers" II, where, on television they denied that he had an affair with Jennifer Flowers. Subsequently, he did admit to the affair, to the shock of very few. Then there was the ongoing matter of Paula Jones's sexual harassment suit, as well as lingering doubts about a number of transactions, including Whitewater, Filegate, Travelgate, etcetera. Perhaps the Clintons truly believed it or perhaps it was politically convenient, but to their mind, a vast right-wing conspiracy existed, with the sole purpose of bringing the president down. To that end, they (the conspiracists) monitored his actions in minute detail. Finally, the president was looking to the future and wished to enhance the stature of his presidency, so that his legacy would be compared favorably to the best of our twentieth-century presidents.

Given all of the above, what in the world could possess the president to do what he did where he did it. If it were his intention to have sexual relations, he could have set up any number of mistresses in any number of pads outside of the White House. There would be any number of people who would front for him by sitting in the parlor while he had his pleasure upstairs. They would consider it a patriotic duty to do so. If you doubt me, recall the woman who said that because of his position on abortion, he could have sex with her anytime. There were numerous assents to that sentiment.

So, why did the president have relations in the Holy of Holies, the Oval Office complex? Where other people were nearby? While his family was in the White House? While conducting government business? With an intern who was approximately the age of his daughter? Someone who, as an intern, was nominally under his charge? I cannot accurately answer that question, since it remains enigmatic to me, but there are a number of possibilities. The thrill of reckless behavior, and even more, the getting away with such behavior, as he had done in the past is one possibility. Arrogance and a sense of superiority over lesser beings is another possibility. A lack of concern for the sanctity of the White House and its meaning to the American people is a third possibility. I suspect that however charming and popular, he exhibits a fundamental lack of character. More than that, it is possible that he truly does not feel the difference between right and wrong—everything is relative, everything can be shaded, everything can be interpreted in light of the needs of the moment. I admit that all of the above is simply guesswork.

Enigma #2: Why is there such a continuing, and even growing, popular support of the president? During all of the yearlong travails, with subsequent and begrudging admissions of lying, his popularity has stayed high. After his State of the Union address, his approval rating rose to nearly seventy-five percent. Why? The first answer given by most is the rising economy with low unemployment and a stock market that just will not quit. This president, and indeed it would be true of every other president, takes advantage of this as well as taking the credit. Actually the pride of place in terms of credit surely would go to the CEOs of corporations, their officers and their boards, as well as the liberated energy of entrepreneurs who have created whole industries where none existed a decade or two ago. Second would be the monetary policy of the Federal Reserve, and only a distant third, the fiscal policies of the president, which is decided in conjunction with Congress. It is only human for the president to claim credit, since good things happened on his watch. The question to ask, however, is how different would the economy and the governmental response to it be if Al Gore, and not Bill Clinton, were president. Not very much I am sure.

It cannot be denied, by friends or enemies, that President Clinton is a masterful politician. He is able to relate to people in an apparently sincere way, making them think that he is serious about their concerns, so it becomes a two-way love fest. He has reached out to minority groups in a way that no president ever has, and these various groups, including an apparent majority of females, have responded with fervor. Add up all these groups and you are dealing with a majority of the population. Throw in programs that appeal to one or another of them and you have a source of popularity for the president that can be tapped for his advantage.

I believe he, more closely than any other politician, reflects the current values and mores of the population. Truth is relative. Self-gratification is all-important. Character, honor, and consistency of values is not of much use. The present is more important than the future. The Ten Suggestions replace the Ten Commandments. I hate to indict a large portion of the population, but this is certainly a possibility for their overwhelming support of him.

A final argument made in favor of his popularity is that he is seen as a charming rogue. Yes he does this or that improper thing, but he means well. He has not committed treason, and the country is doing well, so let's not rock the boat. This reminds me of Boss Curley of Boston, who governed as mayor of the city from his jail cell and, if I am not mistaken, ran a successful reelection campaign from jail.

To me, despite all the reasons given above, I have difficulty understanding why he has all this support, but what I understand even less is the reasons given for the support. It's only about sex, and it is private. The location and nature of the sex suggests that it is something more than just a private affair, ultimately something between the president and his wife. If he is convicted by the Senate, it is a coup d'etat. With the president replaced by his own choice of vice president (who also belongs to the same party)? It overthrows the election results. Isn't that what is supposed to happen, as enumerated in our Constitution?

Such concerns did not enter the public discussion with the pending impeachment of Richard Nixon, who was elected by an overwhelming majority. It does not rise to the level of a high crime. He was only lying because —— (fill in the blank). That of course is the nub of the argument, since in the court of public opinion he is guilty, the only thing to be determined is the nature of his punishment. Finally, what would the reaction be among Democrats if the president were a Republican rather than one of their fellow Democrats? I strongly suspect that it would be exactly the opposite of what it is now. And in all likelihood so would the response of the Republicans. People have a great deal of difficulty in differentiating their principles from their politics.

Enigma #3: Why are the Republicans so dense? It is not a question of right or wrong. In my opinion, they have right on their side. They are also earnest, sincere, and deeply and properly disturbed by the events of the past year and what it has meant for the country. It is really more a question of wisdom than of strict legal interpretation, a quality they seem to be sorely lacking. The goal is first to expose the type of behavior that took place, and which for so long was denied. Far more important than the fate of this president, is the protection of the presidency, and indeed the entire government, from having this happen again. In other words, the punishment must be severe enough to make it unlikely that anyone in the future would consider doing it again.

Were it in the cards, impeachment followed by removal from office would certainly be an appropriate deterrent for the future; however, it seems very unlikely that that will happen. Rather, it appears at this time that he will not be found guilty and therefore not removed from office. Because Democrats need it even more than Republicans, since they cannot be seen as condoning his behavior, some sort of censure resolution will probably be passed. Although well meant, that could be mischievous. It is not in the Constitution. It could be seen in the future as a way to threaten a president, and doing so would erode the concept of the three coequal branches of government.

If, however, a censure resolution is passed, it will have no teeth and will be passed off as part of a right-wing conspiracy. One can be sure that even if the Senate vote fails to force a resignation, it too and the whole episode will be labeled as a right-wing conspiracy. One can also be reasonably sure that Clinton will take no, or minimal, responsibility for his actions. As if not bad enough, it is likely that the Republicans will be pulverized at the polls in the year 2000. What they will have, in all likelihood, accomplished is to fail to convict the president, be blamed for the events of the past year, and be punished politically as well.

The only way to deal with someone like this, someone who has out politicked you at every turn, is to employ humiliation. Humor would be better, but it would be difficult to top what has already been said and written, and it has all rolled off the president. Humiliation on the other hand, particularly if signed onto by both parties, would probably be the one thing that he could not tolerate. There are many forms this humiliation could take, with all falling within his official duties. As President Ford suggested, he could be openly and publicly chastised. He could have been denied the privilege of giving his State of the Union address in person. There are many other ways that would make it apparent to all that his behavior was completely unacceptable to the American people and their representatives. Instead, the Republicans have pursued a course that may well end up hurting them more than the president.

There is really little debate about the crime; rather it is about the appropriate punishment. It seems likely that Slick Willie of Arkansas will slip out of a difficult situation of his own making once again.

Feminists and Politics

Feminists have consistently confused politics with principles and have thereby discredited themselves in the eyes of a large number of Americans. I am referring of course to their total inability to condemn President Clinton in any way, in spite of behavior that would be loudly denounced in other circumstances.

One has only to look at the former Senator Robert Packwood affair and the confirmation hearings on Clarence Thomas for the elevation to the Supreme Court to see an extraordinary double standard at work. Like Clinton, Packwood was a strong advocate of women's rights. He also had a propensity to proposition women and at times to pinch bottoms. When the message to him from his subject was unequivocally no, he desisted. There was never any suggestion of force involved. In spite of his record on women's issues, he had to go, and go he did.

What is even more astonishing is their behavior towards Clarence Thomas during his confirmation hearing. The feminists, with great emotion, claim they "knew" that Anita Hill's version of the story was the true one. How did they "know"? Well, they just knew. None of them claim that they just "knew" that Jennifer Flowers, Paula Corbin Jones, and Juanita Broaddrick were telling the truth, although the story of Juanita Broaddrick involved an alleged rape. That is far, far more serious than what Clarence Thomas is purported to have done, left a pubic hair on a can of Coke and made suggestive remarks.

I don't know whether he did or not, but the level of the purported crime is so low, compared to what happened with Clinton, both in Arkansas and Washington, that it is hard to remember the fury that it awakened. I do not know, nor does anyone else but the two participants know what transpired. I have spoken with two women: one, a former neighbor of Thomas's and the other, a high-level worker at EEOC when Thomas headed the agency. Both emphatically denied that he could have done something like that. They both stressed that he was a "straight arrow" and such behavior would be far from his norm. Could they be wrong? Of course. But it is also possible that this whole tempest was more about politics than about principle.

If you are an organization or an individual with principles, you utilize them in your actions and let the chips fall where they may. After all, it takes no great courage to attack someone with whom you bitterly disagree politically. It does take courage to attack someone with whom you do agree on the basis of underlying principles. Feminists have not exactly shown themselves to be very courageous.

The relationship between Hillary Rodham Clinton and the feminist movement is also somewhat odd. It is perfectly true that she is a political soul mate of many of the feminists. However, her behavior during and after the travails of Bill Clinton is certainly foreign to expected feminist behavior. An independent woman (indeed any woman) should not have to be humiliated by her husband, and in public. She should not be a victim of her husband's behavior. She should not continue in such a relationship. That's the principle but not the performance, either on the part of HRC or the feminists. I am sure that she extracted a suitable price for standing by her man, but that is scarcely a matter of principle.

More recently the Florida secretary of state and a Republican, Katherine Harris, came under bitter attack. The attack apparently centered on, of all things, her wearing too much makeup, but in reality, it was her politics that were under attack. Her achievement in becoming a high-ranking state official was totally ignored by the feminists. Unfortunately for her she held the wrong politics, and thus there was no springing to her defense on the part of the feminist movement.

It seems clear that behind a mask of high principles, feminists are simply carrying out a political agenda, and to a large degree they have become discredited. They will continue to function, of course, but in a diminished role, since everyone will know that they stand for no principles, but simply for their own political interests.

Hillary Rodham Clinton

I must admit that I do not understand Hillary Rodham Clinton, nor do I understand her fervent admirers. When Bill Clinton was first elected, he declared that one was elected but two would govern (slight paraphrase). Leaving aside the dubious constitutionality of such an arrangement, she was placed in a position where she shared in the making of the policies of the administration. There were some good things that happened, and she deserves credit for participating in them. There were, however, an endless series of disasters for which she also must share the blame as a functioning co-president.

In early 1993, she undertook to reform the entire health care system, making up one-seventh of our economy. In ninety days (later changed to 150 days). In secret. With no knowledge of, or contact with, health care other than well-baby care. With no input from practicing physicians or their organizations. If you want a definition of chutzpah, you've got it. One has to wonder here why she did not undertake to reform the legal system, which is badly in need of reform, and about which she presumably knows a great deal. Rather, with the failure of her health initiative, she went from a president's wife who wouldn't be seen baking cookies to symbolically doing just that. She attended countless funerals, ceremonial openings, and international conferences—most meaningless, politically correct, and also endless.

Her insistence on a female for attorney general brought not one but two public relation disasters to the new administration. We found out that she was a miraculous investor making $100,000 from $1,000 in a short period of time. One wonders why she did not continue with her obviously fantastic ability, since there was always an underlying theme of their (the Clintons) poverty. Her billing records from the Rose law firm also appeared miraculously, apparently by immaculate conception, on a table in the upstairs sitting room. Will miracles never cease?

When the Lewinsky scandal broke, she did what she swore never to do—she stood by her man. She could have demonstrated her pain and disgust by leaving, but she did not. Rather, she went on the offensive, claiming that the problem was a vast right-wing conspiracy that did her husband in. She is certainly partially right, but what did her husband in was not the right wingers, but her husband himself.

There seems little doubt that she is bright, dedicated, and serious about certain causes. However, except in the eyes of her fervent followers, her achievements have been slight, she has failed miserably in the one major policy job she was given, and she has consistently done exactly what she had said she would not do—act as a domesticated First Lady and stand by her man. With the breaking of the Lewinsky scandal, she had the opportunity to bring a moral dimension to the presidency, but she did not.

If it is difficult for me to understand her, it is even more difficult for me to understand her followers. Most recently, the idea of running for the Senate from New York may turn out to be successful, but it sounds wacky to me. She has never held elective office (why start at the bottom when you can start at the top). She has never had administrative experience running a large organization (government, business, charitable). Further, she is a carpetbagger, never having lived in New York State. While it is true that New York has had carpetbaggers in the past, that will not make it any less of an issue.

On the face of it, it seems strange that New York cannot find a single home-grown worthy Democrat to represent it but must rely on an individual from outside the state. She could have waited for two years and made her run from her native state, Illinois, but she could not wait. This led to the preposterous statement that she was always a Yankee fan. It is true that pols often put on funny hats and say nice generic things to the audience being addressed. In general, people take such comments with a grain of salt. It is usually just campaign rhetoric, and they discount it. However, publicly it was well known that she was a lifelong Cubs fan, coming as she does from Chicago, but fibbing and the Clintons seem to go hand in hand—not a very nice attribute. Do fibs on small things precede fibs on larger issues? At least the question should be pondered.

I am troubled by her repeated references to a vast right-wing conspiracy. It is of course true that a large number of people on the right despise the Clintons, for their policy beliefs as well as for their behavior. It is also true that people who feel that way do finance efforts to discredit the Clintons. However, the words "vast" and "conspiracy" bother me. If the opposition is vast, then one might reasonably say that there is some merit in their argument. If it is a conspiracy, there has not been to my knowledge a single piece of evidence that this vast army of opponents are being organized and run by a single group, the essential nature of a conspiracy. That this concept is laughable can be demonstrated by substituting Nixon for Clinton. Was Nixon thrown out of office because of a vast left-wing conspiracy or because of his own actions? The answer is obvious but apparently does not percolate down to HRC. There has never been even the faintest hint that they, the Clintons, bear any responsibility whatsoever for the strong feelings against them.

Let's jump to the election and suppose that HRC wins. I see a disconnection between her goals, which probably includes aspirations for an even higher office, as well as changing the world in a fashion that she believes in, and the New York Staters' goal of fixing potholes. They laughed at Senator Al D'Amato's sobriquet of Mr. Pot Hole, but meeting the legitimate needs of her constituents is perhaps a boring, but necessary, part of her work. To accomplish that, she will of necessity have to make compromises, perhaps in some of her core beliefs. Can she do it? Will her fervid supporters stay with her when she becomes just a pol? Stay tuned.

So how do we explain the phenomenon of Hillary and her adoring minions? My guess is that the explanation is twofold. She is nothing if not politically correct, and that is why she is so admired. The second reason is that it is therapy. She was misused by her husband and a Senate seat will correct the hurt. How very new age. How very New York.

Legacy

Recently, much has been made of President Clinton's search for a legacy, presumably one more fitting than being the butt of late-night TV humor. We can always use some laughter in our lives, but that way? To my surprise, the *Washington Post* of 7/7/99 provided just such a legacy, an article about a middle-school group in the Virginia suburbs of Washington, D.C. involved in group oral sex. In the article, the blasé attitude of the kids towards what they were doing was striking. What's the big deal, they seemed to be saying. President Clinton did it, so why can't we? Can anyone doubt, given the pattern of youngsters imitating those older than themselves, that soon will follow widespread grade schoolers employing the same practice?

I don't know which idea will prevail: it is not really sex, or it is sex but it is no big deal? However, I suspect that the parents of those kids and those who have kids in that age group, no matter what their political affiliation or beliefs, are less than thrilled with this behavior in their children. I don't believe that they are amused, and I don't believe they are willing to engage in a philosophical debate—they undoubtedly just want it to stop.

So Mr. President, you now have your legacy. You can quit trying any further. Congratulations.

Pat Buchanan

Pat Buchanan has made waves again with a whole series of issues. He has bolted the Republican party, from whence I believe he will gradually sink into oblivion. Before that happens, however, there needs to be discussed a number of questions about him that have never been fully discussed, for reasons that follow.

The first question about him is whether or not he is an anti-Semite. He is certainly a hater of all people who are different. I believe he is also an anti-Semite. After all, if it walks like a duck, etcetera. Even if you don't buy that argument, you must admit that he is close enough not to have it made any meaningful difference. His empathy for Holocaust deniers and his empathy for Nazi prison guards who were clearly involved with crimes against humanity, if not the specific charges on which they were brought up, is of a piece with the rest.

To my mind, he follows a course started by Father Coughlin in Detroit and Father Feeney in Boston, both filled with vile hate and anti-Semitism and both excommunicated from the church for it. I have always been amazed that the Irish, sorely put upon in both the Old World and the New World, would produce and tolerate people who inflict the same intolerance on others as that inflicted upon them. It also seems to me that there is a lack of empathy on the part of the Irish for those groups who are clearly in need of it. Not all Irish of course, but enough to cause disturbing thoughts.

A second issue is his narrow, protectionist viewpoint at a time when the world is moving at warp speed towards globalism. He has some validity to his concept that some people have been hurt by the dramatic changes in the world economy, but trying to hold back the tide of globalism is something that neither King Canute nor Pat Buchanan can do. It is with equal amazement that politically he allies himself with the America Firsters—isolationists and haters of England—people whom I thought were thoroughly discredited after the start of WWII, but apparently, I was mistaken.

His largest, and most controversial thesis is that Hitler was not such a terrible guy and was one who harbored no grudge against the Western alliance, including America. Had we just let him alone, he would have spent his energy conquering the USSR, and both sides would have fallen back in exhaustion, leaving alone the rest of the world, particularly the Western alliance. His thesis is breathtaking in its folly, completely ignoring reality.

The thesis contradicts what is nearly universal thought: that WWII was a just war fought against an evil totalitarian, which had to be thoroughly beaten. His isolationist assessment (he even uses the words "America First," an organization of figures on the far right of the political spectrum during the thirties that vigorously opposed American involvement in a European war and was noticeably isolationist in its sentiments) is at complete odds with what the overwhelming majority of Americans felt. Yes, the American people did not wish to go to war, particularly with a prolonged depression still present, one that sapped America of its strength. But they also were readily able to distinguish the good guys from the bad guys. There is also a willful misreading of how totalitarians act, that they probe for weaknesses and strike when they find them, no matter what the cost in human misery. Totalitarians can be controlled only by the use of force or the threat of force. We have had many totalitarians in the twentieth century, and none have behaved differently.

Where he really stretches credulity, however, is the belief that the military campaign against the Soviets would have led to mutual exhaustion, making neither a threat to the West. It's not the war; it's the likely outcome his supporters say. There are a number of military outcomes from such a war, all bad for the West. Had Hitler started his military campaign against Russia in June instead of September (he was delayed by a brief campaign to subdue Yugoslavia), it seems likely that he would have conquered Moscow and have all of European Russia in his hands before the start of winter. That would almost certainly have meant the fall of Leningrad (Saint Petersburg), since there would have been no way to resupply it during the winter months.

The following year he would have conquered the Caucasus, leading to a breakout into the Middle East, thus controlling the huge supplies of oil, which he could deny to the West. At the time, America was independent in terms of oil supply, but Britain was not. With just this situation, he would have had Britain forced to sue for peace. Further, he would have then conquered Siberia and controlled the Trans-Siberian railway. This would give him direct access to Japan, importing raw materials from Southeast Asia and exporting finished goods, both military and civilian, as well as technologies and the technicians to direct them, even possibly military forces. It is difficult to see how this situation would help our war against Japan. Many more American lives would have had to be lost to defeat Japan.

By far the most dangerous thing, however, would be that, free of bombing from the West and given more time, Hitler could likely have completed the atomic bomb and the rockets to carry them to the U.S. In spite of heavy Allied bombing, he was still able to fire the prototypical VI and V2 rockets on England before the end of the war. We too might have had to capitulate. What a prospect. Also, do not forget, in addition to the rockets and the bomb, Hitler had jet aircraft years before anyone else. Our air fleets would have become instantly obsolete.

The most likely scenario of leaving Hitler free to conquer the Soviet Union, capture the oil fields of the Caucasus and the Middle East, hook up directly with Japan, and be free to develop his military might up to and including atomic bombs with an appropriate delivery system, is not even mentioned by Buchanan or his supporters. How come?

I believe that the Buchanan critics are naive in stating that one of our war aims was to prevent or mitigate the Holocaust, as well as destruction of Gypsies, gays, etcetera. Not likely, since it (the Holocaust) was known by only a relative few and cared about by even fewer. The farcical conferences at Evian and elsewhere attest to that. What concerns me about Buchanan's thinking is his complete indifference to evil, which had been matched only by the totalitarians of the left, the Soviets. Yes, it would be unfortunate. Buchanan says, but you have to look at the big picture. Millions upon millions slaughtered, tens of millions injured, and none of it moves him.

What Buchanan is saying now is not completely new, although perhaps more explicit. It has been said by him for decades. The reaction of the media is extraordinary, his TV haunts accepting his return with open arms after his political defeat and apologizing profusely for him for what clearly are unacceptable ideas. He is a marginal figure with marginal ideas, and they should be ashamed of themselves for not swatting him down. By and large, they have given him a free ride when they should have been all over his case. One of the less endearing traits of Buchanan is when caught in a falsehood or a clear misinterpretation of facts, he turns boyish and with a choirboy smile, he says he didn't say that, he was only kidding, etcetera. And somehow the media buys it—every time.

Perceptions, Liberals vs. Conservatives

Bitter fighting continuously takes place in Washington between liberals and conservatives. The pettiness, vindictiveness, jealousy, lack of trust, the searching for partisan political advantage on every issue, the lack of understanding of the big picture by both Democrats and Republicans in Washington makes one cringe. More pragmatic governors and state legislators appear to be able to accomplish much while our federal legislators are mired in trench warfare. The people have responded in the only way possible—they have stayed away from elections in droves. The unexpected viability of John McCain's bid for the Republican nomination has been fueled in large part by people who were previously uninvolved in politics because of disgust with inside-the-beltway politics and politicians.

It is not, however, solely a difference between two parties—the Democrats versus the Republicans. It is a fundamental difference in both perception and philosophy. In the past, there was a conservative wing of the Democratic party (largely Dixiecrat Democrats), which in its beliefs and perceptions was closer to that of the liberal wing of the Republican party than to its own left. That has largely disappeared. Clinton claims to be a centrist, but if you look at his deeds instead of his words

("The end of Big Government as we know it") there is a definite leftward tilt to his actions. Now the division of Democrats and Republicans more truly resembles liberals versus conservatives.

Why do they come out differently? At the onset, I should state that I consider myself a conservative in the best sense of the word (conserving the values upon which the republic was founded, maximizing the liberties of the individual consistent with the needs of the larger society, etcetera) but I do not believe that one side or the other has a lock on wisdom, correctness, or any other quality. I do believe, however, that liberal perceptions are, in the main, incorrect.

The first battle is over the proper role of government in general and the federal government in particular. It goes back to the Founding Fathers, as manifested by Hamilton versus Jefferson and those who followed in the early part of the nineteenth century. The debate about the role of the federal government in our lives as an activist government versus a more passive role is ongoing. The preeminence of the federal government versus the status of states' rights was as much a cause for secession and the resultant Civil War as was the issue of slavery. It (states' rights) continues to be a constant topic for discussion.

Following dramatic expansion of the federal government over a fifty-year period, from FDR and the New Deal to the ascent of Ronald Reagan, there now appears to be a countercurrent of the lessening of federal control. Clinton said in his State of the Union address that he foresaw the end of "big government" as we know it. That he didn't really mean it but was only catering to what he perceived to be the mood of the country doesn't matter; he did state it. It is obvious that he really didn't mean it, because since then he has proposed expansion after expansion of existing programs and the development of new programs.

Liberals are much devoted to root causes, all of which can be solved by the application of ever-larger amounts of money—federal money. That often means doing nothing, since root causes are not so easily changed, not even with infusions of more and more money. By stating that one is going after root causes, one may feel good, but that is not the same as doing good. It is necessary at times to accept realities and accept the common sense approach of incremental changes, rather than trying to solve a society's problem in one fell swoop. A reflex reaction of liberals is to attempt to solve a problem by throwing money at it. Virtually all supporters of social problem-solving claim that more money will solve the problem. If it does not, then additional money must be obtained. The pathetic state of secondary education, particularly in the inner cities, is always phrased in terms of lack of money. Yet fifty percent of our tax dollars at the state and local levels go to education. That the inner city schools of Washington, D.C. receive approximately the same dollar per student as the suburbs means nothing to the "more money" crowd.

More money is the panacea for all the ills of secondary education—forget the role of the family, teachers, and principals and Board of Education—just pour in more money and the problem will be solved. Progress is seen as coming from the government, the Fed in particular. Scratch liberals and you will see that they are closet socialists. Despite all evidence to the contrary, despite failures of disparate socialist endeavors throughout the world, socialism is seen as the best economic solution available. After all, it would be run by kind, wise, knowledgeable bureaucrats: in short, people like themselves.

There is a liberal sympathy reflex for the "underdog," the little guy. In many ways, that is admirable, but there are flaws in this way of thinking, including a definition of underdog, and the only solution being ever-larger government programs. There is a striving for perfection, which is also admirable, but anything less produces anger and even rage. There is present among a number of liberals a hostility to America. In any situation, they tend to blame America first. Because we are not perfect? Because from time to time we make mistakes? Because at times democracy is messy and partisan? Because it is being compared to an absolute rather than relative to other nations?

Some or all of the above reasons may explain the hostility to the United States. One thing is certain amongst this group, the U.S. is guilty until proved innocent, rather than the reverse. There is also a certain hypocrisy amongst living-room liberals who lead a very good life indeed but are quick to join a cause—any cause—that sounds politically correct. Finally, I believe there is a fatal flaw to liberalism, because one cannot have a coherent country with the thinking that individual rights trump everything and the community taking a back seat to all. I think it fair to say that there is a liberal characteristic of an overwhelming need to feel good even if it does not lead to doing good.

Conservatives are not without flaws in their thinking. The market place cannot solve all problems. It is clearly necessary for the federal government to have a role in regulation, support of the needy, particularly those who cannot function by themselves and therefore require a safety net, of public works, of military defense, and the like. They are right to fear big government, but they must understand that it does have a role to play. I believe conservatives, however, are more in the right about the balance between the federal and state governments, which would manifest itself in the form of a devolution of power not enumerated in the Constitution.

They are also more attuned to the balance of individual rights with community needs. It is fair to say that conservatives are all too often deficient in caring about those individuals who simply cannot help themselves, in spite of the best efforts of the appropriate agencies. Rather, they should be in the forefront of solving the nation's social problems by means other than big government. All too often they are not. There is a certain smugness present about them, which is not a terribly likeable feature. All too often they also tend to be exclusive rather than inclusive.

The slugfest in Washington, D.C. that so often takes place represents not just mean-spirited partisan politics but also differing ways of looking at the world.

The Political Spectrum

It was so simple. I was a high school sophomore and was being introduced to my first course in social science. The teacher illustrated the political spectrum by drawing a straight line. In the appropriate places, she marked, "Far Left," "Left," "Center," "Right," "Far Right." Far Left and Far Right could not be further apart. Imagine my surprise when a few years later, after WWII, former Nazi officials became Communist officials. Not just a handful. The police, the military, intelligence, the bureaucracy, and many others traded in their black uniforms for brown ones and went on doing the same tasks they had been doing before. How was this possible? Even earlier, the Hitler-Stalin nonaggression pact in which they divided up Poland between them took place. How could the Far Left and the Far Right even talk to each other, let alone sign a pact? There was obviously a lot to learn.

I have since realized that the model of the political spectrum I was shown in high school was flawed. Rather than a straight line, the correct model is a circle with one pole, totalitarianism, and the other, democracy. And the equator, representing the philosophy of the end justifying the means. Both poles use it at times of course, but it is the frequency of its use that is the key. Its greater or lesser use pushes one closer to or further from either pole. The closer to the equator, the more closely the views on this blend.

Each side would hate to have it said, but when two sides of the circle are equidistant from the poles, they represent mirror images of each other. Take for example the Far Left and the Far Right in the democracy hemisphere. They each grade both candidates and elected officials on how politically correct they are. For both, compromise is a dirty word. They would rather be right than get elected with the resultant ability to pass what they perceive as needed legislation. Their way or no way. While it is true that there are some bedrock issues that cannot, and should not, be compromised, most issues for most people, as a fact of life, are open to compromise. All of this is overlaid by both sides with a smug sense of moral superiority. When somebody tells me that his view is not just correct but is morally superior, I just run for the hills.

Take the dispute between Pro Choice (abortion rights) and Pro Life (anti-abortion). Both sides move forward, blissfully unaware that the other side is sincere in its beliefs and unwilling to change them. If only another argument is put forward or another article is published or a demonstration held, surely the other side will see the light. No way. Surely a compromise can be reached that will completely satisfy neither but that would be better than open warfare (not just a figure of speech for the crazies of Pro Choice, who apparently believe that hearts and minds will be changed by bombing and gunfire). I personally believe in President Clinton's formulation: abortions should be legal, safe, and rare.

The dispute between the more moderate groups of the political left and the political right are also mirror opposites. Both sides recognize problems, albeit with different emphasis. One side wishes the federal government to solve the problem, while the other wishes it to be solved by private efforts, or perhaps by government effort at the state level. This cries out for compromise, but judging by our Congress, there is precious little of that.

There we have it. The political spectrum is in reality a political circle, not a straight line, with those on opposite sides of the circle but equidistant from the poles and serving as mirror images of each other. Why people end up where they do in the political circle—family upbringing, environment, individual needs, or pure fate—I do not know. If they change positions, why? And in what direction? A new discipline—political psychology—might help us find out about why people end up where they do and what if anything can be done to change them?

Politics vs. Principles

It is interesting to see people rabidly defend (or attack) politicians with whom they differ on political matters in the name of principle. Of course, in a few cases, it is indeed principle at work, but most differences are partisan politics masking (even to the proponents) the true cause of their high dudgeon.

Watching the petty partisan politics here in Washington, D.C. offers many examples of such partisan politics masquerading as high principles. When Ronald Reagan's attorney general, Edwin Meese, was accused of impropriety, or worse in the WedTech scandal, the Democrats were in full cry for his scalp. However, in a court trial, he was acquitted. It doesn't matter, claimed the Democrats, he should still resign because even the appearance of impropriety was inappropriate in an attorney general.

Flash forward to the Clinton travails. The principle of impropriety was never raised and the calls for resignation were few and far between. I do not doubt for one moment that the Republicans took great pleasure in the discomfiture of the Democrats and would certainly have punished Clinton if they could. However, the Democrats faced not only improprieties but also unacceptable actions by the chief legal officer of the U.S.—the president—lying under oath before a federal grand jury. There were thus two reasons, as a matter of principle, to punish the president, but they made sure that he did not resign and that the vote to remove the president failed. Purely as a matter of principle, of course.

A second example of politics masquerading as principle was the intense, often radical and violent, opposition to the war in Vietnam on the part of the political left. This was a matter of principle; however, when it came to Bosnia and then to Kosovo, the previous sentiments that we were not the world's policeman, people should be left to solve their own problems, it was only a civil war, we are trying to impose our will on the people, war would spread elsewhere, civilian casualties would ensue, etcetera all went out the window. When it became a policy they were in favor of, the exact same arguments against involvement in Vietnam were used in favor of our intervention. High morals and high principles, but bent to fit their politics.

Everyone claims to act in the name of morality and principles. Which of the many bloodthirsty dictators of the twentieth century would admit that their bloodbaths and reign of terror occurred because they simply liked them and needed them to keep power. No, it was a higher principle that drove them. Racial purity, lebensraum (living space), equality of the masses, threats to the regime, and other causes were their motivation. Principles, not their political beliefs, were the reasons for their actions. Of course.

A simple test can show whether an individual's beliefs and actions are motivated by principle or political belief. One needs only to ask the question, how would they behave if the action in question were to be performed by people of similar political beliefs? After all, it takes no great courage to fiercely attack those with whom one disagrees. It does take a great deal of courage to attack on principle those with whom one agrees. If seen that way, it is obvious that we are witnessing theater with people's politics being their principles.

The (newest) trial of the century has just been completed and on both counts—perjury and obstruction of justice—President Bill Clinton has been found not guilty. There are many reactions that seem appropriate to me, even if I don't agree with them—joy that the ordeal for the country is over, pleased that the "bar for impeachment has not been lowered," contentment with our government and with the full functioning of our Constitution. What seems entirely inappropriate is the overwhelming glee and joy of some people. After all, the man did admit to "an inappropriate relationship" (what a euphemism) in the Oval Office complex while he was conducting affairs of state, with his family around, performed with an intern over whom he had a supervisory duty.

Further, as Senator Robert Byrd has stated, every reasonable person would recognize that he did lie under oath and obstruct justice. Somberness at the damage and trauma would be a far more appropriate attitude, but then again, I have been unable to understand many of the arguments put forth during the long ordeal.

The first argument put forth is that "it is only about sex." That's like saying that Watergate was only about burglary. The burglary may have been the precipitating factor that led to the entire Watergate affair, but the fundamental problem was lying and cover-up. In Nixon's case, he misused the agencies of the executive branch (attorney general, FBI, etcetera) to cover up his misdeeds and in the process, tainted virtually everyone around him. In Clinton's case, by lying before a grand jury (please remember he is the chief law enforcement officer in the land), he perverted the judiciary, and by lying to people around them and getting them to go public with false information, he too tainted everyone around him.

The next argument is that everybody lies, and all sorts of examples are given. Perhaps many people do. Perhaps even presidents lie when they feel national security issues require them to do so. None of them are supposed to lie under oath, and our entire justice system is predicated upon people being truthful when under oath. The argument that many people lie about matters sexual, even under oath, is probably true, but that raises the question about what items one can lie about under oath. Divorce? Dividing of assets? Child custody? Are there absolute limits on lying under oath or are they merely relative?

The next argument is that it is a private matter. Refer back to argument one for reasons why it is not completely a private matter. Had he a mistress in town whom he visited regularly, it would have been a private matter, between him and his family. Of course, the press would rapidly have discovered it and publicized it, but it would still have been a private matter. It could be said that lying to the public still kept it a private matter, but once the chief law enforcement officer of the land was placed under oath, the lying should have ceased, not for his good but for the good of the country. Instead, an extraordinary contortion of the English language and of common sense was used to keep him from admitting anything other than an "inappropriate relationship." Further, he was not charged with any of the above; he was charged with felonious crimes: perjury and obstruction of justice.

Gloria Steinem, one of the icons of the feminist movement, puts forth a simple argument about President Clinton's behavior. Yes is yes and no is no. If both parties are consenting adults, then a clear answer of yes or no should be final, and there is no longer a problem. Hence Clinton is blameless and responsible only to his wife. Would that it were so simple. In human relations, particularly in male/female relations, no may be absolutely not—get lost. It may also be yes, but not at this moment.

It may be probably yes, but I need to think about it further. It may be yes eventually, but more stimulation is necessary before beginning the sexual act. Similarly, yes has many answers. Yes, but not now. Yes, but not here. What may appear to be yes may simply be a technique of flirtation. It is far from the simple yes or no that Steinem proposes.

The arguments about Special Prosecutor Kenneth Starr are also quite strange. The general consensus of the Democratic pols, much of the media and the guest TV talking heads, and indeed some lawyers is that Starr abused his prosecutorial privilege. Perhaps that is so. The White House has taken it even one step further and labeled him as part of a vast right-wing conspiracy. Perhaps that too is so. However, to me it is all irrelevant. If the president (and/or one or more of his close associates) is indicted, then Starr will be seen to have demonstrated bulldog tenacity in the face of persistent efforts to malign him and thwart the investigation. If, on the other hand, Clinton is exonerated (due to lack of legal evidence), then the cries of the above noted people would seem to be true; Starr abused his power and harassed Clinton and his associates. The middle does not matter. How it comes out is all important.

Removal from office against the will of the people was an argument often made. In the first place, there was only the most indirect evidence of the will of the people, namely polls and congressional elections. Removal from office was never placed on a ballot with the intent of claiming guilt or innocense. People who make this argument do not appreciate representative democracy, where elected officials try to balance the will of their constituents with what they consider to be their own view of what is right, a phenomenon that is surprisingly rare. A related argument is that the problem is not severe enough to warrant removal from office. Remember, he was charged with perjury and obstruction of justice, not an illicit affair, and surely anyone would take those charges seriously.

Overturning an election of a popular president is yet another strange argument. To my knowledge, this subject was never raised by the Democrats about Nixon during the Watergate proceedings when in the previous election he had won forty-nine out of fifty states. Clinton's programs are vital, some say, and therefore he cannot be removed from office. It is hard to understand how, if Vice President Al Gore were to ascend to the presidency, it would grossly alter those "vital programs." A related argument is that a coup d'etat was attempted by the Republicans. A coup d'etat in which the Constitution was scrupulously followed and in which the vice president, Al Gore, a fellow Democrat, would assume power? You've got to be kidding.

Another argument is that it was nothing more than a vendetta by extreme right wingers. Like all conspiracy theories, this has a grain of truth to it. For a variety of reasons, conservatives despise Clinton, but you have to willfully deceive yourself to believe that Clinton did nothing and conservatives manufactured the case out of whole cloth. The final argument made is that it was terribly expensive, approximately forty to fifty million dollars by current reckoning, and that money could be better used for something else. These people forget—or do not want to know—that Judge Lawrence Walsh spent a comparable amount of time and money investeigating the Iran Contra matter during the Reagan administration. Does it depend on whose ox is being gored? You bet it does.

What is one to make of these strange arguments? It appears that some people are unable to separate their politics from their principles. Others have displaced their anger on Kenneth Starr rather than on whom it really belongs. Finally, it takes no great courage to punish somebody from the opposite party. It was easy to punish Nixon, not only because he was a Republican during a time when the Democrats controlled the Congress but also because he was intensely disliked by both the public and the Democratic politicians. Courage is definitely necessary when a president of your own party is in the dock. While the Democrats did criticize him—harshly—in private, publicly they stood completely by him, both in the House and in the Senate. Not exactly a profile in courage.

Primaries vs. Conventions

We have always had a limited number of state primaries where delegates to the national convention of the Democrat or Republican parties were chosen, but the overwhelming majority of the delegates were chosen by the state political hierarchy and were responsive to the political bosses of the state. Thus the majority of presidential candidates were chosen at the national convention by a series of horse tradings, often taken after ballot after ballot after ballot. Approximately thirty years ago, reformers put in place a more "democratic system," where the overwhelming majority of delegates were chosen by the primary system. It is worth asking whether we as a country have benefited from this more "democratic" system.

The first and most important question to ask is if we have had better candidates from this system than from the previous system. I cannot say that they are worse, but surely they are no better than the candidates previously chosen by convention rather than by primaries. We have forced potential candidates to campaign for a full four years to secure support during the brief primary season that determines who will be the candidate. The support is not merely the obtaining of delegates but securing the financial support to publicize the candidate and his views. This is physically exhausting and ultimately demeaning to potential candidates who, week in and week out, must raise large sums of money to keep their campaign viable. Pandering is essential. Promises made to this group or that are not kept after the election. This leads to a great deal of cynicism on the part of the electorate. These promises are thus taken with no more seriousness than are party platforms. It is truly embarrassing to see good people who have much better things to do trample through the snows of New Hampshire and Iowa year after year, seeking support. Many good people refuse to go through with the process and, as a result, we are denied their services. This process seems to get worse with each passing election cycle.

The national conventions these days are truly embarrassing. We no longer see any vestige of democracy in action, even if it is not pure participatory democracy, since the candidates are already known. Rather, they are purely show business, with all the trappings of Oscar night, and with about as much substance. Even less, since at least the Oscar winners are not known before the evening, only the candidates.

We thus have in place a supposedly democratic system that is extraordinarily long, extraordinarily expensive, and extraordinarily demeaning to the candidates. If we ended up with clearly superior candidates, then it might be worth while, but they are no better than those chosen by party bosses who knew their people and of course put forth the candidate they thought most likely to win. Sometimes they chose wrongly, but no more so than what we see from the primary system, where money and stamina seem to be the most important criteria for success. Finally the conventions have been stripped of all sense of history in the making, and of suspense. They are just professional extravaganzas and boring in the extreme. Perhaps it is time to look back to our old system.

The McCain Phenomenon

At this point, the presidential campaign of Senator John McCain has failed and George W. Bush, Jr. is the Republican presidential nominee. McCain has given Bush a relatively tepid endorsement, and it is not clear what his role will be during the upcoming campaign. Almost certainly it will not be as a vice-presidential candidate—a blessing for both men, given their different temperaments and outlooks. Whether or not McCain will actively take the stump for Bush remains to be seen. Should Bush fail in his presidential bid, McCain would become the titular head of the Republican party, a rather remarkable phenomenon for a senator who held no leadership position in the party or in the Senate and was generally seen as a maverick.

Even more remarkable than McCain's potential leadership position within the party was the splash he made during the early part of the primary season. After all he was a senator from a small state, enjoyed little or no recognition amongst the general public except for the knowledge that he was a war hero (almost an oxymoron for Vietnam veterans), had a short resumé of legislative accomplishments, was the co-author (with Senator Russell Feingold of Wisconsin) of a doomed cause of campaign reform, enjoyed little support among his colleagues, in large part because of his persistent pushing of that cause, and, at least in the beginning, had little financial support. Yet in the space of a relatively few months, he galvanized the country, threw a terrible scare into the apparently anointed candidate and his backers, and pointed the way for future candidates to relate to the voters.

We have witnessed the scary phenomenon (for a democracy) of a progressive decrease in voter turnouts for our national elections, and an overwhelming cynicism about politicians and how the whole national political process functions. Of course, not without cause. This has been a gradual phenomenon with many causes. The disconnect between the functioning of Washington, D.C. and how the rest of the country functions seems to grow greater with the passage of time. In spite of words to the contrary, inside the beltway seems to function as an entity independent of the rest of the country, responding to its own needs and waited upon by its own court of lobbyists, special interest groups, think tanks, political hangers-on, scribblers, and babblers and court jesters, as well as large campaign donors. One can readily see the analogy between the functioning of a royal court, with its retainers, intrigues, and internal politics versus the rest of the populace to see what is happening today in our own national politics.

This has always existed to some degree of course, but in my opinion, never to this degree. Never has there been such pettiness, unwillingness to compromise for the common good, contempt for common sense and decency, and personal vindictiveness and lack of civility as exists now. In the past, bitter fighting took place during working hours (on matters of principle), but after hours these were put aside and civility reigned. It is my understanding that there is precious little of this at the present time. Both sides bear some responsibility for this situation.

The Republican leadership does not seem destined for praise by future historians for its far sightedness, leadership qualities, and ability to compromise for the greater good. Its probity has not been outstanding, as a Speaker and Speaker-elect have been forced to resign because of personal misbehavior (the Democrats have chipped in also with a Speaker forced to resign because of personal failures, as well as a powerful committee chairman being sent to jail). However, new standards of low behavior have been set in motion by the current presidential incumbent, and that is the larger cause of the low esteem held by so many people about the current political occupants of Washington, in spite of an apparent approval rating of the president's politics.

Lying about one thing cannot help being seen as potentially lying about other things as well, even if in the pursuit of what is felt to be a good cause. Winning at all costs, even including the contempt of those bested is not the way to promote comity and compromise; rather, it promotes an attempt at getting even. Skirting the edge of what is permissible, as in soliciting campaign contributions (actually going over the edge?) cannot but produce intense cynicism amongst the general population, even if it is rationalized as being in a good cause. In sum, a gradual phenomenon of a disconnect between Washington, D.C. and the rest of the country has been markedly hastened by the conduct of those currently in power, leading to cynicism, disrespect, and a tuning out of Washington as manifested by an ever-decreasing number of voters, particularly amongst the young.

Enter John McCain. A genuine war hero. Not because he was willing to make personal sacrifices when his country called upon him. Not because he was captured. Not because he was tortured. Not because he was permanently injured as a result of the torture. Because he was unwilling to accept preferential treatment not granted to his fellow prisoners. That is what makes a hero, and the public surely recognizes that. On top of that, the subjects of his campaign ignited the imagination of many. Not just reform of what is generally recognized as a sick campaign system, but honor, duty, patriotism, inclusiveness, a moral code for public behavior. Openness with the public via the press without carefully thought-out positions as a result of focus groups and spin-doctors. Imagine that. And the public responded with fervor. Independents, young people, those who had given up on the current political system all flocked to his side. How ironic to see the children of Vietnam War protesters flock to the side of a Vietnam veteran whose espousal of old fashioned virtues their parents mocked. In the end, such a group was no match for the party organization and the enmity of the ultraconservatives, and he was defeated.

It was said that McCain had flaws, big flaws. He had been tainted by scandal (albeit peripherally), he had a bad temper, he did not tolerate lightly those who opposed him, etcetera. All true, but most important of all, his campaign and the response it elicited offered hope for the future. If not McCain, then someone else.

Tricky and Slick

Given the lapse of a century or two, the misdeeds of Nixon and Clinton will be studied, comparing the differences as well as the similarities. Supporters of each side will emphasize the differences between the two men, but it is striking to me how many similarities there are to each other.

Both men are (were) outsiders to the Establishment. This meant that doors were not automatically opened to them, and they had to work all that much harder to achieve their goals. They both met political failure early on (Clinton in his quest for governor of Arkansas: Nixon in his quest for the presidency), learned from it, and persisted in their quest. When each had finally achieved his goal (president of the U.S.), he worked hard on achieving lasting goals for which posterity would remember him—Nixon in the field of foreign affairs and Clinton in the field of domestic affairs. Finally, each was brought down by a relatively trifling affair—a bungled third-rate burglary by Nixon and a sexual affair by Clinton—each of which blossomed into a full-blown national convulsion.

Both precipitating events could have been isolated by the incumbent and not progress to the situations they found themselves in (Clinton has not yet been tried, but even if he is exonerated, there will always be an asterisk next to his name—the only elected president in our history to be impeached). A full, genuine, early confession of wrong doing and a pledge never to do it again would resonate with the public, who desperately want to believe in the president of the United States. Instead, each chose a policy of lying and cover-up. With Nixon, the cover-up predominated, while with Clinton, the lying was the predominant theme, but each used the two elements. Eventually, each scheme unraveled, and the country was subjected to a tremendous and unnecessary trauma. Why they each chose this course is unclear, but it could conceivably be related to their underlying insecurity as outsiders. An additional question is why Clinton failed to learn from Nixon's experience and embarked on the same downward course.

This brings us to the final similarity: their nicknames. Tricky Dick Nixon and Slick Willie Clinton. Each suggests a character of shading the truth, resorting to illegal means if necessary to stay in power, and lacking those components of character such as honor, principle, and respect for the highest office (the presidency) in the land. Woe is us.

IV

Politics—Foreign

A Play in Three Acts

American actions during and surrounding the Gulf War can be fairly characterized as a play in three acts. The first act, leading up to the war was a disaster. Obviously fixated on the menace of Iran, and needing a counterweight to it in the form of Iraq, our leaders and diplomats failed completely to accurately gauge the intentions and the menace of Saddam Hussein. Whether our policy was stated or implied, Saddam Hussein drew the conclusion from our position that he could invade Kuwait (and at the very least, threaten Saudi Arabia) without much more than a temporary verbal outcry. How wrong he was.

The second act was magnificent. President Bush and his military and civilian advisors built from scratch a formidable multinational force. This force came from a dozen countries inhabiting virtually every continent. He conducted the most intensive air war in history followed by an overwhelming and relentless ground attack. We took minimal casualties, far less than had been anticipated. Wonderful.

The third act started with the cease-fire and persists to this day. Instead of disarming the republican guards (the backbone of Saddam's army and power) and sending them home in their underwear, we let them return to Iraq with their weapons, and in short order, they reconstituted themselves as a fighting force.

When the Shia rebellion started in the south of Iraq, we let Saddam use helicopter gunships to fly over that portion of the country. That spelled the end of the rebellion. It might legitimately be asked whether a Shia triumph would be any better for Iraq and, indeed, the whole region, but surely it would not be any worse.

When Saddam's forces invaded Kurdistan in the north, President Bush's successor, President Clinton ordered some pin-prick bombing in the south. Saddam drew the obvious conclusion that he could get away with things and started the process of forcing the exit of the U.N. weapons inspectors. Who knows what trouble he can cause once he again has weapons of mass destruction and the means to deliver them.

The point is being ever more frequently made that the sanctions, including the oil embargo, has caused untold civilian suffering, and states or implies that it should end. That argument conveniently forgets that it is Saddam, and only Saddam, who caused the sanctions in the first place and that surely there are mechanisms in place for funds from the amount of oil currently sold to alleviate civilian suffering. Without question, additional funds received would certainly not go to the civilian sector but to his war machine, just as it has in the past.

It is a shame, as well as a blot on their reputation, for those whose marvelous second act was preceded and followed by such poor first and third acts. The current U.S. administration has been in place for eight years, so it cannot blame anything on its predecessors. Perhaps this response (or more correctly a nonresponse) represents a lack of will, a lack of understanding of the nature of totalitarians, or something else. It is both the blessing and the curse of a great power that at times it must act with overwhelming force if it is to maintain stability in a still very unstable world. It would be helpful for the future to find out what motivated our leaders in a time of crisis.

Cuba

A sea change has occurred among that section of the American public enamored of Castro and Communism. No longer does anyone volunteer to serve in the Venceremos Brigade and cut sugar cane. No longer does anyone extol the miracles of Marxism, the wonders of Cuba's health care, education, etcetera. Of course, there are still a few Blame America Firsters who put all of Cuba's troubles on the doorstep of the U.S. The truth is that Cuba's economy was and is in constant shambles, was propped up by the Soviet Union with subsidies and direct grants in the billions of dollars. When the Soviet Union collapsed and the subsidies ended, so did Cuba's economy.

Communism, Castro, and the Cuba he has ruled for the past forty years are in their death throes. Virtually everyone realizes that they must go. It is simply a question of how to apply appropriate pressure so that the above do disappear. Also, it is important to do so with the least loss of life possible. Here, reasonable people can disagaree. Some say that the only way to get rid of Castro is to keep up, and even redouble, our pressure. Maintain sanctions. Continuous heavy propaganda via the airways. Foment revolution from within. Perhaps that will all be necessary to unseat him.

Using Central and Eastern Europe as an example, what brought down communism, and the Soviet Union too, was knowledge. The world outside the Soviet bloc was quite a different place from the world within. This was true economically as well as politically. Perhaps it had been one or the other, rather than both, the people would have endured, but they would not endure both. Further, the people knew, through travel, word of mouth, clandestine broadcasts, and of course, the sheer incompetence of the Soviet system, what the real situation inside and outside the empire was. The mass outpouring of rage and frustration was a tide too strong to subdue. Within a very short period of time, an empire toppled.

A similar approach should topple Castro. By all means, let bilateral trade and tourism flourish. When Cubans see what the West is really like, they too should rise in righteous wrath and topple the government. If it worked in Europe, it should work in Cuba.

At least that was my feeling until the extraordinary case of Elian Gonzalez unfolded. The six-year-old boy accompanied his divorced mother, along with others, on a flight by sea to Florida and to freedom. Like so many others who attempted to flee, their escape turned into tragedy. The flimsy raft sank, most (including the mother) drowned. Elian survived and was rescued by a fisherman and turned over to the Coast Guard and eventually to his relatives who had escaped and taken up residence in Miami. From Cuba, the divorced father claimed his son, and an epic battle took place over the disposition of the boy. The astonishing thing to me was the surfacing of American attitudes about Cuba that I thought to be long-dead-attitudes as outlined in the beginning of this essay.

From the beginning, there was a debate about the rights of the parent to bring up a child as the parent saw fit versus placing the child in harm's way by returning him to a vicious totalitarian dictatorship. Not an easy choice by any means, but in the end, I believe a parent's rights to a child, barring negligent or abusive behavior on the part of the parent, trumps all.

The subsequent arguments and attitudes were what amazed me. Over and over, the argument was made that we are a nation of laws and obedience to the law was of the highest order of priority. Wasn't the entire underground railway movement to bring out runaway slaves a violation of the law? Wasn't the entire Civil Rights movement predicated upon the violation of existing law? Wasn't the entire Vietnam protest movement based on breaking the law—sometimes violently? Wasn't the entire sanctuary movement of several years ago—providing sanctuary to those Central Americans who escaped from various right-wing dictatorships—based on breaking the law? Wasn't the civil disobedience expressed by the Miami Cuban community considered to be worthy in the same vein as the anti-Vietnam and civil rights movements? If not, why not for the Cubans?

Let us take a hypothetical case. In 1939, the ship *St. Louis* sailed from Hamburg, Germany, to Cuba, where the nearly 1,000 Jewish passengers thought they would be provided asylum. Politics prevailed, and they were not allowed to disembark. Instead, they sailed fruitlessly around Florida hoping to be admitted to the United States. When they were not, they returned to Germany, where most perished in the concentration camps. Suppose a mother and her son slipped over the side of the ship off the Florida coast. The mother drowned but the boy survived. Would there be a single individual who wished for Elian's return to Cuba insist on returning the hypothetical boy to Germany, even if requested to do so by a relative? Not a chance. They would all be out protesting vigorously against such an act.

What has been lost in the discussions has been why so many people would risk their lives in rickety rafts and boats to come to the United States. They surely knew that many in the past had drowned and become shark food, and yet they persisted in coming. Risking their lives just for economic gain? Perhaps. But then again, perhaps not. Several years ago, the guards in front of a Latin American embassy in Havana were removed for uncertain reasons. In an instant, a reported ten thousand Cubans gathered in the courtyard of the embassy looking for asylum. Many Cubans have attempted to swim or raft to our military outpost at Guantanamo Bay to seek asylum. Perhaps all of these people knew, as virtually all Cubans know, that Cuba is a wicked, repressive, totalitarian dictatorship, with all that that implies. Informants on every block. Children taught to spy and report on their parents. Ceaseless propaganda. Imprisonment for the least infractions. Perhaps freedom was important enough to them to risk all to obtain it. Somehow that possibility is never discussed. Perhaps there are some here who are so blasé about freedom that they cannot conceive of people making sacrifices, even the ultimate sacrifice, to obtain some of it for themselves and their family.

When the boy and his father left for Cuba, I felt it was the right thing, but I felt terribly sad. To me it was a day of mourning, not of joy. How could people cheer about a situation in which a young boy was returned as a propaganda tool to a repressive dictatorship? Why wasn't the subject of a terribly wicked and oppressive dictatorship mentioned at all? The only person I heard mention it was Janet Reno, and she spoke about Castro and Communism as she would about differences between Democrats and Republicans. No outrage about Cuba in her voice. No mention about the evils of Communism by anyone else that I heard. The real reason, I believe, is the same as the failure to recognize and denounce the evils of the Soviet Union, even after it was completely exposed following its fall. I believe now that there is still a subtle sympathy for Castro and Communism.

Kosovo—Pro and Con

We are now nearly a year removed from the fighting in Kosovo (and Serbia), but I admit that I now feel the same as before and during the fighting. Sometimes right (the struggle against the Nazis, the Gulf War against Iraq) is right and wrong (intervention in Haiti) is wrong, but in this case, it seems to me that honorable people can assess the facts and come up with differing conclusions. Let us list the pros and the cons of our intervention in Kosovo.

For those in favor of intervention (and I count myself in that category), there were at least four cogent reasons for going to war against Serbia. First, Slobodan Milosevic was a dictator, and the basic truth about dictators is that they only understand force. Negotiations, concessions, good will, and personal diplomacy are seen only as weakness to be exploited by the dictator. We have seen this over and over in this century. One can deal, but only from perceived strength.

Second, there will be future dangerous situations where NATO and the United States will be called upon to act. Their unwillingness to do so now would have a negative effect on actions in the future. Further, bold and determined action now can serve as a deterrent in the future, preventing, rather than fighting, a war.

Third, there was a real danger (and still might be) of the conflict spreading beyond the confines of Kosovo and Serbia. Through a series of religious, ethnic, cultural, and political alliances, other countries could easily have been drawn into the conflict. Finally there was the ethnic cleansing—right in the heart of Europe. One picture is worth a thousand words, and there were many pictures. TV makes all the difference. The slaughter in Ruanda was worse, but it was not televised. TV is not a passive recorder of war but an active participant, voluntarily or involuntarily steering public perceptions one way or the other.

Those are the arguments in favor of intervention. I find them convincing but so too are the arguments against intervention. Kosovo was part of Yugoslavia (Serbia as the sole surviving state), and the problem was therefore a civil war. An attack on a sovereign nation because of an internecine problem is a bad precedent to set. As has been said so often in another context, we are not the world's policemen. It is true that civilian killings and other horrors took place, but our own bombing necessarily killed civilians as well. We certainly had interests (the peace and stability of Europe, for one) but not vital strategic interests. Europe, however, did have vital strategic interests and, therefore, it should have been the Europeans who took the lead.

As a separate issue, the Europeans showed how unprepared they were for modern war, depending on the United States for their offensive punch. That they were unprepared militarily is their fault, not ours. Also, there seemed to be little gratitude towards us for entering the fray. They have preferred to hide behind an American military shield and spend their money on other things. Finally we have an open-ended strategy with no clear exit strategy. Since these sectarian hatreds have been going on for hundreds of years, how long will we have to be there before they learn to love each other?

Although on balance, I was in favor of intervention, I recognize the validity of arguments of those opposed. However, any reasonable person will recognize that we have become over-involved throughout the world. One can argue whether we have a strategic interest in this or that crisis, but very few could be called of vital strategic interest. The claim could be made that we have a strategic interest in Kosovo, whereas we did have a vital strategic interest in Iraq—a very big difference. With claims of a strategic interest and for humanitarian purposes, we have become involved with our military on virtually all continents. This would include Somalia (where we attempted foolishly to bring about political reform rather than sticking to a voluntary relief effort), Haiti (where again, reform has failed badly and the people are up to their bad old ways, with some new ones, like serving as a large drug smuggling center), Bosnia (where our forces' supposed stay of one year has stretched out to forever), and now Kosovo. To be involved in all these ventures with a military trimmed down so much that they had to ration missiles during the attacks on Kosovo and Serbia makes no sense. You cannot have more and more missions with fewer and fewer resources to carry them out to the fullest.

It is strange to see that many of the people who were violently against the Vietnam War and voted against the use of force against Iraq have pushed for war in Kosovo. It almost seems that they are willing to go to war only if we have no strategic interests. Perhaps the best solution as stated during the Vietnam War would be to declare victory and get out.

Loss of Civilian Lives

Every major war fought in the twentieth century, beginning with the Boer War and ending with Chechnya, has involved the loss of civilian lives. Up until then, two armies faced each other in a field or as attackers and defenders of a fortified position and had at each other. Of course, the victorious army felt free to rape and pillage, but there were no civilians killed as the direct result of the fighting. The weapons of the twentieth century changed all that, and the battlefield was everywhere. Air war caused even more dramatic changes, since collateral civilian damage was almost certain.

Recently the claim has been made that everything and anything should be done to prevent civilian casualties. Of course it is a desirable principle, but how can one carry out an effective military campaign without at least the possibility of civilian casualties? After all, it is not uncommon in the Middle East, for example, to use civilians as a shield. Most recently, Saddam Hussein filled his "palaces" (probably WMD [weapons of mass destruction]) facilities with civilians so as to preclude bombing attacks on them. Hezbollah did the same thing in Lebanon when they set up artillery units next to civilians in a UN camp. An errant Israeli shell caused the death of many of those unfortunates. Israel was then loudly denounced for the killing of civilians.

Our victory over Hitler was possible in large part because of the continuous bombing of his production and transportation facilities. Heavy collateral civilian damage was inevitable, particularly since the only weapons available were dumb bombs. Prior to the Normandy invasion by the Allies in 1944, very heavy bombing was carried out at or near the front, as well as in Germany itself. That meant that tens of thousands of French, Dutch, and Belgian civilians were injured or killed. What if we didn't bomb and the invasion failed? What if we didn't bomb and the Allied troops took tens of thousands more casualties? One must choose between painful options, since in wartime there are no good options, only a choice between bad options. The same holds true for our bombing of Japan during WWII (see "Dropping the Bomb").

So what can we make of those who clamor for zero civilian casualties?—an obvious impossibility in modern war. What is their mindset? I believe that their preference is for avoiding war at any cost—embargoes, sanctions, conferences, negotiations, one-on-one discussions all should do the job. Of course, the military option should be demonstrated but would be no deterrent to an enemy who knew that we would not use it. Therefore a ruthless enemy such as Saddam Hussein can easily exploit civilian casualties to modify our military efforts. Feeling good is not the same as doing good.

The U.S. and Saudi Arabia

It always astonishes me to repeatedly hear how close the United States is to Saudi Arabia. From President Franklin Roosevelt on, every president has, to varying degrees, proclaimed our solidarity with Saudi Arabia. The Gulf War was really more about the fate of Saudi Arabia than it was about Kuwait, Iraqi aggression, etcetera. A truly stupendous effort was undertaken by President Bush to remove the threat to the Saudis, of course at the same time serving our own interests as well.

Yet how close are we really? Our geography is completely separate, as physically far apart as two countries can be. We have a democratic republic; they have a hereditary monarchy. We are predominantly a Christian nation by population but determinedly secular. They are almost entirely Muslim with no separation of Church and State. We are dedicated to Western values, they to Eastern. Our legal and justice systems bear no relationship, one to another. We are a world power and thereby hold a world view, while they are concerned with themselves or, at best, their region. We have been welcoming to immigrants; they have not. We are a nation of minorities; they are not. The role played by women in our society simply cannot be compared to theirs.

There is, however, one overriding equation that appears to cancel out all of the above. They have oil and we need it. Without that we would have no more or less interest in them than in say Nepal or Sierra Leone. One should remember that the next time one of our officials extols the wonderful virtues of Saudi Arabia.

V

Public Policy—Domestic

A Few Simple Questions

As time passes, more and more people are suggesting that recreational street drugs be legalized. Aside from a few libertarians, most people offer the rationale that decriminalizing usage will remove the profit motive and, therefore, the presence of drug pushers. They seem to be saying that if you can't lick them, join them and, at the same time, unclog the legal and penal systems; however, details about what will take the place of the present system are vague, and perhaps a few simple questions are in order. (*Courtesy of Virginia Medical Quarterly, June 1990*)

The first question to be asked is who will be selling the drugs; the private market place or the government? The former is less likely, but if the private sector is given the task, will it be on a monopoly basis or on the basis of competition within the free enterprise system? If a monopoly, who will get it and how will it be regulated? If regulated, by whom? How will prices be set? Will it be regulated like a utility? Or will it be free to charge that the market will bear? Which drugs will it sell? And will it be free to introduce new drugs on its own? If competition is the order of the day, will advertising be permitted, at least to the extent that tobacco and alcohol products are permitted to advertise? If not, and it is legal, why not? Will "specials" be allowed to be offered to increase the user population? Will new "designer" drugs be developed and marketed? Will exports be permitted, to improve our balance of payments?

If, as is more likely, the government takes on the task, will it be in the hands of the local, state, or federal government? If either of the former, won't chaos result from different regulations, different drugs permitted to be sold, and at different prices? Since that is likely to happen, it would fall on the federal government to sell the drugs out of "state stores" as some states now sell liquor.

Now a host of new questions arise. Would the government advertise? Would it sell all drugs or just some, leaving the market for the others in the hands of drug dealers? Would it take the lead in introducing new drugs, such as the "ice" coming in from Japan or the amphetamine "ecstacy," or would it leave that to the dealers? Would it set prices high to discourage use and, therefore, open the market to "moonshiners" who would easily be able to sell cheaper because of less fixed costs (one can imagine the size of the bureaucracy it would take to set up such a program). Or would it set the price low and thereby encourage broader usage? Would it be restrictive in its sales practices, trying to discourage abuse, thereby making it easier to go to your neighborhood pusher? Or would it be lenient, thereby encouraging broader usage?

Obviously, it would not sell to minors, but does anyone familiar with teenagers doubt their ability to obtain the drugs one way or the other? If not sold to minors, would this not leave this entire market open to drug dealers? In the name of "fairness," would the government distribute the drugs free of charge to indigents? Will this become a basic right discovered somewhere in the Constitution? Not if, but when, side effects occur, will it be the responsibility of the government, since it is doing the selling, to provide appropriate care? Will this open the door to a whole new class of lawsuits? If an adddicted or deformed or impaired baby is born, will it be the responsibility of the government to care for it? Forever?

If it is decided to distribute the drugs through clinics run by physicians, new questions arise. Again, will they be limited only to some drugs or to all? Will it be limited to addicts or to anyone who expresses an interest in them? If the former, will not the recreational drug users, who are in the majority, continue to get their supplies from dealers? With addicts, who decides how much is enough to satisfy their needs? If the clinic staff decides, will not many addicts take the pure drug, adulterate these and become dealers themselves, so that they have money to meet their needs, as they and not the clinic determine it? Will addicts be forced to undergo treatment? And if so, is it a violation of their rights as some people would undoubtedly see it? What will be considered an acceptable recidivism rate when requests come to Congress or the state legislatures for refunding? What would be the total costs of such a program?

Currently, those who smoke can do so in smoking lounges or sections of restaurants designated for smokers, while those who wish to imbide alcohol in convivial company and surroundings can do so in a wide variety of bars, taverns, restaurants, clubs, etcetera. Is there any reason, with recreational drugs legalized, why there should not be similar places for those who wish to do the same with drugs? Could we deny the opening of shooting galleries for heroin, crack, and coke bars and the like? Perhaps we could even have a TV sitcom based on the friendly camaraderie that would exist in one of these establishments.

If recreational drugs are legalized, why should we keep intact the elaborate system to supervise the dispensing of controlled substances—narcotics, tranquilizers, and the like? Why should we not sell morphine and codeine and their derivatives over the counter, next to the aspirin, acetaminophen, and ibuprofen? Why should we not sell major tranquilizers and sedatives the same way? Why not all prescription drugs?

A further concern is the educational system we have painstakingly put in place over the past two decades against abuse of alcohol, tobacco products, and recreational drugs. How seriously will anyone take these campaigns when the government passively (and, in effect, actively) endorses the use of recreational drugs? Virtually everyone across the political spectrum agrees that a fundamental role of government is to maintain public safety. What amount of testing will be necessary to protect us from harm?

We immediately think of airline pilots, air traffic controllers, railroad engineers, and tanker captains, but would not everyone who makes decisions that affect our health and welfare be subject to testing? Would this not include all vehicle drivers? What size police and support system would be necessary to screen the roads for drug use in addition to alcohol use? We are aware of the increasing competitiveness of the world economy. Is legalization of drugs likely to improve or decrease our productivity and competitiveness?

There are obviously many more questions to be asked, and the ones asked above will undoubtedly raise many more related ones. However, the greatest questions relate to our ability, and will, to deal with difficult and dangerous problems. Is our solution to such a difficult and intractable problem to give in to it, or is it to devise effective ways of fighting it? If this problem is difficult, aren't also so many of our other social problems? Should we give in to them as we give in to this? The answer depends on where we are going as a society.

Affirmative Action

The problems relating to the government policy of affirmative action are never far below the surface, bubbling up periodically to poison our civil society. After thirty years of such policies, there is a significant and growing majority that feels that such programs are causing more harm than good and should be abolished. Let me raise some of the reasons for such feelings.

There is no chronological end point to the program. It could be stated with some fairness that blacks are the only immigrants to these shores who did not come voluntarily, and Native Americans were conquered and then badly abused. Perhaps a set time period, say a quarter century, should be given to these groups to help them catch up and compete more fairly; however, no time period, other than the appearance of the social millennium in which everyone will be perfectly equal with everyone else, has ever been proposed. Therefore a benefit that is given to a particular group in perpetuity becomes an entitlement that is not lightly given up and is clearly a source of resentment on the part of others.

A black child of two professional parents, raised in an affluent suburb and attending a prestigious secondary school is considered a victim and entitled to special treatment, while a white child of an unemployed miner from, say, Scranton, Pennsylvania, is considered to have been blessed by society and deserving of no special treatment. Such is the irrationality and harm of stereotyping people based only on such criteria as the color of the skin. The same holds true for gender.

The only way to count the success or failure of the program is by numbers, and numbers all too frequently deteriorate into quotas. Also, how does one count? As intermarriage rises and multiethnic adoption rises, is a child who is one-half or one-eighth black, white or black? If a black child has been adopted and raised by a white family, what is his ethnic identity? Who determines it? Is a recent immigrant from the Caribbean or from Africa who is not a descendant of American slaves entitled to favored treatment? These questions are difficult, no, impossible, to answer, so they are never addressed. Instead, talk is always about principles, concepts, glittering generalities, etcetera.

There has to be some stigmatizing of the recipients. Clearly the beneficiaries of such a program are of two minds: grateful that they have been chosen to enter a prestigious job or school, and at the same time, fearful that they have been selected on criteria other than worth.

The American dream has always been that the individual can rise as high as his or her abilities will take them. That this has all too often been a dream and not a reality does not mean that this is not what we should strive for; it is the very dream that has brought millions to our shores and from whom we have benefited so much. The concepts of group merit, of chosen "minority" status upon whom certain privileges are bestowed and of group victimology with benefits accruing from that status is bound in the long run to create exactly the resentments that are present today.

"Diversity" is the current buzzword that has replaced preferences as the reason for preferences. This word implies that it is the institution rather than the individual that benefits and is therefore more acceptable. One can see that there are indeed benefits from contact with people from diverse backgrounds and that, for example, a broader student population would confer benefits on everyone at the institution. Unfortunately, the requisite for benefits from diversity—namely, mixing together—is all too often moving in the opposite direction as "minority" groups self-segregate themselves more and more completely.

On various campuses across the country, separate dorms, separate eating facilities, separate courses, separate campus newspapers, separate student unions, and even separate graduation ceremonies have occurred. One can understand the need for comfort in what is perceived as a strange and foreign world, but where does comfort end and when does it become self-segregation, the very antithesis of diversity? One can readily see that those who are the beneficiaries of such programs are loath to give them up, and fight changes tooth and nail.

The problems are deeper, however, and affect a far wider range of society, as a letter to the *Washington Post* from a tenured law professor at a prestigious eastern law school demonstrates. He wrote in support of affirmative action but rejected the standard arguments in favor of affirmative action, namely diversity and compensatory justice. In their place, he used an argument that he calls a structural remedy. By that he means eradicating the "caste structure," which he claims is endemic in our society. Unfortunately, his arguments produce more problems than the ones he rejects, if that is possible.

Not all blacks (or indeed any other approved group of "victims") are at the bottom of the heap, as pointed out above. Why should they be given preferential treatment? No mention is made of this. He claims that any group currently subordinated by society should be given preferential treatment. How one picks such a group is not commented upon, neither are the problems involved in selection that would be produced. He feels that recent immigrants should be given preferential treatment over resident Americans. Only a professor lost in an ivory tower could make such a proposal.

As in all his discussions on the topic, he never gets past the philosophical aspects. Who decides which groups are included? Who appoints those who decide? What are the criteria for inclusion or exclusion? When does the process end, or is it a never-ending entitlement? None of this is even mentioned. He correctly notices that such a process would cause injustices and grievances, but he feels that sacrifices must be made, by others. He, for example, could leave his comfortable endowed professorship and give the benefits of his talents to a struggling black law school. He could give up his comfortable academic position

136

and teach inner city minorities. Instead, he bravely suggests that others must step up and make the sacrifice. How noble. I mention in detail such peculiar thinking not only because it is so far from reality but also because, unfortunately, it represents the thinking by a large number of our so-called intelligentsia and stands in the way of reforming the system.

All of the above examples do not negate the fact that we have an enormous social problem on our hands. No matter what our view is of current remedies, the problem affects all of us adversely and simply must be solved. If one wishes to do good rather than feel good, then abandon what is considered by a large American majority as another failed social program and look towards new solutions.

Unfortunately virtually all of the discussions about this issue dwell largely on the past and on philosophy. There is little emphasis on concrete steps, which must be taken if we are to develop a system of individual merit rather than group entitlement, with all its pernicious side effects. Most laws, after a quarter-century on the books, get grudging (in some cases enthusiastic) acceptance. Here, the outcry against affirmative action is becoming louder and more angry as time passes. Something is amiss.

Therefore, I propose four questions to try and focus the debate. (1) Will there be an end to affirmative action? If there is no end, it is an entitlement and should be labeled as such. One can make a reasonable case that a leg up is necessary for groups that have been held down through no fault of their own, but when do we revert to individual merit and not group preferences? (2) What are the criteria for ending preferences? Are they based on elapsed time, fulfillment of certain criteria or some combination of the two? (3) Who decides when it ends: that is, that the goal has been met? Is it an individual, a commission, or something else? What is their term of office? (4) Who appoints those who decide? Is it the executive, legislative, or judicial branch?

At this stage, all of the arguments have been made and countered. It is time to move on to the next phase of the process: namely, to put in place a fair and just judging system for school and job applications, which will put an end to the existing system that is at bottom unfair and unjust, as well as undermining a basic principle of our country—each individual should go as far as his talents will take him regardless of extraneous factors such as race, gender, etcetera.

Americans with Disability Act

I have spent my adult professional life treating patients with disabilities. It has always been my belief that we have failed to make adequate use of disabled people in the work force. It is usually their brain we are after, not their muscles or back. In this time of a severe shortage of qualified workers, employment of a handicapped person makes eminent sense, provided of course that "reasonable accommodation" for this person remains just that—reasonable. It certainly raises an individual's self-esteem to be gainfully employed and a contributor to society rather than a dependent of society. It is also beneficial to have a group of people off the welfare rolls and, instead, on the tax rolls.

Something has gone wrong, however, and I believe it began with the Americans with Disability Act (ADA). I believed that the principal problem once the law passed would be resentment on the part of coworkers as well as businesses and corporations for spending time and money on a chosen few. I also felt that the definition of "reasonable," as in reasonable efforts to accommodate the handicapped, would constantly rise, assuming unreasonable levels. What I didn't see, but perhaps should have, was the complete trivialization of disability, so that nearsightedness, back pain, and hypertension were claimed to be disabilities under the ADA, and the "victims" were able to sue for damages if they were not hired. Fortunately for us, the Supreme Court shot down those cases and we hopefully are back to a reasonable definition of disability—a physical handicap that only in part can be corrected but can be modified sufficiently for gainful employment.

If the Supreme Court had agreed to broaden the definition of disability, here are some things that could have conceivably happened. A mailman with flat feet, corns, or bunions would be given a golf cart to complete his or her route. Someone with hemorrhoids would be fitted with a silicone gel pad and his/her own Jaccuzzi. For the obese, businesses and corporations would have to build a gym in the office for special exercises, with a trainer, of course, who would be paid by the employer. These examples may sound really goofy, but they are certainly a logical extension of those cases brought before the Supreme Court. Extension is the key word to understand the Disability lobby.

I should have seen the formidable lobby that would develop around a new law such as this. Attorneys who specialize in Disability law. Social workers. Bureaucrats dealing with disability problems. Manufacturers of disability-related equipment. Foundations and organizations that specialize in helping people with disabilities. Legislators at the municipal state and federal level who have received campaign contributions from one or more of the above groups. They of course do have the welfare of the disabled at heart, but they also have self-interest at heart. Logic and common sense would dictate that their money and efforts should be concentrated on making more mobile, more functional, and more employable those people with true disability. Instead, their economic and social interest is to make the definition of such people as broad as possible, leading to the ridiculous cases brought before the Supreme Court, and the cries of horror from those whose attempt failed.

What about the disabled themselves? What is their attitude? They wish, and of course they are right to wish, that they be treated as other citizens who desire to become productive members of society, with only some modification of their transportation and work environment. Ramps, enlarged bathroom stalls, lower water coolers, special desks, public phones accessible to the handicapped all strike me as reasonable items, which can be modified for the benefit of the student or worker. Even handicapped parking spaces, although the reality of that situation shows the abuse to which a special treatment, an entitlement, can be seen as a reasonable accommodation. Convenient or reduced fare parking are enough of a stimulant for all sorts of abuses, which are frequently reported in the papers. When one gets to public transportation, however, the costs and the benefits really become out of sync. Millions of dollars are spent on buses with special lifts, or on those that kneel, all too often vastly underused. Paying for a taxi to transport people with disabilities would be a far cheaper, and better, use of public money, but is resisted by the disabled. Why?

I believe there are two conflicting urges amongst the disabled. The first is denial. If one can believe that one is just like "normal" people, then one can do everything that normal, or nondisabled, people do. Therefore since normal people ride buses to work, that is what they wish to do, in spite of the cost to society. The other urge is for victimhood. If one is a victim, one can fail with impunity ("It's not my fault. It's because I'm disabled"). One can gain emotionally by being involved in a cause, and one can gain economic power by being able to sue, with the expense of the suit being born by the government. A no-lose situation.

The ADA law makes an attempt to permit a class of people,

people with disability, to become productive, independent tax-paying citizens. On the other hand, the disability lobby, for their own needs, attempts to broaden and trivialize disability by making the definition so broad that essentially all of us would qualify. Those with disabilities who use denial and victimhood to promote their own needs contribute to the problems surrounding the ADA.

Bilingualism

There is a steady push for bilingualism in this country. What is meant by this is twofold: first, all public documents, signs, registrations (as for motor vehicles), and even voting should be done in two languages, and second, the other language should be Spanish. A corollary of this is that initial instruction in the schools should be given in a second language (see "English as a Second Language"). There is at least an implied entitlement to this, that it is our duty as a society to provide this service. To me—this is both disturbing as well as destructive.

The first question to be asked is, Why Spanish? It is true that the largest number of new immigrants speak Spanish, but that is scarcely the only foreign tongue. Indeed, our relatively new immigrants speak literally dozens of foreign tongues. Why should they be discriminated against? Second, although painful, full assimilation into the mainstream of America requires everyone to speak the same language, American English.

Nobody in the world has more experience in absorbing immigrants than America, experience over several centuries. That experience has taught us that children, with some help from the schools, learn to speak English in an unbelievably short period of time, only a few years. Those who have the most desire to succeed and the strongest push from their parents learn the fastest, but all will succeed. It is a far more difficult problem with adults. Basically, adults' familiarity with English breaks down into three classes.

The first group makes no effort to learn. They therefore stay in their own communities, speak only their native tongue, and have little to do with the larger outside community. By and large, they also work at more menial jobs.

The second group does make an effort to learn, perhaps attends night school classes, and is able to communicate in English but certainly not fluently. Their jobs too are more menial, although they may be performed outside of the native community because they can at least communicate in English. The third group learns to speak English fluently. Some have a slight accent, some none. They enter the mainstream and participate fully in the larger society. Their jobs are often more sophisticated and skillful than the others and are not limited to the native community. Which category the immigrant falls into depends on his or her desires and abilities.

It is not as though we are plowing new ground in pushing for bilingualism. Canada has done just that with French taking its place as an equal with English throughout the country. They have taken it one step further. Not only must all of the above situations prevail, but also people who do business with the public must be bilingual. Not because it is just good business but by government fiat. While it might make some sense in Quebec and possibly the adjoining eastern provinces, it makes little sense in the western provinces, where there is very little French spoken as a primary tongue. I am sure that it is honored more in the breach than in the fact, but it still produces a great deal of resentment.

We therefore have a concept that is flawed on all fronts. It delays assimilation and promotion in the larger society (there is absolutely nothing that prevents people from speaking their native tongue amongst their own); it creates resentment amongst those who are not native speakers but are not so favored by law; it creates difficulty and resentment amongst native speakers, and inevitably leads to ever greater demands, such as the requirement that those who deal with the public speak a second tongue. The net result is that we divide people instead of bringing them together. But that won't stop those who push for bilingualism.

The Death Penalty

The pattern is familiar and predictable. A horrific murder or series of murders explodes on us. We are shocked and depressed. Images of the victim(s) and their families are shown repeatedly. Calls are made for the capture of this cruel, heartless murderer. People live in fear. No effort should be spared to capture him, the media says. Then the presumed perpetrator is caught. Almost at once, sympathy shifts. His deprived or abused childhood, his mental capacities, and his skin color, if black, are all brought to bear. If he should have literary or artistic talents, he can't possibly be considered to have done the killing; why that is so is difficult to fathom. If such a person actually did it, he was provoked, and society, not the killer, was at fault.

Once the trial is over, the accused is convicted and the death penalty is invoked, the arguments against the death penalty start. The state has no right to take a life. Revenge is wrong. We are far more cruel than, say, Western Europe or Canada. The death penalty doesn't deter crime. What does one do if the death penalty has been applied to an innocent man?

There are counterarguments. In earlier times, the families, clans, or tribes exacted their own revenge, which in many cases was stylized, ritualized, and proportionate. When the modern nation state took over the dispensation of justice, it was reasonably expected that a heavy price would be extracted from the murderer, not only in the name of the victim but also of the larger society. Whether this should include the death penalty is open to debate, but we should remember that the death penalty was abolished by most states, only to be reinstated in the past two decades by most states. Why is that? I believe that to a large extent it is a question of numbers. If one vicious murder took place in the entire country in a year's time, compassion would prevail and the killer would simply be put away for the rest of his natural life. If there were no more than one such murder per state per year, the same would hold true. But we are dealing with dozens and dozens of murders per state, one more horrific than the next. If the state cannot protect its citizens from harm, it is not truly a functioning state. That is why state after state reenacted the death penalty. Why such a large number of horrible murders occur in the United States—far more than other democratic countries—is a different topic and worthy of further discussion.

The argument against putting to death what may be the wrong man is a powerful one, but let's examine it further. What if someone is incarcerated for thirty or forty years and then is found to be innocent? What if one is murdered in prison and subsequently found to be innocent? What if he is gang-raped and then develops AIDS? All of these are distinct possibilities. Does that mean that no one should go to prison because of the possibility of a mistake being made? Of course not. Mistakes are part of the human condition. Everything reasonable should be done to reduce mistakes to a minimum, but they will occur, in spite of our best efforts. Pilots make errors and passengers die. Railroad engineers make errors and trains crash. Physicians make errors and patients die. Pharmacists make errors and patients die. And so on. We should do everything humanly possible to reduce human error, particularly in situations where human life is at stake. But errors will occur. Perfection in human endeavors is a goal but not a realistic possibility.

However, it seems obvious that all that could have been done, and all that should have been done in capital cases was not done in state after state. The state has an obligation, even if the costs are higher, to provide adequate defense counsel. It has an obligation to run DNA testing if it could in any way produce evidence of innocence. I have not heard a discussion of what should be done to brutal murderers if DNA testing proves beyond a shadow of a doubt that they are indeed guilty of the crime with which they are charged. It should also be remembered that often there is only circumstantial evidence to point to the murderer. That is why we have trial by jury. If the point is made that a man should not be put to death unless there is clear-cut objective physical evidence, then the converse is that he should be put to death if such evidence exists.

The argument about deterrence seems to me rather strange. It would seem to me that the large number of incarcerated violent criminals and the falling violent crime rates are at least in some way related. Certainly for the perpetrators, they are no longer available to commit further crimes. Also, because of the extraordinary length of time between sentencing and execution, the killer is no longer a real person but an abstraction and one can forget the victims and the lifelong devastation of the victim's family.

Can we get by without the death penalty and still have justice for the victims and their families? I believe we can. I personally believe someone can be paroled after fifty years in prison, perhaps to some facility other than a maximum-security prison. I could say the same for someone completing forty years of hard labor. Or thirty years of solitary confinement. The actual number of years could be different providing the perpetrator is put away for a period of time that most people would consider to be a suitable punishment for the crime. The complaints against capital punishment would disappear, and it would even be cheaper for the state, since executions are terribly expensive.

I, and I suspect most people, get no personal satisfaction from an execution. It does, however, seem an appropriate treatment for some of the horrors that have been perpetrated on society. What, for example, should one do with Timothy McVeigh, who blew up several hundred people because of some grudge or other against the government? What to do with the two white men who dragged a black man behind their truck, leaving a trail of body parts? What to do with the men who beat a gay man and then tied him up outdoors in winter time to freeze to death? What to do with the man who raped and murdered a ninety-year old woman? And so on and so on. I have never heard, in effect, from opponents of the death penalty that the above type of murderers should be locked up and the key thrown away.

The problems that arise with punishment less than the death penalty are redemption and rehabilitation. As soon as the death penalty is abolished, cries will come for lessening the sentence of those who have been redeemed and/or rehabilitated. Now, I don't pretend to know who has been truly redeemed and/or rehabilitated and who has not, but I strongly suspect that there will be a large number of convicted killers who will claim redemption and rehabilitation, perhaps many more interested in reducing their sentence than in finding God and truly recognizing their antisocial behavior. If sentences are significantly reduced, society breaks its contract with the victim and their families. Surely their needs should surpass those of the killers.

Death Taxes

Inheritance taxes, colloquially called death taxes, is again a hot topic. Several bills are working their way through Congress.

President Clinton has promised to veto them, but since the first bill was passed by an overwhelming number of Republicans as well as approximately one-third of Democrats, it would seem that some form of legislation would resonate positively with the public and would in all likelihood be eventually passed, if not in this Congress, then the next. Here are some of the arguments against and for such legislation. It should be noted that the arguments both for and against are often somewhat disingenuous.

First against removal: When the bill was first passed, nearly a century ago, there were only an infinitesimal number of people who had any estates of any significant size, and it seemed fair that these few families should pay some intergenerational taxes. After all, there was essentially no income tax at the time, and there was concern that just a few families would accumulate inordinate amounts of wealth and the power that goes with it. During the House debates, the figure bandied about was that only two percent of families qualify for the taxes after the exemption. Here is the first disingenuous argument. Since the last decade of extraordinary prosperity, literally millions of people, many of them relatively young, have accumulated estates large enough to be subject to the inheritance taxes, and whereas before it was fine to see the Rockefellers and the like hit with enormous potential taxes, now it is much closer to home, and it hurts.

Second, it is seen by some as undemocratic that wealth should be obtained and then passed on to heirs.

Third, the government needs the tax money. Of course governments always need tax money. It is just a question of how they are going to obtain it.

Arguments for repeal: Wealth production and accumulation involves active effort. Tax avoidance requires active effort. It would be wiser to put energy into the former rather than the latter, with better results for society. When individuals go into a tax avoidance mode, decades may go by before their demise, and many are in a holding, not accumulating, mode—not a benefit for society. This argument would be bitterly opposed by estate planning attorneys, accountants, etcetera, but so what? Whereas before it was only a small exclusive club, it now is a much, much larger club of people who have climbed into the estate tax "problem," and it will continue to grow. In that sense, it is very democratic. It is a large group of people. It is nonexclusive, and it includes peoples of all political persuasions and all ethnic groups. No wonder a significant percentage of Democrats voted for the bill. Those congressmen who favor repeal are somewhat disingenuous too when they talk about the sale of the family farm or small business because of a lack of cash to pay the taxes. While it certainly happens, a far larger number of people have their funds in equities or commercial real estate, and they can sell out for cash. The question is, should they?

In a strange way, a lot of people will be facing for the first time the problem of large sums of money to be passed on to the next generation and will have to face the consequences and the downside of that. I believe it is true that unearned money is unappreciated money and families will find a number of heirs who lack the desire to generate assets further. They may even lack the desire to lead productive lives at all, behaving like European royals. However, when enough families see this happening, they will then take the next step and either directly donate large sums of money to charities or set up a Family Foundation to do the same thing, making the heirs comfortable but not enough to prevent them from being productive members of society.

In this sense, it will be far more democratic than what we have now, where a handful of politicians, bureaucrats, and activists direct the debate as to where the government should spend money on social programs. Rather, it will be literally millions of individuals and foundations, who will, by their funding, decide which social programs are worthy of support. The role of the government will not end, of course, but it will not be the sole source of funds and, therefore, will not exclusively set the rules. A good thing too.

There is a problem of the loss of tax money, money that will have to be made up somehow. I have no problem with some modest tax on inherited money, enough so those heirs realize it is not a free ride but not enough that their energies go to tax avoidance. The bigger problem, however, is underlying attitudes among some about wealth accumulation, and of course we are talking about honest accumulation, a result of hard work and perhaps some luck. The attitude is of jealousy and distrust. Those who hold that attitude seem to feel that there is something fundamentally wrong with being wealthy; it is just undemocratic, and it should not be allowed to stand. That seemed apparent in the House debates. The second attitude is that the government knows best, and individuals should not be involved in decision making about the dispersal of their money. That should be left in the hands of experts.

Drug Policy—Further Thoughts

It is difficult to overstate the amount of corruption that exists in Latin America, particularly in Colombia, Panama, and Mexico. From top to bottom, virtually all entities of government are hopelessly corrupt, in large part due to the drug trade. Incredible wealth exists alongside grinding poverty, a sure sign of civil strife in the future. These countries claim, with justification, that it is the U.S. that consumes enormous amounts of drugs, and it is that consumption that leads to enormous wealth for the drug dealers that breeds the corruption. There has always been a great deal of corruption in these countries, and it

149

cannot all be blamed on American drug consumption, but certainly a lot of it can. With enormous amounts of money at stake, it must certainly be true that there is widespread corruption in the United States as well, although except for a few cases, there has not been a great deal of publicity about this. It seems almost inconceivable to me that corruption does not exist amongst those individuals and institutions that come in contact with drug money. These would include banks and bankers, judges, lawyers, and enforcement officers.

We are terribly upset about the use of handguns, and wish them to be banned. We seem more ambivalent about the use of hard drugs, which destroy far more lives than handguns. Could it be that because many of our societal critics are or have been drug users themselves? It is certainly true that sixties-style liberals, who openly used drugs themselves, find it difficult to criticize their offspring when they do exactly the same thing. Personal pleasure (do whatever feels good, no matter what the consequences) rather than abstinence because of communal needs is the driving force. Actually, there are no communal needs, because we no longer have any communal standards. We must be completely nonjudgmental about everything.

Hollywood seems to be made up of moral midgets (they are available to fight all causes except those where they can make a difference) in their personal behavior as well as in the films they make, filled with gratuitous violence, cigarette smoking, hard core drug usage. In truth, the behavior of the sixties' liberals is both immoral and destructive and not only of the fabric of this country but of Latin America as well. That is a heavy burden to bear.

The sterile battle between interdiction and treatment goes on endlessly, although why it has to be one or the other I do not understand. I believe, however, that neither one will win the war on drugs. The most important element is societal disapproval. When a clear, unambiguous message comes from society at all levels that such behavior is unacceptable and simply cannot be allowed to stand, then both interdiction and treatment would have a greater chance of success.

Education

Historically, free public education has been one of the glories of America. Generation after generation of immigrants, many completely unlettered, have come to these shores, have received their free public education, have absorbed the principles on which America stands as well as their basic educational knowledge, and have gone on to achieve what their ancestors from their homelands of origin would be astonished to see—most of those having been fettered by a strict caste-based society. It should be noted in passing that the G.I. Bill after WWII did the same for higher education that free education did for secondary schools: namely, to provide literacy and a passport to a better life for people who would not even have considered higher education. It is therefore the shame of America to see the status of public education today, and that is why people place the problem so high on their list of concerns.

It is difficult now to realize that in times past, it was our cities where the best educational systems existed. Now the cities are for the most part a wasteland for education, but it must be admitted that problems galore exist in suburban schools as well. It is critically important at the dawn of the twenty-first century to realize that knowledge is the key in the information age, with a particular emphasis on science and technology. Those who have it will succeed. Those who don't will fall further and further behind.

The first task is to replace the wasteland, which is inner city education, with a functioning system that provides the basic educational tools needed for survival. The problems have gone on long enough and are serious enough that falling back on the old war cry, just give us more money, is simply not enough. New solutions must be looked at with an open mind. Some solutions will undoubtedly fail, but some will succeed and can be applied on a larger scale. Failure is a means of learning and should not be looked at as a total waste of time and money.

The teaching establishment should be in the forefront of change, but all too often, they place obstacles in the course of change for a variety of reasons. Fear of something different, bureaucratic inertia, clasping the past rather than looking to the future, fear of failure, fear for their own future, and undoubtedly many more things. It is thoroughly unfair, however, to place all of the blame on the schools, the teachers, and the administrators. Although society places one of its most challenging and important tasks, educating the next generation, in the hands of teachers, it does not seem to adequately respect them, and I am not just talking about salaries.

No longer do the best and brightest of our young people aspire to be teachers. Rather, they look towards other fields—other professions, business, etcetera. A recent report on the results of a test given to new teachers showed astonishingly bad results—not much higher results than would be expected by grade-schoolers. A vicious cycle of relatively poor salaries, looking down upon initiative, and little respect leads to better people fleeing elsewhere, which leads to a lower quality of people aspiring to being teachers. This can be reversed by putting teachers on a twelve-month contract (placing schools on a twelve-month year), requiring an M.A. for teaching starting with those teaching math and the hard sciences, eliminating undergraduate teachers' colleges or limiting those schools and programs to provide only M.A.s, and above all, respecting innovation. With a twelve-month year (granted, relatively few students would choose the summer months for school, and there would be an up-front cost for air conditioning the schools), fewer teachers would be required, and those kept could be paid more, or, at the very least, class size could be reduced. More pay means harder work, but that is the fair trade-off to be made.

There are essentially no professional groups that do not require a graduate degree, and teachers should be no different. Knowledge has grown so much that an undergraduate degree is simply not enough. This is particularly true in the hard sciences and math.

The problem of inner city schools cannot be blamed solely on deficiencies in the schools—facilities, equipment, teachers, administrators, boards of education, etcetera. The parents bear a direct responsibility as well. It is not lack of education on the part of the parents or impoverishment or crowding and a lack of privacy or lack of time to supervise studies due to the necessity for working long hours that accounts for the poor achievements of inner city students. After all, each and every one of those conditions was present when the inner city schools were the pride of the nation. Rather, it is the lack of an overwhelming commitment towards education as a means of self-improvement and a willingness on the part of the parents to sacrifice the present for the future that made education so successful in the past. When that changes, so will the achievements of the students.

By and large, suburban school systems are better than inner city schools. Not only is there a greater commitment on the part of parents and more funds for enrichment than is present in the inner cities, but aspirations of both students and parents are higher. However, when compared to the world scene, our students do not achieve at the top level, particularly in science and math. Yet, we should. However, this cannot be done without sacrifice. If we are to take our place as the leader of the new technological age, then more hours have to be devoted to study and more funds committed to better training and equipment for science. Perhaps there will have to be a lengthening of the school year. That inevitably will take away time from other things—enrichment, extracurricular activity, free time. Are we willing to make the sacrifice to achieve this? Time will tell.

What about the states' departments of Education and the federal Department of Education? They appear to function like all other bureaucracies, setting up projects, determining the rules for receiving the funds, and monitoring the recipients. They would do far better functioning as enablers and facilitators. Their emphasis should not be on disbursing and monitoring money but on the creation of new ideas and new ways of doing things. Seed money for innovation of all types should be made available, and they should then supply expertise when needed. Those ideas that fail should be discarded but only after it is determined how and why they failed. Those that succeed should be expanded, in an orderly fashion, to see if they function as well on a macro as on a micro scale. Publicity for those projects that succeed and those that fail should be spread widely, via meetings, reports, the web, etcetera. Those individuals with new ideas should be brought together to brainstorm further. They should encourage a bottom up, rather than a top down, process of innovation. This of course is in direct contradiction to their instincts to maintain control, and that instinct must be fought.

Education in America is a mixed bag. In the more affluent suburbs, a good public education is available, although perhaps weak in the hard sciences and math. This is reflected in the relative paucity of Americans in graduate programs in these subjects. In the inner cities, it is nothing short of a disaster. Why should hard-working taxpayers feel that only by way of private schools can a child get a decent education in large parts of the inner cities? I see no point in affixing blame, since there is plenty to go around and it is not a profitable exercise. Clearly, changes must be made. Many resist it for a variety of reasons, but it must come about. All changes that do not directly threaten the Constitution should be fairly considered and tried. If it fails, it fails, and it then should be discarded, but not before. A change in attitude on the part of everyone but, most particularly, the teaching establishment, is necessary. Few things are more important than a well-educated citizenry, and we as a society have every right to demand the best for all of our citizens.

English As a Second Language

We are a nation of immigrants. For over two hundred years, people have migrated here to obtain a better life. In the beginning, the immigrants were predominantly English-speaking and Protestant. Gradually, as migration patterns changed, fewer and fewer were native English speakers. That has never been a major problem for the young, who, having an overwhelming desire to assimilate and become "American," learned the English language in an extraordinarily short period of time. My own father, who immigrated here as a young boy, learned to speak flawless idiomatic American English and, like so many others, went on to college and graduate school.

I remember speaking to a young lady a few years ago who was translating for her grandmother, who spoke no English. When I asked her what she was going to do the coming year, she mentioned a prominent eastern college as her future school. I then asked her how long she had been in America, and she told me, three years. She spoke flawless English. It is undoubtedly more difficult for adults to learn a new language, as well as new customs, but it certainly can be done and has been done, in the millions. With the past as prologue, why are we now having such a to-do about learning English? English as a second language (ESL) studies have appeared and persisted in spite of the lack of any evidence that children tutored that way learn English any better or any faster than throwing kids into the water and swimming for themselves (and swim they will). Yes, there will be a painful year or two, but after that, they should do quite well.

The first question to ask is, in what languages are they to be taught, since people have recently immigrated from dozens and dozens of countries with dozens and dozens of different languages? Next, why are they not learning English, when immigrants did learn to speak English fluently throughout our history? The answers are multiple. An ESL bureaucracy has grown up, and, like all bureaucracies, they will defend their turf fiercely. Then there appears the argument that we are "forcing people" to be American. That seems to be an oxymoron because that is why people immigrate here, isn't it? There is a fundamental misunderstanding underlying the thinking that we are somehow denying their heritage if they learn proper English.

The truth is that we all live in at least two societies: one, the large public place of American society and, the second, the more private place of racial, religious, and national origin. In the second society people congregate to learn and reinforce their traditions, eat their ethnic foods, celebrate their own holidays, speak their mother tongues, and in general, let their hair down. There is no effort that I know of to deprive people of their private place. Indeed, we all celebrate and benefit from the existence of such places. The public place, however, is where we learn and where we work, and those who do not learn are therefore unable to compete for better jobs and are doomed to be at the bottom of society.

Certain groups are not doing well economically and socially, and we are therefore making a well-intentioned but, ultimately, a failing attempt to teach kids in their native tongues. This is primarily true among Hispanics but also has become evident in schools trying to have children speak English as a second language by teaching them in Black English, or "Ebonics." It is hoped that that pitiful attempt to solve fundamental problems has died an early and permanent death. With regard to Hispanics, the danger that they will not progress beyond Spanish is, in my opinion, a danger to the country. We can only see what is happening to our Canadian neighbor regarding language to do everything possible to prevent it from happening here.

I do not deny that there is considerable pain in assimilating new culture, new customs, and a new language. Fortunately the pain does not last forever, and young people have the advantage of learning naturally and rapidly. Indeed, it is the desire to succeed and the pressures from peers that cause children to learn thoroughly in a short time what adults may only learn, if even partially, over a lifetime.

Finally, there is the problem of stoop labor. Every modern industrial society needs people who will do the tasks that the rest of society shuns: migratory stoop labor to pick the crops; general laborers to dig ditches and lift heavy objects, sweep the streets, and collect the garbage; unskilled laborers to bus restaurant tables, wash the dishes; and many more. It is necessary that we have those jobs performed, and I am afraid that those in ESL programs will be the ones doing it.

Flag Burning

A constitutional amendment against desecration of the flag is again working its way through Congress. Rightly angered by those who would desecrate our national emblem, those in favor of such an amendment are motivated by patriotism, but I fear that their effort is doomed to failure. Here is why.

An endless stream of items have an American flag motif, from actual flags to beach towels, T-shirts, undershorts, coffee mugs, plates, and many more. The first problem is to define what is meant by a flag. If the above items are red, white, and blue and have stars and stripes, are they flags? What if an article looks like a typical flag but has the wrong number of stars or stripes. Is it still a flag? Can underwear truly be considered to be a flag? What about objects such as a coffee mug. Can it truly be seen as a flag?

What about desecration? Is burning your own underwear a crime against the Constitution? What if you break some crockery that is in the pattern of a flag? What if you cut a beach towel that has a flag pattern? I recently saw a picture of a model plane painted in the pattern of a flag? What if it crashed? Would that be considered defacement of the flag? What if you wore a flag T-shirt and splattered sauce on it? Is that flag defacement?

It (flag defacement) would produce endless jokes and, even more important, endless attempts by individuals and organizations to see how far they can go in making the law and the people who support it look silly, as well as vitiating the content of the bill. Rather than a new amendment to the Constitution, there should be strong and even overwhelming community disapproval for flag desecration. That will deter some but not all of the people. The second thing to do is to ignore or minimize as much as possible the publicity surrounding the act, because in most cases that is the real reason why the act is being carried out.

This is the greatest country on earth. There are more personal freedoms than ever existed anywhere in the globe, anywhere in history. Why would somebody enjoy all the blessings of liberty but still act in such an irresponsible fashion? There appears to be more than one reason. Perhaps a transient moment of fame. Perhaps self-aggrandizement. Perhaps a lack of judgment or self-control. Perhaps the thrill of pushing the envelope to see how far it will go. However, I believe that the most important reason is a complete unconcern for the feelings of others. Some people demand sensitivity and understanding for their own feelings and beliefs but are unwilling to grant it to others.

Free Speech

Free speech is a precious right. Indeed, it is a cornerstone of our democracy, a freedom that permits us to speak out in favor of unpopular causes and against what is considered by the speaker to be an unjust action by the government. This basic freedom is denied or curtailed in far too many countries in this world. At the same time it is a privilege, a privilege of being a citizen in a country that grants this precious right. Therefore, along with rights come responsibilities. These responsibilities are spelled out below and, to my mind, are as important as our rights if we are to have a stable, civil society.

We all recognize, or should recognize, that there are limits placed on our right to express free speech. It is commonly said that one cannot cry fire in a crowded movie theater. By that, it is meant that free speech cannot be used when such speech can cause harm to others, in this case by their being trampled to death in the rush to reach the exits. It is also recognized that one cannot preach sedition, which is harm to the state. There are also some gray areas.

Included in the gray areas are limits to where one can use free speech. Admittedly some of these are judgment calls, but that is all right, since we are constantly called upon to make judgment calls. In the academic environment, free speech is limited, or should be limited, to ideas that have intellectual validity, since respectability for the idea is given by having it discussed in an academic environment. Presumably, given that an idea has intellectual validity, all ideas and all viewpoints are welcomed and are open to serious consideration by the academic community.

Nothing of course could be further from the truth. Unpopular, particularly politically incorrect, ideas are given short shrift on college campuses. Not just that, it is thought to be proper to drown out speakers who have been invited on campus to express such ideas. Apparently even listening to a politically incorrect idea is enough to cause behavior that is against the very concepts of a university. Isn't that behavior the equivalent of book-burning. If you burn the book, you destroy the idea. If you drown out unpopular speech, you destroy the idea. No real difference.

Further, rule upon rule at campus after campus are promulgated the dictation of appropriate speech codes. Those who violate such rules are punished severely, even expelled. On at least one campus the offender was forced to recant and then sent for reeducation. Isn't that exactly what happened in Vietnam after the war, where people were sent to reeducation camps? Indeed, in all communist countries? One would think the faculty, mindful of the importance of exposure to differing points of view as the sine qua non of education would be up in arms, unreservedly condemning such behavior and such rules, but in actuality, they are often the initiating forces in such actions.

So much for the wisdom and judgment of college faculties. Whatever happened to the idea of disagreeing with ideas but defending to the death the right to express them. These very same faculty members are often writing op/ed and scholarly pieces about the evils of censorship, without even a hint of irony.

In the public square, essentially all ideas, those that have and those that do not have established content are open for discussion. The modern day version of the public square is of course the Internet. Pretty much anything goes, since it is so difficult to limit "speech" that comes in over the airways, literally from anywhere. However, there is still considerable discussion as to what is proper for children to receive via the Internet and how parents can block access to what they consider objectionable content. A very difficult task indeed.

TV falls in between academia and the public square. Some TV (a relatively small part) mimics academia and presents differing ideas for discussion and edification. Most of TV tends towards speech at the level of the public square. There is no question that over the years there has been a coarsening of discussion and a dumbing of ideas. While carrying the banner of free speech, more and more TV has been appealing to the baser instincts of people and their apparently insatiable demand for excitement and titillation. Sex, violence, foul language, public humiliation, and more are all considered valid forms of free speech on the public airwaves. If it is mentioned that these are indeed public airwaves and the use of them requires some discretion on the part of the broadcaster, one is immediately accused of censorship. We are again faced with the problem of how a parent controls what is appropriate for his or her child to view. The V-chip is one attempt, but I have no doubt that the children will, in short order, figure out a way around such attempts.

There are certainly some major problem areas regarding free speech, verbal and written. The first is hate speech. Here it seems to me that we can and should offer the widest latitude for this type of speech as long as it is not a call to violence. John Rocker, the Atlanta Braves baseball player, may be an ignoramus, but just because his speech is most unpopular, should it be punished any worse than anyone else? There is also a clear remedy for this problem. This remedy includes exposure so that all know the vile content and the ability to vigorously counterattack with facts.

Next is sick speech, such as child pornography. I personally think there is no place for this, anywhere, anytime. However, with the Internet, it is impossible to stop, at least at the present time with the present technology. The next type of speech is vile speech. There clearly has been a coarsening of language; what previously had been considered unthinkable of uttering is now commonplace. It certainly shows the limitation of the mind and of the imagination to express oneself only with an endless stream of vulgarities. Here we can use the concepts of time and location. What is appropriate in one setting and at one time may be entirely inappropriate at another.

The next form of speech is dangerous speech. This includes books, pamphlets, and the Internet on techniques of how to make firearms, bombs, and explosives, how to assassinate people, and even how to make an atomic bomb. The argument in favor of such information is that it is available elsewhere in public places—libraries, Internet, etcetera. True. One can also learn these things by joining the army, belonging to a terrorist group, or by theft of national secrets. The real question is whether publishers or Internet sites are behaving responsibly in collating, organizing, publicizing, and distributing such information? Aren't great responsibilities the necessary counterweight to great freedoms?

There will never be a final answer on the extent of, and limits to free speech. We will always have an opposite trend. Increasing freedom will lead to increasing licentiousness, while limiting of freedom will lead to increasing censorship. It seems to be human nature to seek the extremes rather than striving for moderation. Therefore, there cannot be absolute rules, but rather, the existence of many gray areas, which will need to be solved on a case-by-case basis. These cases can be solved on a local level, for example, the school boards or by the courts, depending on the circumstances. The feelings of the community can lead to the passing of local ordinances that indicate how far the community is willing to go on a specific free speech problem. The courts will always be available to those who wish to challenge the judgment of the community.

In general, I believe that free speech is so basic that it should be allowed to the maximum, but it need be clearly understood that everything has its price. Unpopular as well as popular ideas will be expressed. Parents will lose some control over their children. Vile and disgusting "speech" will seep into our homes. At some point and on some issues, the community will rise up in righteous wrath, and such speech will be censored. In such an important freedom, conflict over its extent is normal.

Government Social Programs

Since the time of the New Deal, the federal government has become increasingly involved in treating persistent social problems. Hunger, poor housing, lack of jobs, lack of job skills, lack of education, deficient public health are all serious problems that have to be addressed. Like the once annual arrival of a new Broadway musical or a new hotel in Miami Beach, there used to arrive each year a bewildering array of new social programs. The New Deal, Fair Deal, Great Society were only the programs with names. Many, many more programs were put into effect. Money was poured into each and every one of the above, but billions and billions of dollars later, it is difficult to say that the problems being addressed have disappeared or, even, significantly improved. The one exception is welfare reform, where a clear shift in perception on the part of most people has taken place.

Improved social policy does not come without some pain, but in the main, everyone has benefited by placing in jobs people who were formerly on the dole—the recipients, the local, state, and national governments, which provided the funds, and society in general. I do not doubt that there are some people who are incapable of working and will become permanent wards of the state. Others, however, have started to crawl out of the hole of perpetual dependency, and that is truly heartwarming. Their stories of feeling like a participating member of society, and the psychological benefit that accrues is terribly important. Frankly the only people who have not benefited from the massive reduction of people on welfare are the bureaucrats who administer the program.

Given the fact that this new approach to social problems has worked, while others that persist have not, one would think that people would look eagerly for new ways to solve societal problems—but one would be wrong. The reiteration of the same failed policies, coupled with the plea for larger and larger sums of money, is scary.

Government Syndromes

I have served in three separate government agencies and have had a chance to observe them closely. Although they differed markedly in quality, the same basic characteristics were observed in them all and distinct syndromes were seen.

More and Better Syndrome

All organizational problems can be solved with more personnel, more money, better facilities, and so forth. Somehow it seldom works out that way. More expansion leads to new directorates; therefore, the organization functions less efficiently than before. More time is spent on internal problems (parking privileges, vacations, turf wars, for example) than on solving the external problems for which they were created. At one agency in which I served, a decrepit aging facility was replaced with a new one, but no real change in function or in attitude occurred. The opposite of expansion is downsizing, imposed by those outside the agency. One would think that the people in the field, those who actually inspect our food, check the safety of our water supply, of our energy supply, and so forth, would be immune from downsizing. However, all too often, it is the central office personnel who are protected and the workers in the field who pay the price of downsizing—losing their jobs.

Leaning-Hard Syndrome

The premise is that when problems occur, one leans hard on people and things will get done faster. It may be true in the short run, but it is self-defeating in the long run; people do not function well under a constant whip. Anxiety and bitterness are not long-range tools for productive work. The diversion of energy and personnel to accomplish the task decreases energy to perform other tasks, and as a consequence, they suffer from a lack of attention.

Get Along/Go Along Syndrome

It is easier to get along and go along than it is to fight the system, even if one feels that the system is not functioning as it should. This leads to groupthink and punishes original thinking. Government is not the place for iconoclasts, even though original thinking about a problem, provided it is not in excess, can only be beneficial.

Problem-Solving Syndromes

Meetings: The standard approach to a problem is to call a meeting. Everyone wishes to protect his turf so he/she wishes to be included in the meeting. Because of the resultant enlarged size of the meeting, less is accomplished and yet another meeting must be scheduled. The meetings themselves become the object, rather than the means, to solve the problem.

Attitudes: One can count on someone at the meeting to say one or more of the following things. "It won't work." "It is too difficult." "We've tried it before." "It's too expensive." It is a lot easier to raise reasons why something new cannot work than expending energy on making it work. The objections frequently have no relation to the problem at all but rather relate to the individual's feelings of insecurity, to personality clashes, to turf wars, and so on.

The question arises as to whether the same things happen in the private sector. Of course they do. It is the nature of organizations and how people function in them. There is, however, a fundamental difference between the private sector and government. If things go wrong in a private organization, the CEO (often a new CEO) and the board of directors will do whatever is necessary to right the ship—layoffs, closing, containment of expenses, and so forth. Unfortunately, these things do not happen often in government organizations.

Gun Control

There has been more than enough senseless gun violence the past few years to drive sensible people to seek help, any help, to bring it to a halt. Hence the Million Mom march to stop gun violence. They raise the not unreasonable proposition that a few ideas, such as gun locks to prevent child misuse,

166

appropriate background checks on prospective purchasers, and limitations on the number of gun purchases an individual may make at one time might limit the amount of violence. The proposition is reasonable, but the expected results are extremely unlikely for the following reasons.

Before getting to the reasons for the likely failure of the initiatives, let us look at the reaction of the National Rifle Association (NRA), a reaction that was entirely predictable. They claim that any effort to limit or modify sales of guns, however necessary and sensible, will inevitably lead to confiscation of all guns. This is as highly dubious a proposition as the claim of supporters of the First Amendment that any effort, however sensible and necessary, to limit the First Amendment will have a "chilling effect," which will lead inevitably to the taking away of all of our First Amendment protections. Both are completely wrong, are based on the theory of the inevitability of the slippery slope, and give no credit to the common sense of the American people. In a delightful irony and without any understanding of the implications of what they are proposing, the leaders and supporters of the march, largely First Amendment stalwarts, are saying that the Bill of Rights can be appropriately modified when the need arises, ignoring the fact that others will say that the supposedly untouchable First Amendment can also be modified when the need arises.

Leaving the above aside, what about the benefits of the proposed changes to gun manufacture and gun purchase? With all of the incidents of gun violence caused both by adults and children, only an infinitesimal number (surely less than one percent) of the population is actually involved in violent gun incidents. They certainly cause a lot of damage and destruction, but why do those people act the way that they do? Many of the episodes have been perpetrated by people who are clearly unstable mentally. They have been in and out of mental institutions, but have not stayed where they could be supervised and forced to take their prescribed medication. Instead, our laws prevent people from being committed against their will and from staying in if they appear psychologically stable (that is, they are on regular doses of their medicine). Here is an interesting dilemma. Dozens upon dozens of people have been killed because dangerous psychotics have been let loose in the general population. Can we infringe upon their civil liberties in order to save others? There is certainly no easy answer, but the Million Moms didn't bother to raise the disturbing question.

While ninety-nine percent of the population can handle the violence that pervades our pop culture—movies, videos, music, etcetera—there appears to be a small number who mistake what they see and hear for the real thing, and act accordingly. Shouldn't there at least be a discussion and then a program, of action that limits the amount of violence that surrounds us, to protect us from dangerous actions taken by the few? The Million Moms didn't bother to raise the question.

Guns are scarcely new in our society, so why are we only recently seeing such an explosion of their use in a violent fashion? Is there a permissiveness that pervades our society and permits people to act out their feelings, even violent feelings? Is there a lack of a sense of societal judgment about what is right and what is wrong, which fails to inhibit violent actions? The Million Moms didn't bother to raise the question.

By and large, the Million Moms were middle-class and upper-middle-class moms from the suburbs and the better urban neighborhoods. I would guess that not only were their children not killed or even threatened by guns, but that they did not directly know of anyone who was. The problem facing their children were and are alcohol consumption and its complications, such as drunk driving, the use of illicit drugs, group sex by not only older teens but early teens and even subteens, sexually transmitted disease and teenage pregnancy. Having failed miserably in controlling and solving all of the above problems, they focus on a problem that is deeply disturbing but certainly not in their neighborhoods.

We all understand that people, including children, including very young children, can obtain all the alcohol, cigarettes, and illegal drugs they want. The only thing necessary is cash. Why would anyone believe that the obtaining of guns would be any different? "Well," the Million Moms reply, "we have to do something. We have to try." All very well, as long as it is understood that doing something, anything (that is, feeling good), is not the same as doing good. We have to address some of the troubling questions raised above if we are going to make a dent in the slaughter we read about on a daily basis.

Hard Drugs—No Easy Choices

I start with the premise that recreational drug use (herein called drug use) has become a scourge to our society. This is not a self-evident statement, since there appears to be a segment of our society that feels that drug use is not all that bad; at the very worst, it is a victimless crime. As a physician who in the course of practice has had contact with families in which there is a drug user and has seen the devastation this use has caused, it is perfectly clear to me that this is not a victimless problem. To me, drug use is an extraordinary waste of resources, human and material; it fosters corruption at many levels of society; it promotes crime; it interferes with productivity; and most important, it produces personal and family grief that is painful, destructive, and unnecessary.

Our current methods of combating this scourge are terrible. One can only hope that recently introduced measures by the Office of National Drug Control Policy will ameliorate the situation. However, even though the current system for combating drug use is bad, the proposal for legitimizing drug sales and usage makes little sense to me (see "A Few Simple Questions"). Born out of frustration and anger rather than rational thought, it is highly likely to substitute one set of problems for another and, in all probability, will be infinitely worse (ref).

Drug use in this country is not new. In one form or another, most of the naturally occurring drugs, as well as the synthetic ones manufactured from an opium base, have been used in our country either licitly (over-the-counter sales and by prescription) or illicitly. There are significant differences, however, between the current wave of drug usage over the past quarter-century and those that came before.

The first difference is the prevalence of drug usage. Whereas once there were relatively small pockets of usage of the various substances, now we are dealing with an enormous number of users.

The second difference is the use of polypharmacy. Whereas, before, it was largely a case of an individual using one drug, with or without addiction, now, see people experimenting and using multiple drugs, often at the same time. Most important, the current wave of usage is largely among our children and our young adults. If our society is incapable of acting in an effective manner to protect our children, then it is questionable whether we can call ourselves a worthy society.

By nature, human behavior is flawed and, therefore, the society, which is the totality of human behavior, is flawed. Our behavior as individuals is often contradictory and irrational and, therefore, so is that of society. Discussion about an effective approach to the drug problem often degenerates into scoring debating points, directing attention to how this substance or that policy is treated in a different fashion from that substance or that policy, and this or that point is therefore irrational. It may well be, but that should not prevent us from coming up with reasonable solutions to the problems at hand.

The substances most frequently compared to drugs are alcohol and tobacco. An attempt will be made to show that each one is different, although of course, with certain similarities. Some approaches to the drug problem will be offered. I speak only as a concerned citizen and not as an expert in the field, if indeed there are any, since at bottom, this is a societal problem, not a police (legal) or a health problem. If we can change societal beliefs and perceptions, we will be left with a much smaller and more manageable problem.

Alcohol

The use of alcohol is buried in antiquity. It was in use in virtually all cultures and certainly throughout Western civilization. Nearly all fruits and grains as well as other products, such as milk, have been fermented to obtain alcohol. In Western society, it has been and continues to be employed in a wide variety of religious ceremonies, civil functions, and for virtually all social occasions. The reason for its widespread use throughout society is that, unlike other substances, it promotes sociability, and sociability is a very necessary human need. Because of this positive aspect of alcohol use, it is clear that abolition via the Volstead Act was a hopeless aberration and doomed to fail. It is perfectly true that people abuse alcohol, but so too do they abuse pets, children, and spouses and yet nobody is suggesting their abolition.

There are some clear areas of progress in dealing with the major problems of alcohol abuse. Recognition of alcoholism as a disease rather than simply a human weakness has led to research on its underlying causes as well as to improved treatment. There have also been positive changes in societal attitudes as well. The friendly drunk is looked on more with pity and embarrassment than with humor. No longer will people with evidence of drunkenness be permitted to endanger others on the highway. Society has been willing to sacrifice a small piece of its personal freedom for the common good by permitting police to stop and test people whose driving leads to the suspicion of driving under the influence. Education by Mothers Against Drunk Driving (MADD) and Students Against Drunk Driving (SADD) chapters have been helpful as well. If one looks at old movies or early TV shows, one could see a clear difference in the portrayal of people drinking to excess, driving under the influence, and so on, from what one sees now. The same is true for the smoking of cigarettes.

Despite progress, major problems remain. There is still too much glorification of drinking to excess. In a recent college alumnus magazine article, one of the creators of the movie *Animal House* bragged about drinking not as an adjunct to having a good time but of the glories of staggering, falling down, throwing up drinking. If that is the attitude of some adults, is it any wonder that teenagers will mimic them. The whole area of teenage drinking, at both the high school and college level, is a matter of concern. High school kids are still under parental control. The continued reports in the newspapers and word of mouth indicate an enormous excess of usage by high school teenagers. Parents must either have little concern about it or lack the will to control the problem.

On the college level, where parents are absent and schools no longer act in loco parentis, drinking is a major problem on college campuses. I have been assured by several college health professionals that the problem is no worse than when I went to college forty-plus years ago. They certainly did not state that it was any better. Indeed, the current national statistics show thirteen percent of males of college age and five percent of college age females to be alcoholics (ref). Even if no worse than that of decades ago, it is hardly a picture of which we can be proud.

In spite of progress, there is still a great deal to do. New information as to why some people become alcoholics, while others who drink just as much do not is just coming to the fore. If a genetic defect is responsible for this, then better treatment plans can be formulated. How to make drinking alcohol pleasurable but with responsibility is a social, not a medical problem. The basic mechanism will have to be peer pressure. How to generate that peer pressure is our great challenge.

Tobacco

The history of tobacco usage is interesting because, unlike alcohol, its use in Europe, Asia, and Africa was unknown before Columbus. Initially, it was used for medicinal purposes. Another century or so passed until it was cultivated, marketed, and used as we do now. It plays no role in religious or civil ceremonies (other than its historic role among American Indians) and, in contradistinction to alcohol, is used primarily for personal pleasure and personal gratification. If there is a socialization role, it is purely secondary.

As physicians, we have known for decades the harmful, deadly effects of tobacco and have not required the ultimate in statistical analysis to know it. We have also acted upon this knowledge. The AMA has long since ceased to accept advertising in the *Journal of the American Medical Association (JAMA)* for tobacco products. Years ago, one entered a medical meeting room only to be enveloped in a blue haze of smoke, where the nonsmoker did not have a chance. That has changed completely and not only in medical meetings.

There has been a dramatic change in attitude about tobacco, which I believe preceded the drop in its use. The clear disadvantages of tobacco usage, coupled with its no longer being seen as a sign of sophistication and worldliness, has lessened its usage, at least among white-collar people. This apparently is not true among blue-collar people, and their usage of tobacco has continued unabated. Education has of course been helpful but if not translated into societal and peer disapproval, its use would not have dropped. Finally, the fitness craze has played some role, but it would seem limited, since both alcohol and drug usage interfere with athletic performance, and their usage has not appreciably dropped. The clear-cut change in attitudes, at least among the upper classes, towards tobacco usage and the resultant drop in usage may be used as a paradigm for our approach to control drug usage.

Drugs

As has been pointed out, illicit drug usage is no newcomer to Western society, with pockets of usage of all major drugs present, but not throughout society. Beginning with the 1960s a significant change in drug usage appeared—widespread usage throughout society, waves of different drugs sweeping through, receding but never disappearing, the use of polypharmacy, and most important of all, principal usage falling among children and young adults. The famous words of Timothy Leary, "turn on, tune out," seemed to exemplify the attitude for such usage. As with tobacco, the principal purpose of drugs is not increased socialization (with the possible exception of cocaine) but personal self-gratification.

It is not clear what needs are being fulfilled by this widespread usage of drugs, and this would appear to be a fruitful area of investigation. Is it youthful rebellion, alienation from society, excessive concern with self-gratification at the expense of society, or is it perhaps too much disposable income? Is it all of these or just some? Are there other factors not mentioned here? The problem is probably multifactorial, but if some dominant causes emerge, strategies for combating them can be developed.

Politicians, editorialists, commentators of all sorts, and the public at large have proclaimed that we have embarked upon a war. It is useful to remember some things about war, lessons that should have been learned from Vietnam. First, we should not declare war unless we have the intention of winning. Second, war demands sacrifice from its citizens, and third, a war cannot be fought without suffering casualties (primarily to our civil liberties). Exactly how much sacrifice and exactly how many casualties we are prepared to take is up to the people to decide, but we should have a fairly good idea of this before embarking on a war.

A tremendous amount of time and energy is being spent in determining whether we should concentrate our efforts on supply or demand. I personally feel that anything and everything we can do is helpful, but we should remember that decrease in supply is the role primarily of government but decrease in demand is the role primarily of the citizenry. How we as citizens can modify behavior to decrease demand is what needs to be discussed.

Decreasing demand can be done by both positive and negative enforcers. The most commonly mentioned positive enforcer to alter behavior is education about harmful effects. One cannot be against education, and there can never be too much education. Of course it does have a role to play in the long term. Bitter fights take place over the dollar amount allotted to supply versus demand, which is largely interpreted as meaning education. Yet education as done by volunteer groups, as part of schoolwork in the classroom and at assemblies, and as public service announcements is relatively inexpensive.

I am suspicious, however, that those who pronounce education to be our answer to drugs may have the idea of setting up an enormous bureaucracy with vast programming and with the hiring of counselors (and their staff) for each school, and elsewhere. That did not take place with education about tobacco and was not necessary. Ultimately, the limitation of education is that the population being addressed by educational means is the young, and they believe, whatever the evidence to the contrary, that they are immortal. Bad things can happen to those to the right and to the left of them but never to themselves.

More important than education per se is a change in attitudes and perceptions on the part of our society. Education may of course contribute to this, but it is not the whole answer. How to do this effectively is the question, but perhaps we could learn from the tobacco paradigm and attempt to apply it to drug usage.

In addition to the positive motivators, the negative motivator is punishment. Such punishment must be considered separately for dealers and for users. It is in the area of punishment where society must determine what sacrifices of individuals' rights we are willing to make in wartime (we have, after all, declared a war on drugs) to further communal needs.

In past wars, we have recognized the sacrifice of individuals' rights (everything from the draft to rationing) for the sake of the common good. These did not result in a permanent loss of freedom, for when the war was over, our rights were restored. If anyone would say that there is a danger in giving up liberties, he would be correct. However, there is a clear and present danger facing us as a society today. Eternal vigilance is the price of liberty, and liberty must be restored as soon as the danger has passed.

I make no case for punishment for dealers other than the current one of a prison sentence. Perhaps that is all that is necessary, although, obviously, we will have to continue to build more and larger prisons. However, if one were to suggest mandatory life imprisonment for pushers to children, the licensing of bounty hunters for known dealers, or permission for the police to shoot to kill known dealers, or indeed any other measure, I for one would be willing to give it a fair hearing.

With regard to users, punishment has been a sometime thing, unusually harsh for one drug in one community and unusually mild in another community. The majority of consumers of illicit drugs are middle class (certainly this is where the money that fuels the drug trade comes from), are recreational users, and are nonaddicted. They blithely put their own pleasure and gratification above all the harm that befalls society as a result of their insatiable appetite. To me, the proper punishment for the middle-class recreational drug user is not prison but a combination of economic pain, humiliation, and community service.

Economic pain can be applied by the imposition of huge fines, with impoundment of personal property if the cash is not available. Humiliation for middle-class adults is the publication of their name in the local newspaper, preferably accompanied by a picture. If it is a minor who uses, the appearance of the minor and his parents at a school assembly, impressively flanked by police officers, might have a salutary effect on other parents to be more observant of their children.

Those who recognize the problem with their children and assist them in seeking counseling should be praised. Those who turn a blind eye or prefer to pretend that nothing is wrong should be punished. Finally, community service is an appropriate way for the individual to pay back society for the trouble and expense the individual has caused.

A more difficult problem, if that is conceivable, is dealing with inner city or lower class users. The previously mentioned sanctions would in all likelihood not have the desired effect. This group is less status-oriented, less future-oriented, and tend more to think of the here and now rather than of the future. Rather than sanctions, efforts might be directed to a restructuring of the family (both nuclear and extended), instillation of the work ethic and participation in, rather than alienation from, the larger society. A tall order no doubt, but a necessary prelude to getting a handle on inner city drug use.

When a social problem is difficult, painful, destructive, expensive, and intractable, well-meaning, but wild and woolly, approaches for dealing with it are put forth. One of these, drug legalization, is dealt with elsewhere. Others range from the libertarian approach (that is, let people do what they want, and if they kill themselves, so be it) to the ultraliberal approach (which emphasizes the role of government in education and medical treatment).

When thought about carefully, these approaches emphasize the vague and the philosophical, dealing with glittering generalities, while ignoring the hard and practical realities. The devil is indeed in the details, and once the details are pointed out, these theories do not hold water.

There are two concepts that should be remembered about our drug crisis. First, it is an epidemic, and one of relatively recent origin; therefore, it has the potential to be reversed. Second, more than any specific measure or combination of measures taken, it is the will of society that will determine whether this epidemic can be overcome. Given the will, we can develop the measures necessary to fight the epidemic. Unfortunately, at this time, we do not have the will (indeed, we have too many prominent people participating in drug usage and seeing nothing wrong about it); therefore, the battle will not be won.

Conclusion

I conclude where I started. Drug use in its current form and extent is a clear and present danger to our society. What we have done thus far is not very promising. Worse than that, our programs have been confusing and contradictory. It is hoped that we will be doing better. If not, hard choices will have to be made about the kind of society we want, what we are willing to pay to have such a society in terms of sacrifice, of our dollars, and our civil liberties.

References

Zohn, D.A.: Legitimizing Drugs—A Few Simple Questions. *Virginia Medicine,* June 1990.

Meilman, P.; Gaylor, M.: *Substance Abuse in College Psychotherapy.* Guilford Press: New York.

Humiliation—An Underused Tool

Absolute control by the state leads to tyranny, but absolute individual rights leads to chaos. The struggle has always been to give maximum individual freedom and still meet the overall needs of the society. Sometimes, solutions tilt one way and sometimes the other, but it is clear, at least to me, that the pendulum has tilted too far to the needs of the individual, ignoring the needs of the larger society. Most observers would, I believe, recognize that in spite of our unprecedented economic progress, something is terribly wrong with our society. We have an essentially value-free society, money being the only value. Wisdom, age, knowledge, and achievement are looked upon with benign neglect. If he's so ——— (fill in the blank), why isn't he rich, people say.

Crime is the curse of all cities, preventing the redevelopment that would remake the city the vital center of the region. Yes, crime statistics are down, but we don't know yet whether this reflects an increased number of police and improved policing techniques, increased incarcerations, or some other combination. We also don't know whether this reflects a trend or is only a temporary downturn, as drug and alcohol abuse amongst teenagers and younger are abnormally high. There is also a reluctance of the citizenry to become involved because of time constraints on the family, as well as the overwhelming fear of lawsuits.

Before getting to the reasons for the breakdown, let me say that there was a time when things were very, very different—the thirties to the fifties. I do not wish to idealize those times because there was much to criticize, but teenage alcohol and drug use was virtually nonexistent. Fear of personal harm was extremely low. As a young teenager, I rode the subway to and from Manhattan, at night and alone, with absolutely no fear. Our family sat in the park, and strolled along the avenues on warm summer evenings with no fear.

Many families did not even lock their doors during the day. As bizarre as it sounds, even gangsters behaved well when not involved in their work. People knew what they, the gangsters, did for a living, but they could still interact with them. During the day, my uncle's small candy store (a shop selling newspapers, photography film, and candy and soda fountain services) was protected by them, and my three female cousins were safe with them. Larger neighborhoods were also protected by mobsters. Crimes against individuals did exist, but they were extremely rare. People often relied on them more for their safety than on the police. Lawyers were counselors and not sharks. A decade ago, the country had a good laugh about Dan Quayle's family-values campaign. Such a bizarre notion. How could he have come up with it? Now it has become a mainstream idea with which pols and the public feel quite comfortable.

Why have we had this civil breakdown? The answers are multifactorial. Authority and authority figures have been cast aside—the cop on the beat, the teacher, the principal, the family physician—all figures of authority have been cast aside because individual rights cannot be trumped by anything, certainly not the safety and well being of the community. We have become nonjudgmental, therefore, youngsters do not know right from wrong. Without an underlying system of values, restraints on individual behavior are no longer in place; therefore the only criterion is if it feels good, do it. Sacrifices of the present for the future is not seen as a worthy idea. The selfish idea that individual needs are far more important than sacrificing for the community is rampant. The lack of community in role-modeling and in keeping an eye out for potential trouble makers among the young has resulted in the large-scale break-up of the nuclear family and the scattering of relatives all over the country. If Mom and Dad weren't around, Uncle Charlie or Aunt Jane or Grandma Bea were, and there would be no place for the miscreant to hide. They would also provide role models for the kids to emulate. Approval or disapproval could be given or withheld, and the child would clearly know the difference. Standards of public behavior were set.

Adults tried to meet those standards (or themselves face ostracism) and these served to be role models and to restrain asocial behavior. Individual responsibility was important. If I cut off my finger with a lawn mower due to my own carelessness or tripped and fell because I was not looking where I was going, I did not rush to sue everyone in sight, implicitly stating that someone else was at fault, not I. Of course, I except those cases where negligence is clear-cut—the only lesson for those people and companies is an economic one. Even those individuals whose asocial behavior causes them to commit absolutely horrendous crimes become, in time, to be seen as victims.

The idea of self-choice for everyone, with resultant responsibility for those choices, seems foreign to many. Recently, there has been a spate of books based on the generation that fought in WWII, both as soldiers and civilians, portraying them as being far superior to the current generation and enabling the free world to survive and prosper. I don't believe that is the case.

They were perfectly ordinary people with exactly the same strengths and weaknesses that people exhibit today. What they did have was a powerful sense of patriotism, which they were not ashamed to exhibit, and a willingness to sacrifice their own needs for the good of their country. How very different today.

Given the deterioration and the coarsening of society, what can be done to protect ourselves? Prison may be an answer for some, particularly the violent predators. Reformers say that they are worse when they get out because they learn about bad things, but what else would you do with them? I believe the larger prisoner population has much to do with the fall in national crime statistics. Doing nothing (giving him a second chance) or sending him to school are really not solutions for anything but soothing the minds of those that propose them. We can, and should, reinstitute behavior control by means of public humiliation. This was done rather crudely in the past by shunning the individual malefactor ("sending him to Coventry" in the British parlance) or by more physical means—the stocks, the scarlet letter—in our colonial times.

In modern times, humiliation could be both public and economic. A heavy fine plus publication in the newspapers of the offender and the offence would serve, at least for some to prevent relapses in the future. For children who abuse alcohol or drugs, a high school assembly with their parents present, and their misdeeds publicly read out, as well as publication of the family name and the offense in the newspaper would surely stimulate parents to be more observant of their children's behavior. A heavy economic fine on the parents would also be appropriate. I rather suspect that it would not take too many assemblies before parents got the message. Raising children does involve sacrifices as against the many benefits that accrue to parents having the children. If one doesn't want the necessary sacrifices, that's fine—just don't have children. Don't have them as status symbols or trophies. While each family has the absolute right to do what it wants regarding their children, it can be the feeling of the community at large that having children involves sacrifices as well as pleasure.

Humiliation alone is not enough. A positive program keyed to the community and its needs is necessary. A change in perception about the community and putting it into better balance with the needs of the individual is essential. What I have been talking about, namely the role of public humiliation, applies to the middle class, but I am not at all sure it would apply to the lower classes. Diversion of some of the middle-class funds obtained from fines to lower-class help may be one way of helping, but I don't delude myself that it would solve the entire problem. Such a solution must come from within the community.

Immigration

We are a nation of immigrants. I am a child of immigrants. Every day I give thanks and gratitude to America, both for being a wonderful country and for taking in my parents and grandparents nearly a century ago. Had they not, it is unlikely that any of our family would have survived WWII. It is pointless to argue who was worse, the Nazis or the Communists. Both were incredibly evil, and one or the other of them would in all likelihood have done us in.

I am therefore committed to immigration. But it should be recognized that significant changes have occurred since the mass migrations that started after the Civil War and extended until the 1920s. A series of more and varied migrations occurred after WWII. At the beginning of the first migration, the country was vastly underpopulated, with enormous areas of the country having little or no population. The railroad, and subsequently the automobile were able to more closely link different parts of the country, enabling settlers to relocate to more distant parts of the country with relative ease. Further, we were at the dawn of the industrial age, where able-bodied people could readily find employment in burgeoning industrial enterprises. For those who preferred farming, there were vast tracts of open land to be farmed, with the railroads providing a way to bring harvests to market.

There was also great ferment in the various cities, with an enormous investment in infrastructure—bridges, tunnels, roads, subways, aqueducts, and dozens of other projects—all providing employment for new, unskilled immigrants. An explosion of projects in the charitable sector brought new building in the cultural arts, universities, hospitals, and research centers. Finally, new private enterprises were expanding, with many opportunities for employment there. In short, America was undergoing a transformation from a small, rural, agriculture-based society to a much larger industrial society, one that required many able-bodied, if unskilled, workers, provided in large part by the immigrants.

A century or so later, our needs have changed. There are still vast open spaces of course, but the population density of our metropolises have caused havoc with our transportation system, which cannot keep up with the growing populace. Further, suburban sprawl has made the problems of transportation, environment, conflict with nature, and so on even worse. In spite of that, we need an influx of new blood, new skills, and new ideas. As a bonus, new immigrants are far more appreciative of the wonders and benefits of America than most native-born, who take the benefits they have from citizenship matter-of-factly. But now we are at the dawn of the postindustrial society, where education and job skills are what is needed. Bringing in raw, unskilled, illiterate labor, who in a generation or two might obtain the skills required by this society, or they might not, is not the answer.

There are also differences in attitude between prior and current immigrants. The earlier immigrants wanted nothing more than to rapidly assimilate into the larger American society. Nobody wished to be seen as a greenhorn. Everyone internalized the American ethos. Now they wish to keep their own culture. Diversity is rightly praised and brings much to society, but too much diversity will lead to chaos. What if we are unable to communicate in a single language understood by all? No country in the world has had more experience and more success in absorbing immigrants from all over the world and integrating them successfully into the larger society, and yet people, completely unmindful of our past, insist on teaching in their native tongue, not in English.

There is an accompanying idea that integration into the larger society will eliminate the culture of origin. Nothing could be further from the truth. We all live in at least two cultures, the dominant American culture and the smaller original culture. There is every indication that people pass back and forth between the two with ease: the dominant culture in the public world and the original culture when individuals can let their hair down, speaking their native tongue, eating native dishes, mixing with friends and relatives, and participating in ceremonies. These original cultures have greatly enriched America and will continue to do so, but we cannot have a cohesive country if in their public life, they do not absorb the dominant culture. It is clear that for some groups, it is more difficult to absorb the mainstream culture than for others.

The only argument that resonates with me to bring in unskilled labor is that we, like all industrial societies, need unskilled labor to do the menial jobs that natives will not do. Stoop labor in the farms and fields, general laborers, bus boys and dish washers are all tasks that need to be done, but it is rare that native Americans will take on such projects, even as a first step. Unskilled immigrants would provide the pool of workers necessary for doing those jobs. It is my feeling that, however unintentionally, English as a Second Language programs widens that pool, since inability to function in the larger dominant society means low-wage unskilled jobs for many.

I believe we should bring in unskilled labor, but on a temporary basis; they would be called guest workers. However, they must leave the country after a specified time and children born here should not be considered American. They should, however, be given priority on a waiting list for entry into the country on a legal basis. With adequate unskilled labor, there should be no reason (except to pay starvation wages) to hire illegal migrants, and those doing so should be punished severely. The illegal migrants who come should be deported when caught and denied any future chance to migrate here legally.

Many people face a dilemma. They wish to save our open spaces for all to enjoy, but they also favor open immigration, which will inevitably lead to more and more crowding and less and less open space. The demands on our natural wonders, our transportation system, our farming system, our forests, our conflicts with wild animals, and in general, our quality of life are bound to deteriorate if our population is allowed to grow completely unchecked. Yet these people continue to think in logic-tight compartments, arguing in favor of diametrically opposed goals.

I am in favor of continued immigration. But it should meet our needs, which is for ever-higher levels of knowledge and skills. Those with such skills are the immigrants we should welcome on a permanent basis.

OSHA and Ergonomics

The Occupational Safety and Health Administration (OSHA) has just made a fool of itself again. After suggesting that it would consider going into homes to regulate working conditions for those who worked from the home, it backed down when opposition became intense and, probably, when it realized that it was an impossible task to perform. Would they mandate that throw rugs would have to be removed because they were unsafe? Would they insist on brighter lighting in the room? Would they insist on rearranging the room or getting new furniture if what was present did not meet their ergonomic standards? The possibilities are endless. If mandated to pay for such changes, what employer would continue to allow people to work from their home?

Before this episode, OSHA had been in the midst of other fierce disputes. They published thick manuals that detailed to a nauseating degree the requirements for equipment an employer must use. Detailed descriptions of tools, fire extinguishers, even the number of rungs on a ladder were written down and mandated. More recently, they have detailed ergonomically correct equipment in the work place.

One might reasonably ask if it can't be helpful to reduce, as much as possible, injury in the workplace. Of course it is, and everyone would benefit from it. The problem arises as to how OSHA goes about achieving that. Obviously believing that the people they are dealing with are simpletons and charlatans, unconcerned about employee health, and themselves oblivious to cost/benefit decisions (obviously the definitive way to reduce workplace injuries would be to have the worker stay home but still get paid—that would reduce workplace injuries to zero) that employers have to make all the time, they make incredibly detailed, one-size-fits-all rules that everyone must obey.

A far more sensible approach would be to serve as a resource that could readily be accessed and used to great benefit. Studies could be funded and distributed regarding one procedure or piece of equipment versus another. Alerts could be issued when there appears to be more than the normal number of accidents or injuries. Meetings could be sponsored and the results disseminated. Experts in the department could be made available to safety officers at corporations. The list is endless.

It will never be done because advising and counseling is not the same as power.

Racial Profiling

The problems and benefits of racial profiling have recently been in the news. It is a technique used by all law enforcement officers but particularly customs officers and state police. There is no doubt a war is going on: namely, the war on illegal drugs. It would be won in an instant if users, particularly in the United States, would stop using drugs, but that is a different story. Federal Interstate 95, running from Maine to Florida appears to be one of the main highways for the dissemination of drugs from South America to the Caribbean to Miami and then for dispersal throughout the Northeast. The same is true for handguns, which are purchased in the Southeast and then transferred to the North. These guns are not for sportsmen but for the furtherance of criminal activities.

By far the best interdiction technique is the use of informants. Every police agency makes use of them. They are looked down upon, sneered at as "snitches," often murdered, but completely necessary for effective police work. For ongoing enforcement and interdiction, profiling, including race, offers a further means of control, by knowledge of which ethnic groups are likely to be involved in which particular form of drug (and gun) trafficking. Without it, there would be a lessening of effectiveness in drug interdiction. It is known that different ethnic groups control different drugs. If, for example, word is received that a shipment of amphetamines is about to occur, and it is known that this drug is controlled by white bikers, wouldn't it make sense to watch closely, and to stop suspicious white biker groups? It would make little or no sense to stop other ethnic groups in order to intercept that shipment.

I have no doubt that some police officers are racist. I have no doubt that some enjoy harassing minorities, but that is not the purpose of the policy, just a side effect. Eternal vigilance is the byword, and punishment for law officer offenders is necessary if they violate the law. I suspect that some of their behavior is due to ignorance, poor judgment, poor training, and fear—some justified and some not. Further training and education for them is essential. Appropriate apology to an innocent when a mistake is made is also essential. However, there is no way to tell an innocent from a criminal without stopping them. If criminals and their wares are not interdicted, there will simply be more death and destruction in the destination communities. How could that possibly help the law-abiding citizenry?

It is the reaction of the minorities who are profiled for particular drugs that surprises me. The immediate reflex action is to claim racism. There may well be some of that, but that is not the motive or the driving force of the policy—drug interdiction is. These drugs (and illegal guns), which help destroy their own neighborhoods as well as others, need to be confiscated. Rather than focusing on racism and on their own discomfort, they should be focusing on the shame that the criminals have brought upon them and the harm they have done to their community. Their criminal behavior has reflected adversely on the whole community, and the community itself needs to step in and take action to lessen such antisocial behavior. Unfortunately, it is a lot easier to just cry racism.

Separation of Church and State

The concept of separation of church and state is an American gift to the world and firmly embedded in our psyche and preserved in our First Amendment. The exact interpretation of what it means in day-to-day life has, however, been a subject of controversy from the start of the republic to this day. With all due respect to our legal scholars, I do not believe that the Founding Fathers wished religion to be abolished from all public life. They, after all, were English gentlemen very well grounded in what had been to them relatively recent bloodbaths between the Church of England and the Catholic Church. They were very well aware of the battling between the two warring religions—imprisonment, beheading, burning at the stake. They rightly wanted no part of it and made sure it was not present via the First Amendment (the establishment clause).

They were, however, perfectly comfortable with religion (at least nondenominational religion) as being integrally tied in to the daily functioning of public life. How do I know this? The Declaration of Independence attributes our rights as being endowed by our Creator. Our currency proclaims that in God We Trust. Our presidential oaths of office are taken upon a Bible and preceded by invocations by clergy. The sessions of Congress are opened by a prayer from the chaplain. Our testimony in courts of law is (or was) taken by an oath upon a Bible. The Supreme Court opens its sessions with a mention of God. Our oath of allegiance declares that we are one nation, under God. And so on. Of course, it is true that none of the founders could possibly have imagined the diversity of belief we now have in America, since all were Christian, primarily Protestant with a Catholic contingent from Maryland.

In spite of that, the basic principle was that there was to be no established church in this country, but that religion played an integral part in public life. There was relatively little questioning of this in the early days of the Republic, but there has been increased questioning on all fronts in our most recent past and up to the present.

That this rigidity against any manifestation of religious expression by governmental figures was not present until the most recent past was shown during D-Day, June 6, 1944. Then President Franklin Delano Roosevelt and virtually all publicly elected officials offered up prayers for the success of the invasion and the well being of our troops. Shockingly, the Republic survived the commingling of church and state. Earlier FDR and Winston Churchill met on board the cruiser *Augusta* to make plans about the war effort. Unselfconsciously, they held Sunday church services and sang "Onward Christian Soldiers." Again, the Republic survived, and we did not establish a national religion. Either they were very politically incorrect or they knew that their heartfelt prayers in a time of need would not presage a fundamental change in our basic philosophy. Perhaps something can be learned by the holders of our current rigidities.

Attacks on all religious aspects of public life from the most mundane (an invocation by a clergyman at a high school graduation or the presence of a congressional chaplain) to the more significant (public school prayer) are on the rise. Why this should be so is probably in part due to our religious diversity and in part due to hostility to religion, but I believe it is primarily because of the inability of our various minorities to come to terms with this not being a Christian nation but a nation that is overwhelmingly Christian. They claim that they do not feel comfortable with manifestations of religion that because of the makeup of our population is often Christian. This is particularly true at the Christmas holiday season, when the symbols are particularly rich and particularly plentiful.

Some of the more overt symbols of Christianity can be uncomfortable to non-Christians, but should everything be under attack, from signs proclaiming Merry Christmas to the National Christmas tree? Besides, what about the comfort level of the overwhelming majority of our citizens? Don't they have rights too, or is it all a one-way street? Are people unable to distinguish minor discomforts from major affronts of their liberty? (see "Holding One's Nose"). Some declare that the majority should act with greater sensitivity to the feelings of minorities, but is that too a one-way street? Don't the overwhelming majority of our citizens have feelings and needs to be met? One would not think so from the complaints of so many.

It has been proposed that we have in our schools one minute of silent prayer. Students may think about their Creator or what they will do on the weekend. The ridiculous argument is made that this will somehow lead inevitably to the establishment of a state religion. To see how ridiculous it is, one need only to turn the argument around. If we don't have a moment of silent prayer, it will lead inevitably to the destruction of all religion. Both arguments are ridiculous and show how far people are willing to go to make their point.

It is a blessing that we do not have a state religion, as so many other societies have today. Those who do not properly believe are relegated to a lower class. However, we have problems aplenty in determining the role of religion in our public life. One would expect to see eternal vigilance in guarding against such an establishment, but at the same time, there is nothing wrong in permitting religious thoughts (and utterances) to be present as they have been since the establishment of our Republic. A fine line, to be sure, but one we have navigated successfully for over two centuries. Tolerance, sensitivity, and respect for the feelings of minorities must be matched by the same for the feelings of the majority. Otherwise we shall not be able to survive as a unified society. It seems to me, to do otherwise, is placing childishness and selfishness behind the mask of high-minded idealism. God bless America.

Space Exploration

Every now and then there is a rumble that NASA should be run without astronauts. These critics claim that robots can do as well in exploring the universe, and perform it cheaper as well. There are at least three reasons why, to date, NASA has rejected the idea of limiting space exploration solely to robots. First, we are getting medical information about humans and the state of weightlessness, which will undoubtedly be helpful in the future. Telemetry, for example, which is now so routinely performed throughout hospitals and elsewhere, was largely a creation of space exploration.

Second, those who criticize having men in space do not understand the unquenchable curiosity of man, which has pushed inhabitation by man to the furthest reaches of the earth. Mankind's history has been one of exploring their environment and beyond. It is not a recent phenomenon, neither is it limited to the white race. Look at the Polynesians, exploring (and settling) the vast Pacific, into the unknown and uncharted seas in little more than rafts. Extraordinary. In more modern times, with new technology, we have explored the depths of the ocean, the heights of the tallest mountains, the ice-covered poles, and every nook and cranny on earth. Exploring the universe is only an extension of that need, that yearning.

A third reason for human exploration of the universe is the survival of the species. The earth's population is expected to double in the next hundred years. Who knows what it will be after that. We also now have the ability to wipe ourselves out with modern technology. Such crowding and such aggression by man against man with modern technology could lead to terrible consequences. Also, although the odds are long, an object such as a meteor could crash into the earth and extinguish all life, as apparently happened during the age of the dinosaurs. Colonization of our universe should be seen as essential to the survival of our species.

Today astronauts and robots each have a series of missions for which each is best adapted. That is the way it should be.

VI

Public Policy—Foreign

Cold War Battles

Now that the Cold War is over (although peace has not exactly been initiated all over the globe) and we have had a decade to reflect on it, it is apparent that we in the West, with our steadfastness and courage, have won a stupendous victory over the forces of evil, namely communism. Enormous sacrifices, of blood and treasure, were necessary to achieve this victory so that we and our descendants, as well as the people and the descendants of our former opponents, can live a decent life free from the ever-present fear of annihilation.

It is interesting to reflect on the numerous and complex facets of the forty-five-year struggle, which, in total, made up the Cold War. There were two major battles, mistakenly called wars, in this struggle: Korea and Vietnam. Both were fought, with different outcomes but for the same reason, containment of the communists. In neither case did we fight for colonies, trade concessions, mineral rights, or any other benefit. We did it because it was in our own long-term interest and because we were the ultimate protectors of the free world. Korea was not really a victory except in the sense that we repelled the invaders. However, after forty years, peace has not been reached, and our troops are still in place and in harm's way. In Vietnam, we failed in our mission and lost the battle. However, we won the larger war. World communism has been defeated, America is the sole remaining superpower, and Vietnam is struggling mightily to become a third-world nation.

Another type of battle fought was against communist insurgents. These took place in Greece, Malaya, the Philippines, and throughout Central and South America and Africa. The insurgents liked to call themselves "freedom fighters," but they terrorized and deliberately killed civilians in order to control them. Thus, their struggle was more about subjugation than about freedom. Some of these struggles, for example in the Philippines and several Latin America countries, are ongoing, but most have been resolved with the defeat of the communists.

A different type of battle was a direct confrontation without actual open warfare but in which such warfare could break out at any moment. The Berlin blockade was the first of such confrontations with such potentially deadly serious overtones. Another confrontation was in the Pacific, where the United States Navy faced off against the Chinese communists over the two tiny islands of Quemoy and Matsu. These islands were part of Taiwan. A third and perhaps most dangerous confrontation was the Cuban missile crisis, in which the United States mobilized its military and instituted a blockade to prevent Soviet nuclear missiles from being installed in Cuba, only ninety miles from the U.S. shore.

Intelligence battles were also fought. These included human intelligence (spies), both native and imported, and electronic intelligence, monitoring by plane and satellite, as well as monitoring the airwaves. Intelligence analysis and attempts by both sides to fool each other was part of the intelligence "game." Propaganda battles were also fought, primarily via the airwaves, although the West, with a free press, was subject more to misinformation than true information. The West, via Radio Free Europe, Voice of America, and the BBC attempted and, I believe, largely succeeded, in getting their message across. Domestic political battles were constantly being fought, some honorable and some not (for example, Joe McCarthy and his crowd). Some of these battles reflected a loss of courage among some segments of domestic society, but in the main, we persevered and won.

Domestic battles were probably the most difficult. We had relatively few, but some very influential people, known then as fellow travelers, who seemed capable of believing throughout the entire forty-five years of the Cold War that we, the United States, and the Western allies, were wholly or in large part responsible for any confrontation that occurred, to say nothing of standing in the way of lasting peace. At an instant, they were ready to march, protest, picket, or campaign against any policy we undertook against our Cold War antagonists. Apparently they felt that the communists offered a brighter tomorrow, no matter how much that conflicted with reality.

In sum, after forty-five years of struggle, the good guys won. Communism was shown to be hopelessly evil, economically inefficient, and indifferent to the aspirations of its people. It fell of its own weight and from the steadfastness and courage of the West, led by the United States. A decade has gone by, and there still has been no recognition and no apology from those whose beliefs were clearly shown to be false.

Dropping the Bomb

Approximately five years ago, on the fiftieth anniversary of the dropping of the atomic bomb on Hiroshima, the Smithsonian Institution's Air and Space Museum dropped an exhibit on the use of the atomic bomb when howls of outrage appeared from many sources, particuarly from various veterans' groups as the text of the exhibit became known. Although multiple reasons were put forth by those responsible for creating the exhibit as to why we should not have done it—that is, dropped the bomb—it boiled down to immoral behavior on the part of the Americans. For my part, I believe that nothing could be further from the truth.

For four long years, we were engaged in a brutal and difficult war on two fronts, a war that was not of our choosing but forced on us by the Germans and the Japanese. Many casualties were sustained. In 1945, after the Germans surrendered, shiploads of troops were in the process of being sent to the Pacific from the European theater of operations, preparing for the invasion of Japan. Okinawa had given us a taste of what an invasion of the mainland of Japan would have in store for us, since it (Okinawa) was not territory conquered by force but an offshore province of Japan. Resistance was fierce on both sea and land. Kamikaze attacks on our fleet produced incredible damage. On Okinawa itself, there were essentially no surrenders, with the Japanese fighting to the death for each position or bunker held. Here too we took very high casualties. If this was what it was like on Okinawa, what would the fighting be like when the Japanese homeland itself was invaded? Without question, enormous casualties on both sides would be sustained.

As a former army officer, president of the United States, and commander in chief, Harry Truman's primary concern, after meeting the military objectives, was the lives of his troops. In effect, if the invasion went forward and we had not used the bomb, which was available. Truman would have had to write a letter to the relatives of the slain serviceman thus: "We regret the loss of your (son, brother, husband), but it was more important that your ———— die so that Japanese people will live." Unthinkable.

But what of the Japanese themselves? Wouldn't lives have been saved if the bomb was not dropped? The evidence is to the contrary. Many of Japan's buildings were made of wood and burned fiercely. The Allied bombing of Tokyo caused a firestorm that destroyed more people than the atomic bomb did on Hiroshima. It would have been unthinkable (except perhaps in the minds of a few revisionist historians) not to have preceded the invasion with attacks on essentially all the major cities of Japan, just as we did against Germany. Without question, the death toll among Japanese civilians (to say nothing of the material damage) would have been far, far higher than the death toll from the dropping of the atomic bombs on Hiroshima and Nagasaki.

I happened to be at Los Alamos, when they honored the bomber squadron, which included the *Enola Gay*, the plane that dropped the first atomic bomb. Among the supporters present was an Asian woman with whom I spoke. She told me that she was from Mongolia and was extremely grateful that we dropped the bomb when we did. The Japanese were starting to slaughter her people, and as an educated woman, she knew that her days were limited if the war persisted.

Well, here we have it. The war was shortened. Heavy American casualties were avoided. People conquered by Japan were saved from destruction. The destruction of the Japanese population was less than it would have been if subject to heavy preinvasion bombing. The horror of the bomb was exposed for all the world to see. The demonstration of its awesome power must have been successful, since fifty-five years have elapsed since the bomb was used, and its use has not been repeated, at least, not yet. Everyone should be happy, but they are not. Revisionist historians (as well as others) believe America was immoral to drop the bomb. I cannot fathom why they consider Japanese lives more important than American lives, but they do. Even further, why were Japanese civilians considered more important than American civilians who happened to be drafted for the war. I cannot understand why the above-mentioned benefits from dropping the bomb are not seen by them, but apparently they are not. Thank goodness Harry Truman was made of sterner stuff.

Foreign Intervention

With the end of the Cold War, wars were supposed to end and people were to turn their attention to matters of peace and prosperity. Exactly the opposite has occurred, and there are conflicts, small and large, internal and external, in an unprecedented number across every continent. This has raised the question of when and under what circumstances the United States, as the sole remaining superpower, should be involved in these conflicts, and how we should be involved.

There is a spectrum of viewpoints of how and when we should be involved, with what means, and under what auspices. At one end of the spectrum are those who feel that we should be involved, irrespective of our interests, when values such as human rights are involved. A few of those holding this approach appear to believe that the less interest we have as a nation in the problem, the more we should be involved. In other words, the more altruistic we are, the better. At the other end of the spectrum are those who feel we should maintain a strictly hands-off policy unless truly vital national interests are at stake.

There are many weaknesses to both viewpoints. The "values" people would surely not want us to intervene militarily against formidable foes such as the former Soviet Union or even present-day Russia or against China, even though gross violations of human rights have taken place in both countries. Therefore, the strength and size of the opponents, rather than the degree of violation of basic human rights becomes the issue. On the other end of the power spectrum, there is a plague of the grossest violations of human decency and human rights throughout the world in small and relatively weak countries. Should we intervene in all of them or only in some of them? Which ones and how? Should we put Americans in harm's way in places where admittedly we have only the most marginal of interests? Should we reduce the effectiveness of our military, with its dwindling resources, by scattering our troops all over the world, making them less effective if a major threat to our interests arises? Are we willing to back up our wishes with increased resources for our military by means of significant increases in funding?

Those at the other end of the spectrum have an easier task. When a clear threat to our vital interests are at stake, our course should be clear. Yet even here, as was in the case of the Gulf War, when a brutal dictator threatened to dominate the oil resources needed by the Western nations, there was a reluctance to draw the obvious conclusion and to do what was clearly necessary. Support for the actions taken by President George Bush just barely passed the Congress. A whole basket of alternatives were proposed to avoid what was clearly necessary, including the use of sanctions, which are still in place today, a decade after the war was fought and supposedly won.

In addition to fighting the ambivalence of the public for appropriate forceful action, waiting for only the threat to our vital interests before taking action fails to permit us to be proactive and to be only reactive. We are unable to practice prevention, up to and including limited military force. It is clear in retrospect that the Israeli military strike against Iraq's nuclear plant at Osirak, rather than being an object of bitter criticism, was an act of enormous benefit to the world. A powerful (in Middle Eastern terms) Iraqi military with nuclear weapons at its disposal could have led to terrible consequences for the world, and not just for Iraq's opponents.

There is a large middle ground where the U.S. has interests, although perhaps not vital ones. If one cannot see what truly vital interests are, then perhaps a new prescription for glasses is in order. These interests, not necessary vital, include peace, stability, the future of supranational organizations, such as NATO and the U.N., and prevention of small problems becoming very big ones. Here the problem is much more murky and more subject to individual interpretation. It is here, too, where the nature of the interventions; that is, military versus sanctions or other methods short of war, and by whom and under what auspices (national or supranational) it is appropriately debated, including whether the behavior of a miscreant nation can better be controlled by contact and persuasion or by no contact—that is, isolation.

I wish there were some nice, easy formula for determining how and under what circumstance action should be undertaken by the U.S. To me, waiting for a direct threat to our national interest before taking action will often end up being more costly than will prevention. At the other end of the spectrum, intervening in dozens of brutal conflicts around the world where we have no significant interests other than that of maintaining a peaceful world raises more problems than it solves. Needless to say, contributions of humanitarian aid are desirable and necessary, but international forces under the umbrella of a supranational organization, such as the U.N. or NATO, are needed for true peacekeeping, not pacification. An interesting suggestion was made for the use of mercenaries for pacification, since it is so difficult to get nations to contribute troops for wartime purposes. I do worry that they could pacify the country and then decide to take it over for their own purposes. Sierra Leone, with its diamond mines, is a good example of such a potential action. Then how would the world get them out?

A further problem, demonstrated in Kosovo, is that no country or combination of countries other than the U.S. has the military wherewithal to conduct a modern war against a reasonably well-equipped enemy. Therefore, if military action is to be taken, it is the U.S. that will have to provide the lead, particularly from the air, if the action is to have any basis for success. A similar problem exists with regard to land and sea forces. In other words, the U.S. will have to provide the shock troops to get the job done. However, there is no reason why others cannot be the pacifiers and peacekeepers after we have provided the bulk of the initial attacking force. This is something that should be agreed upon beforehand, and U.S. forces should be largely withdrawn (some symbolic troops could remain) after the initial phase of the attack has been completed.

It is therefore the middle ground, where we have interests, which if allowed to propagate could lead to harm to our vital interests, where good judgment is necessary. I believe that the guiding principle for action should be enlightened self-interest. Obviously, people will disagree strongly about exactly what our posture should be to serve that enlightened self-interest, but at least one can step back and say that the action proposed is indeed one of enlightened self-interest, and not just one to make a person feel good. That would at least be a start.

Kosovo vs. Vietnam

I have always believed in our involvement in Vietnam. We sought no territory. We sought no raw materials. We had no desire to corner the fishpaste market. What we did hope for was an independent South Vietnam as a free and reasonably democratic state that would be on good terms with all of its neighbors, particularly North Vietnam (in reality, if Korea was to be used as an example, there was little hope for this). We also hoped to contain Communism, by any standard a cruel and ravenous form of governance.

If the idea was noble, the execution was ignoble. President Lyndon Johnson cynically used what turned out to be a mistaken belief of an attack on U.S. naval vessels in the Gulf of Tonkin to pass a congressional resolution that permitted the dispatch of ever larger numbers of troops to Vietnam. He claimed we could have guns and butter, but we couldn't. There was no frankness with the American people. We failed to understand that people who can't or won't help themselves cannot be saved. I am not picking on LBJ alone, since Kennedy and Nixon share some of the blame. As time passed, the American participants in Vietnam (civilian and military) became increasingly cynical, considering Vietnam nothing more than a ticket that needed to be punched on the ladder to promotion.

Scenes from our first TV war did have a profound adverse effect on journalists and media types. Ultimately, it had a profound negative effect on a segment of our population, whose protests grew ever more hostile and ever more violent. I am sure that more than a few, however much they disliked our role, regret aiding and abetting the enemy. Most probably regret the vicious and unconscionable treatment of the troops upon returning from Vietnam, troops who, after all, answered the call of their government and risked their lives and their health at the behest of their government, while others did everything possible, honest and dishonest, to avoid the draft.

Lost in all the prattle was the incredible cruelty of the North Vietnamese and their Viet Cong subordinates. After all, some two to three million Vietnamese Catholics and tens of thousands of others fled to the South. This wasn't for their health or for a job search. Dwellers in villages and hamlets in the countryside of South Vietnam were treated with extraordinary acts of cruelty to keep them in line. After the war, a large number was sent to reeducation camps—really, concentration camps—where cruelty and barbarism reigned. So much so that we had the era of the "boat people," a romantic name for despicable acts. People were sent out in flimsy craft into the South China Sea, an ocean rife with pirates and sharks, with no passport, no money, and no destination. That was cruel enough, but there was a subset of boat people who voluntarily chose to leave via these boats with all of the above problems rather than live under North Vietnamese rule. To me, that says all.

This of course does not mention the incredibly cruel way our captured military were treated. A lean diet comparable to what the population of North Vietnam has is one thing. Beatings, torture, exhibition to the population of prisoners in cages, and more were all used by the North Vietnamese without significant protest from those who were passionately against the war. Why not? Even the Nazis allowed Red Cross visits, food parcels, etcetera. To top the above, the Communist Cambodians (Khmer Rouge) made the North Vietnamese look like just naughty children who misbehaved. Still no protests.

And what was the outcome of this terrible behavior of taking the lives or disrupting the lives of millions of people. If after a quarter-century or so, Vietnam emerged as a prosperous and reasonably democratic country, one at peace with its neighbors and the world in general, one could make the argument that to make an omelet one must break eggs. But nothing of the sort happened. Communism fell, collapsing because of its multiple failures. Vietnam itself is still a despotic state struggling to become a third-rate nation. In desperation, it has welcomed back the U.S. in hopes of receiving some governmental and nongovernmental aid in the form of investments. In the meantime, the U.S. has become the world's sole superpower and an economic colossus.

It is now a quarter-century later, and the wheel has turned. Kosovo was a cruelty that could not be permitted to stand, but every argument used against involvement in Vietnam was used in favor of our military involvement in Kosovo. When President

Clinton talks about the potential danger to Albania and even Greece and Turkey, what is he talking about but the domino effect, a concept that was considered ludicrous by some during the Vietnam War? We are not the world's policeman, the opponents of Vietnam claimed, but here we are in the Balkans, where we have little or no interests. It is only a civil war, they claimed about Vietnam (but it was much more than that—a clash of two very different ideologies), but now people are willing to intervene militarily in what is clearly a civil war. Bombing of cities and the resultant civilian casualties was felt by some to be a form of barbarism, but they appear to greet with great equanimity the same situation in Serbia/Kosovo. We have also not had delegations going to Belgrade and protesting on TV of the terrible harm inflicted on "innocent Serbs." Oh, Jane, where have you gone?

Although we did not have military casualties, the prospects of the same did not arouse fierce disapproval on the part of many, as it had during the Vietnam War. When our military came home, they were treated as heroes, not lepers as were the Vietnam vets.

I never dreamed that I would be able to justify the Vietnam war in my lifetime. Rather, it would be left to future generations to reconcile the good motives of this country with its appallingly bad execution. This was brought out several years ago by the publication of a book by former Defense Secretary Robert McNamara. The book was primarily a mea culpa, and it did little more than open old wounds. I saw, in all the discussions, commentary, interviews, and so on, no softening of position, no apologies for acts that were clearly beyond the pale (abusing our vets, giving aid and comfort to our enemy by doing propaganda for them, no horror for the brutality exhibited by the North Vietnamese both during and after the war), just a reiteration of old positions. It therefore told me that Vietnam as an issue was alive and well, although, for the most part, hidden from view. And then came Kosovo.

Proportionality in War

I have never understood the concept of proportionality in war. The enemy does one thing, and you in turn react, but only in proportion to what he did. By doing no more than what the enemy did, you are somehow being nobler than your enemy. I suppose that at some point the return destruction can be redundant, superfluous, and unnecessary to the pursuance of a war, but otherwise, with people's lives at stake, as much power as possible should be mobilized to defeat the enemy and bring the war to a speedy conclusion.

Let us take the recent conflicts in the Balkans. An entire village is captured, the men executed or sent to concentration camps, the women raped and then shot along with all the children and older people, and the village razed to the ground. What exactly is the proportional response to that? Do we do the same thing to the other side? Hardly. Then how many bridges, power stations, and so forth need to be destroyed to make our response proportional to the horrors perpetrated by the other side? Who decides what is a correct proportional response? Isn't the best way to deal with people who behave in such a fashion to use overwhelming force to bring the fighting to a speedy conclusion and then bring the criminal perpetrators to justice? The people we have fought and struggled against since World War II have been such brutal dictators that nobility and forbearance would be completely lost upon them. Hitler, Stalin, Saddam Hussein, Milosevic, et al are hardly swayed by observing damage to their people. Indeed their own people are completely expendable in the search by the leaders for the successful attainment of their goals.

This is not to say that there are not rules of engagement. Civilians should not be deliberately and randomly killed. POWs should be treated in a humane fashion. Force that is not directly needed for the war should be avoided. Once the goals are accomplished, force should be avoided. However, as much force as is necessary should be brought to bear for a speedy and successful conclusions to the fighting. That is what will limit casualties, and not some abstract idea of proportionality. War is a brutal endeavor that brutalizes the participants. It should be concluded as speedily as possible.

Vietnam

As shocking as it may sound, I have long believed that Vietnam was one of our nobler wars. Take this man away, quickly! In my opinion it was a selfless war, in which we sacrificed blood, treasure, and domestic tranquility for a people who reached out to us. We had no desire to obtain additional territory. We had no desire to corner raw materials; there were essentially none. We had no desire to corner trade. What exactly would we do if we cornered the fish paste market? Enlightened self-interest necessitated that Communism must first be contained and then defeated. Over a period of a half-century the strategy worked very well, with a climax in 1990 of historic proportions—the virtual demise of Communism, certainly in the West. We could of course have done what has been done all too frequently, denounce the North Vietnamese, force through a General Assembly resolution (it would not have gotten through the Security Council) to the same effect. We could have put in place toothless sanctions, since the land routes to Vietnam, via China, were still open. It would have saved a great deal of trouble, but all that would have happened would be that the North would have conquered the South fifteen years earlier.

As noble as the basic cause was, the execution of the war was, in a word, despicable. There was a failure by the politicians to clearly articulate our goals. Approval by Congress (Tonkin Gulf resolution) was not for an unlimited and open-ended war. President Johnson proclaimed that we could have guns and butter, but we couldn't. We understood neither the nature of the enemy nor the type of warfare being carried out. We knew little of the customs of the people and none of the language. We were fighting a war in which we were unable to tell soldier from civilian, friend from foe. We had no clear-cut exit strategy. Finally, we took over the fighting instead of serving as a source of supply, training, and rearguard. I believe it is a basic fact that you can't help those who can't or won't help themselves. We failed to take that into consideration.

The military shared in the deception. Their tactics were, for the most part, geared to the open plains and spaces of Europe, as during WWII. They were unsuitable for the geography of the jungle, where there was no front line and where we couldn't tell civilians from military and friend from foe. We also underestimated the fighting capacity of the Viet Cong and the Viet Minh. How could a bunch of guys in coolie hats and armed with light weapons stand up to the mighty U.S. military? In that respect we mimicked the French who couldn't believe that the Vietnamese could bring heavy artillery to bear in the remote, hilly area of Dien Bien Phu. They were wrong, and the loss of that battle led to the evacuation of the French from all of Indochina. We failed to understand the changed nature of this war, the tenacity of the enemy, their willingness to take heavy casualties and carry on, and their determination and devotion to ridding the country of colonialism and uniting the country under communism.

As time progressed, cynicism overtook patriotism throughout the troops, because it was felt that the civilian masters were sacrificing them for larger political gains. To satisfy the civilians, "objective" parameters were set up. These included the number of defectors, the number of hamlets and villages subdued, and of course, the infamous body count. These were first subtly and then blatantly distorted and even falsified. Vietnam became a ticket to be punched for military people who wished to rise in the ranks. Frustration, fear and the cruelty of war led to My Lai.

The civilians involved (such as the CIA, AID, State, and others) had a more amorphous and difficult task—pacification. It was not long before they too regarded Vietnam as a ticket to be punched on their way up the ladder. Cynicism and safety soon replaced patriotism and sacrifice.

The reaction of the public, particularly the left, was in a word, despicable. Not only did the educated dodge the draft, leaving the fighting to the lower classes, but also they were merciless in their criticism, failing to understand the larger meaning of the conflict. I cannot but feel that some of the anger exhibited was in part at themselves, recognizing that they were safe while others did the fighting and dying. After the war, whether the war opponents were right or wrong, their treatment of the returning Vietnam vets was contemptible. These were, after all, draftees who served their country as commanded. To be cursed, spat upon, and vilified for doing that is incomprehensible. One can feel that way about the leaders, but the grunts? Again, perhaps an element of guilt existed: they went on with their lives while others served and died. At any rate, there was a festering sore which still exists among the Vietnam vets. It has been ameliorated by the Vietnamese memorial, as well as other acts, but it is still there—witness the Rolling Thunder motorcycle parade every Memorial Day and the persistent clamoring to find MIAs who almost certainly cannot be found.

The moral dimension of the conflict has been completely overlooked. Some two to three million Vietnamese Catholics and tens of thousands of others fled the North after the country was partitioned. Why? The incredible cruelty that the Viet Cong used in the hamlets and villages to obtain cooperation is well documented. After the war, this was clearly demonstrated in the reeducation camps (read concentration camps), where proper Communist doctrine was inculcated, with no small amount of death and destruction meted out. Most shocking of all were the quaintly named "boat people." For the Vietnamese government to send people in small craft out into the South China Sea, with no passports and no money, in pirate- and shark-infested waters, denotes incredible cruelty. Even worse, however, were those who volunteered to do just that. It is hard to imagine how bad the new regime was for people to think that the better option was to put to sea under the above conditions. Also, one cannot forget the behavior of the Cambodian communists, the Khmer Rouge, as an example of bestiality on an incredible scale, harking back to the worst of the Nazi and Soviet excesses. There was surprisingly little protest in the U.S. about all of this.

So who lost in Vietnam? Conventional wisdom says we did. On the surface it would seem to be so. The North conquered the south, and we fled with our tails between our legs. Yet everything is not as it appears on the surface. In hindsight, the picture looks different, at least to me. The entire Soviet Union fell, and we became the one remaining superpower. There is clear evidence for those who want to see it, that in this struggle we were the good guys, and the communists the bad. The countries surrounding Vietnam had time to put their houses in order to prevent their being overtaken by the Communists. A sounder military doctrine emerged, which has served us reasonably well to articulate the goals and have in place an exit strategy. Vietnam has to be thought of as a battle, rather than a war, in the larger context of the Cold War. With that perception, we were the clear winners of the cold war, in spite of losing the battle of Vietnam. At the present time, we are the sole undisputed superpower in the world, and Vietnam is struggling mightily to become a Third-World country.

What to Do About Iraq

The Clinton-ordered four-day bombing campaign against Iraq has come and gone with little change except for one thing: it is now our stated objective to remove Saddam Hussein from power if we possibly can. It certainly won't be easy, and every plan, even the good ones, have major drawbacks. I would propose a different idea, completely predicated on the finding of a group of people willing and able to help themselves, given the means to do so. One of the lessons I take from Vietnam (and, I believe, the Israelis take from the failures of their Christian allies in Lebanon) is that in the long run, people who cannot, or will not, help themselves, simply cannot be helped. If energies are squandered in internecine warfare, if corruption is endemic, and if the leadership is all about power and nothing else, then we would be very foolish to get involved in what would undoubtedly be a losing venture.

Assuming that the above is not the case, a new and different plan might emerge. One might consider putting a new Iraqi dissident army on the ground in the western desert of Iraq. It is sparsely populated and relatively lightly soldiered. Initial efforts would be to secure the area and set up training camps and supply trails. These could come through Turkey but would have to be clandestine. Another route, again clandestine, would be to unload supplies in Haifa and truck them across Israel and the northern part of Jordan to the troops in Iraq. Landing strips could be built to supply by air. Undoubtedly Saddam Hussein would attack, but airpower from Kuwait and ships in the Persian Gulf, as well as ships in the eastern Mediterranean, would prevent anything larger than a jeep from being brought to bear. The area would also be made a no-fly zone, so that air power could not be brought to bear either.

When the area appears secure, the political elements would be brought in to what would be called Free Iraq. For our continued support, some steps towards democracy would have to be taken. One cannot move directly from totalitarianism to pure democracy in one step, but surely a written constitution, an elected parliament, an independent judiciary, and limits on the power of the chief executive would be necessary. The parliament should include all ethnic groups that make up modern Iraq. We would be able to closely monitor their actions through CIA and state department personnel. Reversion to more typical Middle Eastern behavior would mean our abandoning them to their fate, something that should be explained to them at the beginning. Assuming that all proceeds according to plan, they could start setting up a complete government in exile with all basic agencies in place for their assumption of power.

As they secure the area under their control, they would gradually seize control of land to their east, towards Baghdad. At the same time, they would seek to encourage defections from the Iraqi armed forces and secret services. It should be few in the beginning but more and more if the Iraqi people see that they are truly planning a coup, that they are viable, and that they are not just another version of Saddam Hussein. Coordination between them and the Kurds in the north and the Shiites in the south would be useful. Their very presence would open up another front, spread out Saddam's forces and lessen the threat to both the north and south. This would permit more organization of resistance forces in both these areas. As they grow stronger, defections should rise, and the likelihood of a coup would increase, since some might wish to depose Saddam and then negotiate with the Free Iraqis, rather than be executed if Saddam loses power.

There are no easy solutions, and I am sure this proposal has its share of problems; but it is also possible that in the end it would work and Iraq would have the kind of government it deserves, we would hope.

VII

Social Issues

Abortion Controversy

A chronic, savage war still rages over abortion. It is indeed a war on multiple fronts—mass movements, rallies, propaganda, passive resistance leading to jailing, as well as despicable hot-war elements, firebombing of clinics and assassination of physicians who work in these clinics. It is a take no prisoners, zero-sum game war, because it is played as an absolute zero-sum game—if we win you lose, and vice versa. Both sides claim that their position, although at opposite poles, is absolutely the high moral ground. How can that be?

Both sides claim that their position is a right to be found in American jurisprudence. They trot out the advantages of their position, but neither side mentions its liabilities. For Pro-Life forces, there is no doubt in my mind that most would indeed have an abortion if the pregnancy was the result of rape or incest, or if the fetus was so badly deformed that anything approaching a normal life would be impossible. For the Pro-Choice forces, abortion would be to some merely a family planning tool, aborting fetuses because it is less than absolutely perfect or even because it is the wrong gender.

There are hidden agendas for both as well. Pro Choicers use this issue as part of the larger question of women's rights, while Pro Lifers wish everyone to adhere to their views of morality in all areas. Each side taunts the other. Pro Lifers stage demonstrations, get arrested as an act of civil disobedience, and of course, put fear in the hearts of Pro Choicers with firebombs and assassinations. Pro Choicers taunt their opponents with clinics on main highways and thoroughfares, in shopping malls, etcetera. Their argument that, otherwise, people desiring to have an abortion could not find the clinic is ludicrous. Before Roe v. Wade, women who desired an abortion were able to find their way to any back alley abortionist, in this country or overseas, with no great difficulty. No, it is really showing the finger to the other side, the Pro Choicers.

The basic underlying problem is that both sides have unalterable ideas about the total correctness of their cause and are unalterably against any argument proposed by the other side. They are therefore in perpetual conflict and constantly mobilize resources, using any means possible to gather support for their view. Adopting legal measures via the legislature or the courts is a fool's game. To believe that one side will capture the hill and the other side will declare itself the loser and, therefore, change its point of view is not reasonable. Rather, it will mobilize all its forces to recapture the hill. It will be an eternal struggle, with battles won and battles lost, but no final victory.

To take this divisive issue off the table means that both sides will have to compromise, compromise that will no doubt be extremely painful. Each side must realize that the position taken by the other side is sincerely and deeply held, unswayed by any appeal to facts, logic, etcetera. Pro Choicers will have to accept that Pro Lifer positions are deeply held moral positions while Pro Lifers will have to realize that their own morality is not shared by people with opposing views. Both sides will have to restrain the extremists whose views prevent any meaningful compromise.

The media will have to demonstrate restraint as well, not fan the flames of differences between the two sides. Finally, there is the problem of public (government) funding of abortion for the indigent. Rationally, it would make sense to lessen the number of children having children, most without a clue as to needed parenting skills. Having Pro Choicers fund much of these clinic costs would remove at least some of the animosity. Pro Choicers could assist even more with adoption as well as paying some of the expenses if a child needs to be institutionalized. All of these steps may not be much, but they seem at least to be a step in the right direction.

Ben and His Flawed Logic

Ben Cohen of Ben and Jerry's Ice Cream is obviously a good employer, a good citizen, and a reasonably successful businessman, at least until recently, when his policies led to business losses, with the result that the company is on the block. It is not his success or lack of it as a businessman, however, which is the topic of this essay, but his recent newspaper article. This article serves as a textbook example of flawed liberal thinking; thought processes that are half a century old and still flawed.

The first fallacy that he demonstrates is that if federal money is saved (usually from the military), it will automatically go to the projects he favors. Nothing could be further from the truth. Money saved will go to wherever Congress says it will go. They may agree with his position and put it where he wants and expects it to be put or not agree and put it elsewhere. While being prudent with money and saving as much as possible is desirable, there is no one-to-one ratio of money saved for favorite project.

A second fallacy is that money will solve problems and throwing more money at a problem will solve it better and faster. Of course, most social programs require an infusion of money to maintain the basic well being of the recipients and to construct the basic infrastructure—for example, adequate housing, adequate schools with nourishing lunches for those who get their only decent meal of the day, adequate recreation centers to counter the pernicious use of drugs, and so on. As I have said, these ideas have been floating around for a half-century or longer, and they haven't made much of a dent in the social problems that afflict the recipients. The only program to date that has succeeded to any large degree in changing a social problem has been the welfare reform program, a program that flies in the face of politically correct thinking as evidenced by Ben Cohen.

A third feature of politically correct liberal thinking is extreme dislike of the military. A certain distrust of the military is of course in order, but what we see at times borders on hatred. The call for further cuts in the military are accompanied by ever-widening involvement of the military in peacekeeping as well as involvement in fighting. It doesn't make a great deal of sense unless one recognizes that there is a visceral dislike of the military on the part of liberals (see "Physical Authority").

One cannot but wonder why bright, successful people keep thinking in the same rut, as social program after social program fails and then is rewarded with ever more money. One would think that they would try and come up with different solutions to these problems, but they don't. And I believe the reason is that these programs, although failures, make them feel good. Not doing good but feeling good is the watchword.

High Priests

Who said religion was dead? It is alive and well although present in new forms—namely, First Amendment worship and Second Amendment worship. Both are fundamentalist or Orthodox in outlook. Both have more similarities with each other than differences. They both have high priests. In First Amendment worship, it is the ACLU, while in Second Amendment worship, it is the NRA. The congregants are true believers who seldom if ever question the wisdom of the high priests who lay out the one and true path. Theology is absolutist in both religions. It is absolute truth divinely revealed by the Constitution. It is conveniently forgotten by both religious sects that this Holy Writ was created by man and can be altered and interpreted by man. As an institution democracy is not so fragile that it cannot recover from what, in hindsight, would be seen as an assault on it. In these religions, no compromise is accepted, because if compromise is reached, disaster will be sure to occur. If common sense is brought into play, disaster will occur. If recognition of needs beyond those of the parochial is reached, then disaster will occur. No credit is given for the common sense of the nonworshipers. All are dummies who need guidance from the high priests. Never mind that American democracy, the oldest democracy in the world, has survived for over two hundred years, often in spite of, rather than because of, the high priests and their religion.

The rituals employed by the two religions are also similar. These consist of rallies, marches, articles in papers and magazines, web sites, professional lobbyists, congressional testimony, and so forth. What is true is that each is completely predictable on any issue. Thinking by the congregants is not required; the high priests will point out the real truth.

What are some of the reasonable measures that each religion could employ?

For Second Amendment worshipers, the mantra is "guns don't kill people, people do." Absolutely true, although it is hard to deny that the prevalence of guns permits them to fall in bad hands. Of course knives and bombs also kill, but they are not as easy to use as pulling a trigger. One answer would be more stringent and national licensing or registration rules.

217

After all, we license or register our houses, cars, spouses, businesses, pets, everything. Why not guns?

One would think that honest gun owners would favor such measures, particularly since they are knowledgeable in weaponry and have no intention of using them for violent, illegal purposes. Further, what communal purpose do "Saturday night specials" serve? They would not be used by gun enthusiasts, only by criminals. For that matter, what communal purpose is served by individuals having automatic weapons, machine guns, bazookas, and other military hardware. If a tiny handful of people are deprived of the thrill of firing such weapons on the farm or in the woods, so what. We all obey laws established for the common good, whether we are happy with them or not.

The First Amendment worshipers are exactly the same. Reduction of child pornography in stores and over the internet would appear to be a reasonable community goal, but it can never be attained when any measure proposed will have a "chilling effect" on the First Amendment. Virtually every step against wretched excess, a process that harms rather than helps the fabric of a community, is deemed to have a chilling effect. Some congregants in the media apparently believe they have an inherent right to falsehoods and libel, but punishing them would have a chilling effect.

Second Amendment worshipers have the same thought. You start with licensing of guns and end up taking their guns away. In other words both believe in the slippery slope, which to them is apparently inevitable. Such nonsense.

One would think that the two fundamentalist religions, having similar structure and theology, would avidly support each other, but nothing could be further from the truth. Each ignores the other's position or actually fights against it. There is intense dislike, bordering on hatred between the two. "Your Bible (constituional amendment) is not as important as ours. We are the one true faith." It cannot but remind one of the wars between

Protestants and Catholics of a half-millennium ago, the wars between the Sunni and Shi'ite Muslims of a millennium ago, or the current wars between Muslims and Hindus throughout the entire Indian subcontinent.

There is one feature of First Amendment worship that is different from Second Amendment worship. It is not just feeling that their cause is right, exclusively right—after all, we all believe that our position is right. No, it is the overwhelming sense that their position is morally superior to any other position.

In summary, we have two absolutist religions, based on the Holy Writ of the Constitution. They mutually, and with a passion, hate each other. Together, they lack two things. First, any hint of common sense or compromise, and second, any true comprehension of the larger needs of society. The individual is all. His wants, needs, acts are absolute, while the corresponding needs of the community are as nothing. I believe that both religions in their current form are a menace to society.

Holding One's Nose

We are an extremely large and extremely diverse society. It is therefore inevitable that we should have diverse opinions, often very strongly held, about virtually every issue. These opinions inevitably are in conflict with each other. How can we function and keep a civil society? Often, unfortunately, we cannot, and very uncivil behavior takes place, up to and including violence and even murder.

Violence has recently taken place in Seattle, with protests against the World Trade Organization. Violence, including arson and assassination, has been carried out by Pro-Life adherents. In the relatively recent past, violence in the form of bombing and murder in the course of robbery was carried out by antiwar protesters. Southern anti-civil rights people also felt that bombing, lynching, and murder were appropriate actions for their cause. All of these groups apparently believe that if they feel strongly enough about something then any behavior is justified, including murder. Of course, if those who believe exactly the opposite about the same issue do the same thing, then that is simply terrible and cannot be allowed to continue or to go unpunished. The proponents of these acts also apparently believe that these violent acts will somehow favorably influence people's attitudes towards them and their cause. How bizarre. In general, there is no reason for violence if there is redress via the ballot box. If there are ballots, there should not be bullets—that is, if one believes in the democratic process.

Recently a series of nonviolent actions have been undertaken by blacks against those Southerners who wish to honor their ancestors. Removal of Confederate flags, removal of statues of Confederate soldiers, protesting the inclusion of General Robert E. Lee on a mural in Richmond, honoring prominent Virginians, and the removal of the names of Washington and Jefferson from schools because they had been slaveholders, as well as a protest against a Virginia Confederate history month have all caused confrontation.

It is difficult for me to understand how people can ask for and expect sympathy for their needs and their causes if they are not willing to grant it to others. It is also difficult to see how a healing process can take place if sympathy and understanding is strictly a one-way street. This is scarcely an argument in favor of slavery, a truly wicked institution. But that is not what Southerners are honoring, and that is not what most Southerners were fighting about. Rather it was the issue of states' rights, and that they fought honorably for a cause they believed in, with many making the ultimate sacrifice.

How are we then to function under such difficult circumstances? Is there to be nothing but continuous warfare? Here are some ways that perhaps we can function as a civil society.

First, we are a democracy, and the way to overturn onerous appearing laws is by the ballot and not the bullet. In places where there is no such redress, it may then be necessary to take up arms, but not in this country. Second, it is certainly important to remember the past, but the focus should be on the future. Third, compromise on most issues is possible. Instead of playing a zero sum game, in which if one side wins the other must necessarily lose, a win/win situation is far, far better, if far more difficult to achieve. Having both sides get something with neither side getting everything should lead to an end result of a lessening, rather than a propagation of, bitterness, and a return to civility. Virtually every existing conflict we deal with today can be handled as a win/win situation.

Finally one must separate the vital from the relatively trivial. It is worth struggling for the vital, even essential to do so; but for the trivial, it is possible to continue functioning and just hold one's nose.

Hollywood Daze

The other day I saw a movie in which everyone, male and female, young and old, smoked. Conspicuously. For a period of time, say the thirties to the sixties, this was a common accompaniment to the character portrayed. One cannot imagine Humphrey Bogart or William Powell (*The Thin Man*) without their being bathed in clouds of smoke. Another convention was the happy, lovable drunk. Weaving from side to side and speeding through traffic, often on the wrong side of the road, was considered hilarious. The depiction of alcoholics and their antics in a humorous fashion while under the influence has not returned to the screen, but cigarette smoking has. It never completely disappeared, but for several decades it was not a prominent feature of the movie. Now it has become a fashion statement again, an act that suggests sophistication and pleasure.

So why has it returned with a vengeance. Can it be that people in Hollywood do not know the multiple health problems caused by tobacco? Hardly. Are they not concerned about the images they produce and its effect on young people? I am sure they are completely aware of it. So why do they do it? My impression is that there is no more cause-oriented group in this country. Wherever the Brie hits the Chablis, there will be a Hollywood fundraiser for a cause, any cause. So why do they, in effect, promote an expensive and extremely harmful habit?

It is not the only problem that is essentially ignored by Hollywood. Since having so many of their own who use and abuse hard drugs, and many of those die from such use, one would like to think that they would be on the cutting edge of opposition to illegal drug use. Yet they remain strangely silent. They are very active in demanding gun control but continue to show an incredible amount of gun violence in their movies and TV programs and music. Such overexposure to violence may or may not be a deciding factor in whether or not people act out their sick fantasies, but it is hard to see how it helps.

So they actively promote cigarette smoking by making it look attractive and sophisticated, make no impression in the fight against illicit drugs, and decry guns but make liberal use of them in their movies. How to explain this? I believe that in spite of their devotion to causes large and small, worthy and unworthy, they are, at heart, business people. They may decry business in general and business ethics in particular, but they behave in exactly the same way as other businessmen. Violence sells, so they produce it. Smoking seems to add some degree of sophistication to the character, so they use it, knowing full well the long-term consequences of smoking illicit drugs are a menace to everyone but there seems to be no determination on the part of Hollywood to do their best to slake the thirst. I consider it likely that many of them participate, and therefore, would find it difficult to condemn. What would one call these actions? Hypocrisy would not be a bad starting point.

Hostility to the U.S.—Why?

I have never understood the hostility of our intelligentsia to the U.S. This waxes and wanes, but is always present to some degree. It reached its climax in modern times during the Vietnam War, and then the Civil Rights movement. Although it has faded a bit, it is still present in its various manifestations, as noted below. More than any in country in the world, we have enormous personal freedoms, a classless society, a meritocracy, with ability being the ultimate criterion of success. It is, by and large, a welcoming society, and most of the intelligentsia are only one or two generations removed from a very generous immigration policy that permitted their forebears to come to these shores. Had these forebears stayed where they came from, many of their descendants, particularly those from Eastern Europe and China, would have been killed, never been born, or lived under the yoke of tyranny. Eternal gratitude to this country and what it has offered them should be the norm, but it is not. It is perfectly true that America is not the idyllic picture painted above, but it is a work in progress, constantly changing, and, for the most part, improving.

The best example of wrongheaded hostility to the U.S. was the long and painful Cold War. Far too many of our intelligentsia were quick to blame the U.S. and forgive the Communists for each and every clash between the two societies. Marches, protest rallies, writings, and speeches, all were directed against America. If only we had (or had not) done something. Communist behavior would be completely different. And then, with startling suddenness came the end of the Cold War, the collapse of the USSR and its East European vassals. Even an early and superficial reading (as time passes, more and more information comes out confirming our initial impression) of the situation showed us (America) to be the good guys and them (the Communists) to be bad guys.

The change was so great that only four Communist states remain, China and three backwaters, North Korea, Cuba, and Vietnam. One would think that having been so terribly wrong for nearly a half-century would bring out object apologies, but nothing would be further from the truth. At a time of great joy and relief throughout the West, there was either silence or a plethora of revisionist history, blaming the U.S. for everything from dropping the atomic bomb, which abruptly ended WWII, to every foreign policy initiative during the Cold War. A few even pointed to the U.S. as keeping the Cold War going; if only we had followed certain policies, the Cold War would have ended earlier. The same ploy was used following the Vietnam War, when the ravages of the brutal Khmer Rouge in Cambodia was the fault, not of the Khmer Rouge themselves, but, you guessed it, the U.S. It didn't work then, and it won't work now, but why make such ridiculous assertions at all, assertions, which fly in the face of reality?

The reasons for this behavior, from simple ingratitude to outright hatred of the U.S., are difficult to fathom. One reason is that they claim that they are only trying to make America a better society and to correct the wrongs that clearly exist in America. Fair enough. We are less than perfect, although unlike other societies we are constantly self-corrective. But what are they comparing us to? Perfection? If compared to other societies that actually exist, we are less than perfect but stack up favorably with all—something for which we receive little or no credit. If something is wrong in the world, we must be responsible. Apparently they want everyone in the world to love us. If they do not we must be responsible for that.

On top of that, however, there is an underlying hostility and mistrust of this country which is not limited to an attempt to improve society. There is also an enormous difficulty in admitting one was wrong, terribly wrong. I am referring specifically to those who found us, in all ways and on all occasions, to be wrong about the true nature of the Cold War. When it turned out beyond all doubt that we were the good guys and the Communists were the bad guys, there should have been abject apologies, but there were none. Admitting they were wrong was simply too destructive to their self-image.

In addition to the above, I believe that there are two reasons why our intelligentsia so fundamentally dislike America. The first is that many of them dislike capitalism. They are frequently risk-averse, often choosing employment in lieu of entrepreneurship, business, or finance. Those few who do embrace capitalism all too often act like capitalists but think like socialists. Although socialism as an economic model, in all its various forms over the past century, has proven that it does not work, they believe it is the model towards which we should strive. I believe they envision a socialist world, where everyone is equal, and society is run by wise, fair, kind, and knowledgeable people—in other words, people like themselves.

Accompanying the economic model of socialism is a desire for nationalism to disappear, to be succeeded by an amorphous supranational entity, again, to be run by people like themselves. Thus the dislike of America can be seen as a dislike of democracy as it exists, not as in theory, especially since the country is run not by people like themselves but a ragtag group of politicians who are not necessarily the smartest people in the country and who often operate from the basest of motives, not the noblest. Now, if they were in charge. . . . But they are not. Hence the dislike.

We thus have the strange phenomenon of people being part of the greatest society in history, one that is looked upon as a model to the world—warts and all—one that people literally die in the effort to get in, and yet, we have a small subset of people who appear to be eternally hostile to it.

Immigrant Absorption

It is universally recognized that effective absorption of all racial, religious, and ethnic groups into the mainstream of America is of vital importance to all of us. It is obviously of importance to the individuals involved, but it is equally important to all of society. There is a moral failure in the country when one or another group is left behind and out of the American dream, but there are enormous direct and indirect costs to society as well. Loss of tax revenues from nonproductive citizens, extensive social welfare programs, and crime control costs are obvious. Less obvious is the need for America to have a well-educated and productive society if we are to compete in the global economy and keep well-paying jobs at home instead of looking overseas for people to fill the jobs.

Although the nature of the problem is well recognized, there appears to be an aura of bewilderment amongst many people about how we are to go about accomplishing this task. Yet no country on Earth has had more experience in absorbing such diverse groups, with the possible exception of Israel. There are four simple rules that have been applied by each immigrant group to accomplish the task of reaching the mainstream in two (or even in one) generations. It should be noted that each of these rules depends upon the behavior of the individual and the group of which he is a part, and not the government. Of course, the government has a role, an important one, to play, but it is not central and cannot accomplish anything without adherence to the four rules that follow.

Sacrifice

It is impossible to advance in this society without a willingness to sacrifice for the future. The sacrifice may be by an individual or by an entire family unit. The Korean family unit comes readily to mind, but it is hardly the only ethnic group to do that. The sacrifice of deferring present pleasures for future gain may last years or may even extend over a lifetime, with the benefits realized only by the next generation. Those who are unwilling to endure the pain for the sake of the future gain will surely be left behind.

Family

Whether it is a nuclear family, extended family, or one-parent family, no child can develop and grow without careful nurturing from a family, any more than can a garden. The family is there to help set goals, to set limits on behavior, and to set examples. It is also there to stimulate, to supervise, to criticize, and most important of all, to love. If the family is too distracted, too disinterested, or too incapable of providing the above, the child will wither on the vine or find an outlet outside the family, such as a gang.

Community

Just as the child cannot survive without a family, so the family would find it difficult to survive and thrive without a strong community behind it. The community provides a sense of stability and a sense of belonging. Its members provide role models to emulate. In time of need, it provides practical help in the form of loans, jobs, and support in the home when untoward things happen, such as death, illness, or loss of job. A strong community is a safe community and a pleasant place to grow up, even if the community is not affluent. Fond memories of childhood places make the child turned adult wish to recreate that environment.

Education

The first three rules provide the background needs for the individual, but education is the key for moving up and out. It is no longer a desirable option but a necessity, both for the individual and for the larger society. In this postindustrial age, a high school education alone basically permits one to survive in the modern world and to work from the neck down. There is nothing wrong or unrewarding about that, but unfortunately, in our global economy the routine, passive neck-down jobs (e.g., assembly lines) that permitted people to get by with a secondary education and even to live quite comfortably have, to a large extent, fled to other shores. Those who choose to work with their hands, such as skilled tradesmen, craftsmen, and farmers (completely necessary in our society) still need an education to use modern work tools, such as computers, that are necessary even for these jobs.

Those who are to succeed in America in the twenty-first century will have to acquire the educational skills for neck-up jobs. Some groups have realized it and are willing to make any sacrifice for the sake of a good education. These groups are moving up into the mainstream. Others have not and are lagging further and further behind. It is vital for this country as well as for the groups involved that they be pointed in the right direction.

Conclusion

The above four rules are universal and have been employed, to a greater or lesser extent, by every immigrant group coming to these shores. Needless to say, there must be in place equality of opportunity so that an individual from a group employing these rules knows that he or she can go as far as his or her talents or abilities will allow. The government can help but only in addition to, not in place of, the four rules. It is time for us to get back to basics and to employ these rules, which were used by every immigrant group that came to these shores for the benefit of us all.

Physical Authority

There is a distressing refusal to respect and obey authority in this country. This includes such authority groups as parents, teachers, principals, physicians, clergy, and so forth, but nowhere is the resentment of authority deeper and more hostile than against what I call physical authority—the police and the military. This resentment, bordering at times on loathing and despising, is a feeling primarily of the liberal left but also of some minorities. It is certainly nothing new. Kipling wrote feelingly about it "The Ballad of Tommy Adkins," where "Tommies" were looked down upon and despised until their services were needed in a war; then they were lauded by all. But in spite of that, such an attitude still continues to amaze me. After all, what is demanded of the members of these groups is their willingness to put their lives on the line for total strangers, and for relatively minimal compensation and often even less gratitude. Shouldn't they be accorded respect until they prove that they are unworthy of it? But they are not.

The first complaint about them is that there is a lot of

waste. This is particularly true of the military, but it applies to both, and it happens to be true. However, it is true of virtually all bureaucracies. Social program bureaucracies waste just as much money as the military and police departments, but this is seldom brought up. When the military tries to save money by closing unneeded bases, a hornet's nest is aroused. The local population, the local pols, and, it seems, everyone else cry that this cannot be done—close someone else's bases; leave mine alone. The same is true of military purchases of weapon systems. If purchased at one location, they would probably be cheaper, but the contract must be spread around so that influential pols will have a stake in supporting financially and politically such a weapon system. Building of new projects is more dependent upon the right congressional district than the right, best location.

A second complaint is that they are "fascists," which means that they exert their authority forcefully and people are expected to obey. This is directed more against the police than the military but applies to both. It is probably true in a few cases but certainly not in most. Although some people despise them, they would not hesitate for a nanosecond to call upon the police to risk their lives for what to them is a complete stranger when a crisis develops. Neither would they hesitate to send the military in harm's way when the need arises.

I find it difficult to understand why some Americans so thoroughly despite the military and the police. It is probably a historic feeling, and I suppose in some sense good, since worship of the military (as in South America) can produce unpleasant results. Caution and skepticism, yes—outright hatred, no. This feeling about the military was held in check during WWII and following the war up until the time that President Nixon abolished the draft. During the war and the early Cold War, "them" was "us," and criticism was muted. Since then, with an all-volunteer army, "them" is clearly "them," as opposed to "us," and they are a fair target for attack.

It has to be said that the military does more than its fair share of embarrassing itself. From faulty procurement techniques to cost overruns to scandals of all types, the military keeps kicking itself in the nether regions. Although the code of military justice says otherwise, it is difficult to see why sexual misconduct in the military is considered such a big deal, when the general public in the Clinton scandals overwhelmingly say that private matters don't impinge on how the individual functions is his/her public life.

The same holds true for the police, whom many people cordially and not so cordially despise. Why? I suspect that there are a number of reasons. First, police prevent people from doing just what they want when they want to do it. Second, there is a resentment of the power (authority) exercised by the police. There is a lack of respect, which is certainly often a two-way street. It cannot be denied that some police officers, sometimes, behave, and evince attitudes that are less than sympathetic to the people they are policing. The most important factor behind that, I believe is, that policing is a sometimes brutal and brutalizing business where force is necessary. It is far more common now than it used to be when most people respected (not necessarily liked) the authority of the police and obeyed (even if reluctantly) what they were told to do. The act of physically subduing a suspect, often caught on film, in the face of life-threatening danger is not pretty to look at. It is necessary, but in some people it evokes a feeling of revulsion.

The question arises as to why certain people select the military or the police (sometimes both, in sequence) as their career path. To generalize, they are people who prefer physical activities to intellectual activities. Many were high school athletes where the sports they participated in were relatively straightforward. This in no way implies that they are not bright,

231

but things are often seen by them in black and white with no nuances. They may have street smarts, but they are not sociologists and not expected to be. They are very patriotic and have a strong sense of right and wrong. They are deeply offended by the flouting of the law and the avoidance of punishment by means of the manipulation of the legal system by people who are obviously criminals. There is still strong respect for what is right and what is wrong. Sensitivity and caring are not their strongest suits—obedience to the law is.

I make no excuse for misbehavior. It should be punished swiftly and proportionately, but it should also be recognized that the police and the military are what stand between us and barbarism. The work they do is dangerous and life threatening. Split second decisions must be made, to be dissected at leisure by others, who often have an axe to grind and have other agendas. It would be foolish to think that they are not affected by a steady drumbeat of criticism and lack of respect without any balancing of the dangers they face on a day-to-day basis. Like everyone else, they need respect, and when it is not received, they turn inward. It is reasonable to ask if all those who look down their noses at the police have ever taken the time to thank the police for the difficult job they do. Some groups exhibit great sensitivity for the "oppressed," but do they ever give a moment's sensitivity and thought to the people sworn to protect them?

Wouldn't it be helpful if some of those neighborhoods that are so vocal and hostile to the police held a neighborhood party to thank the police for the protection they provide and the risks they assume? Don't police need positive reinforcement just as do all of us? Soldiers go into battle for a limited period of time, and then they have long periods of time when they are in barracks. Police are on the front line of danger all the time, and, as mentioned before, it is far more dangerous than it ever was before. If sensitivity and caring are considered terribly important, then let the critics have their own children join the police or the military, then the police work would change—into a social service agency.

Various police forces around the country have been accused of brutality and racism. There is of course some justice to some of the charges. Some of the attitudes of the police, however, are simply a reaction to the ceaseless violence that they see on a day-to-day basis. Restraining violent people who do not respect authority of any kind—indeed, they do not seem to respect themselves—is not a job for the faint of heart. And often it is not pleasant to see. As in other cities, New York City was slowly descending into a state of anarchy and lawlessness. Vigorous police action brought life back to the city, but there seemed to be no gratitude for the work they did. Constant criticism brought about a lack of response by police when they were asked to act on violence in Central Park during a Puerto Rican day celebration. The critics do not understand, or care to understand, that the police feel damned no matter what they do; if they don't act, they are criticized, and if they do, they are accused of racism or worse. Better do less and wait out your pension. A terrible and dangerous reaction. If and when New York City again slowly sinks into lawlessness, the critics will not have a clue as to their own role in such a process.

A final point about the military. There are some who are so hostile and irrational about the military that common sense never seems to intrude. If our entire military consisted of two Coast Guard cutters, one patrolling the Pacific and the other the Atlantic, they would propose that only one cutter be used, six months in the Pacific and six months in the Atlantic.

Overall, it is probably healthy to see a lack of worship of all authority figures, and in particular, physical authority figures, but not a lack of respect. They respond to respect exactly as do the rest of us. It should never be forgotten that ultimately they are our shield and our protectors.

Racism—Where We Are Now?

There is a constant drumbeat of claims brought up with each episode, which seems to demonstrate the claim, that America is a wicked, unrepentanly racist society. There is of course some truth to the claim; there is indeed racism in this country. Some of it is overt and hateful, some latent. However, what exists today bears no resemblance to what was present before, and to deny and understate the overwhelming progress that has been made is to present a terribly skewed picture of what is present today regarding discrimination and, more specifically, racism.

I have seen with my own eyes the extraordinary changes that have taken place. When I first came to Washington, D.C. in the early sixties, it was still a sleepy southern town. There was both de jure (school segregation) and de facto segregation, with the black community functioning as a separate society, completely invisible to the larger white society. Their presence was not seen on the social scene, in restaurants, the newspapers, commercial enterprises (except as menial laborers), or even on the professional sports teams in the area. Then came the turbulent sixties with the Civil Rights wars. The changes that started shortly thereafter were vividly brought home to me when I was having lunch in a restaurant in a Virginia suburb of Washington, in, I believe, 1970. Seated at one of the tables were three army men, a sergeant, a warrant officer, and a captain. Two were white, one was black. It was the first time I could recall seeing a black person in a restaurant I frequent, and certainly the first time that black and white people were sitting at the same table. I remember my feeling of astonishment, since it was the first time I had seen it since I came to Washington. By the way, it was the captain who was black, and the other two who were white. The army clearly preceded the civilian society in terms of race relations. Since then, the changes that have occurred are so astonishing that any fair-minded person would say that we were not living in the same world as existed in the early sixties or before. A perfect world, no, but a very different and better world, yes.

Why then is there this constant drumbeat of complaints of persistent racism without any corresponding recognition about how far we have come as a society? One factor is that there are definite benefits to victimhood, as discussed elsewhere (see "Victimhood"). Another is a heightened awareness to slights, real or imagined. Everyone has the need to be appreciated and even loved, but the really important things are equal opportunities in jobs, housing, education, social advancement, and so forth. If those needs are met, then the real or imagined opinions of the larger white society are far less important, since, by choice, the two societies, to a large degree, function each in their own world. To my mind, there is nothing wrong with wanting to be amongst your own, provided it is by your own choice, and not forced upon you by society.

In my opinion, the black community has been very badly served by its leadership. These individuals are constantly looking back rather than ahead to tomorrow. They see and emphasize only the bad, not mentioning the good. They compare the existing situation to perfection, not to reality. All too many of them can only be described as bigots. They lack sensitivity to the needs of others, particularly those who see things differently, and finally, they call on others, government, the larger white society—not themselves—to correct the problems within the black society. The truth is that there are two black societies (see "Two Black Societies,") and the first has deserted the second for a better life in the suburbs, at least until recently. Surely there must be some guilt about that.

If you are a victim, you do not have to see things from the viewpoint of others, but white society has its own complaints, and it would be worthwhile to heed them. When people are constantly told how wicked and racist they are, there naturally exists a tendency to resent it and to tune out the complaints. Guilt in small doses may be helpful, but in large doses it tends to paralyze.

The problems that exist in the second black society, including poverty, drugs, crime, etcetera, are quite real and cannot be ignored. It is unfortunate but understandable that whites do not differentiate between the two black societies, and the first suffers for the second. It may be hurtful that a cab driver will not stop for a fare from a member of the first black society, but somehow he does not want to give up his life to prove that he is not a racist. There is a spectacular failure to criticize themselves for the obvious flaws that yet exist in black society. If an outsider does it, that is ipso facto evidence of racism. Not a very constructive way to look at things.

Until very very recently, there has been a failure to take the lead in correcting the overwhelming problems that exist within the second black society. If the lead is taken, I am sure the black community would be astonished at how much the white community would pitch in to help. Government can help, but it is no substitute for self-help.

Finally, there is little or no emphasis on criticism of black racism. Some make the ridiculous claim that it is not possible for blacks to be racists, but for those who admit it, they avoid criticism because of the supposed good that is done by these individuals or groups. What kind of argument is that? Should Hitler not have been criticized because he brought Germany out of a depression? Mussolini because he made the trains run on time? Stalin because he industrialized Russia? The one factor has nothing to do with the other.

It is true that this is a less than perfect society, but unlike

236

many others, it is a work in progress and constantly correctable. It is so far better than it was forty of fifty years ago with regard to race that there is literally no comparison. Even further progress can be made by being positive rather than constantly critical, recognizing the good as well as the bad, looking forward rather than looking backward, and taking responsibility into one's hands rather than expecting it all from others.

Rage and Violence

Let's be honest about it. In the past, there was more than enough rage and more than enough resultant violence. However, it was nothing compared to what we are seeing now. Violence as a personal, physical assault on an individual, as well as rage, which leads to violence, is largely a latter quarter of the twentieth century phenomenon. It is so different from the mid-portion of the century, when I grew up, that even the apparent drop in violent crimes, which we are now seeing, still makes it far more serious than it was in an earlier day.

I am not being starry-eyed about an earlier area. Crime was certainly present, but the lack of personal security was not. It seems incredible today, in an era of gated communities, more security guards than policemen, and extraordinary security for residences, cars, workplaces, and so forth, that in the not too distant past, nobody, neither parents nor children, urban or rural, thought about it. Homes and apartments went unlocked during the day. In more rural areas they were not locked at all, neither were their cars. In cities, children rode their bikes everywhere, essentially without fear. Families walked the streets of the city at night and used the parks day and night without fear. Of course there were certain neighborhoods where it was not a good idea to go, but it was certainly true in the main. I remember as a young teenager riding the New York City subway at night. My parents never gave a thought to my safety, never gave a thought to violence, nor did I. One should not forget that economics were bad then, including of course the Great Depression, and supposedly bad economic times lead to crime, including violent crime against individuals, but that did not happen.

In those earlier days, generalized physical violence was not socially acceptable, even amongst gangsters. Of course, they were brutal in executing each other, and they were remorseless in harming businessmen whom they wanted to own and who owed them money, etcetera. Yet the assault on civilians not involved in the above was extremely rare. My uncle owned a candy store, a New York phenomenon; it had a soda fountain in addition to selling candy, newspapers, photography film, etcetera. He had three daughters who helped in the store, since it involved very long hours. The local gangsters hung about the store, helped at times with the customers and wouldn't dream of harming my cousins. Indeed there were some neighborhoods where gangsters did the job of policing. The idea that children and the elderly could be assaulted with impunity was foreign to these men.

Road rage is certainly well known and common now. Something propels people to behave in extraordinary fashion on the road—everything from tailgating and speeding to playing tag, riding on the wrong side of the road, and actually shooting at people for supposed slights. School rage has made itself known with shooting after shooting of students and teachers by junior high and high school kids. It is widespread throughout the country and cannot be attributed to any local school problem. Workplace rage in its common form consists of harassment and rudeness. In its uncommon form, it leads to shootings. The postal service has been a frequent beneficiary of that, but it is not the only place, as the shooting in an Atlanta Day Trading office recently demonstrated. Domestic rage manifests itself in domestic violence and sometimes death, while shoot-outs with the police, previously only by desperados, are now fairly commonplace.

Rage occurs during the playing of organized children's games, if one can believe it. Parents against umpires, even teen-aged umpires (many sports organizations take out attack insurance to protect their umpires) as well as parents against parents. There was a recent altercation between parents that resulted in the death of one of the parents. Finally, rage by the political extremes is manifested by violence. It was the method of the radical left during the Vietnam War and now the radical right. Many people, mostly innocents, have paid the price for this phenomenon.

On the surface, there is no reason for it. We have unprecedented prosperity at home, and there is virtually full employment. There are no external enemies to threaten our existence. Yet rage and violence continues unabated, with a striking number being juveniles. This has continued in spite of a record number of criminals incarcerated and a falling crime rate, suggesting that this is not a criminal enterprise but a societal failure. What might that failure be? I doubt very much that there is a single explanation for this. I do not know all the explanations, but here are some that I believe are major contributing factors.

One factor is sociologic. Families are scattered across the U.S., getting together only for holidays and special events. This prevents a sharing of parenting among siblings, aunts and uncles, grandparents. It also limits family members from serving as role models by their behavior for children to emulate. A loss of authority by authority figures, such as teachers and principals, ministers, police, physicians, and parents, means that children are not at all fearful of their disapproval. Young adults do not see positive role models that they can emulate. Learning, wisdom, honesty, age itself are no longer considered to be valuable commodities in our society. Net worth is. An extreme example of the loss of authority, and the terrible results that ensue, is in the inner cities, where children have children, with no parenting support system in place, and with all too many ending up as male predators and female breeders.

Physical violence seems more acceptable now. There were plenty of killings that took place in the past, but most were just business decisions—killing off gang rivals, eliminating cheating gang members, unresponsive business people, and so forth. Fear of random, personal violence was nil, even in the crowded big cities. People felt so safe that house doors were left unlocked during the day, there was just one lock and not a half dozen, families went out day and night in public places, and children went nearly everywhere in the city without supervision. There were bad neighborhoods, which people learned to avoid, but otherwise, personal safety was not a high priority.

Now it appears that a certain amount of personal violence is normal and to be expected. If under that threshold, it will be tolerated; if over, a severe crackdown will ensue. For heavily Democratic New York City to elect a Republican, Rudy Giuliani, twice as mayor suggests that the crime problem had reached intolerable levels. Why zero tolerance for violation of personal safety is not the norm is an important question. Why individuals should not feel perfectly safe in their homes, schools, and streets is another related question. The current situation, after all, is not the long-term norm in this country.

I believe one of the most important factors is the total concern of individuals for themselves, and not for the community. Self-fulfillment, dedication to the here and now rather than the future, unwillingness to sacrifice anything for the common good, total devotion to the pleasure principle (and current pleasures at that) mean little is left for the community and for parenting either in the nuclear or extended family mode.

There are two other factors that seem to me to play a relatively minor, but real role in the epidemic of violence and rage we are currently seeing. The first is the inability to incarcerate mentally ill patients. A poorly thought-out program to discharge patients from mental hospitals and to prevent them from being hospitalized against their will has placed on the street maladjusted, sick people who all too frequently act out their fantasies of violence. Sick veterans at the post office, conspiracy nuts such as Buford Furow who attacked children at a community center in Los Angeles and killed a Filipino postal worker (and who, incidentally, volunteered to be admitted to a mental hospital and was turned down) and many others should be committed or actively followed but are not.

The second small group are those on the extremes of left and right, whose thought processes are quite similar (see "Political Spectrum"). They exhibit a general unhappiness with the country: those on the far left unhappy about capitalism and wealth, those on the far right unhappy with the government, particularly the federal government interfering with their life. Both have "enemies" lists, and both are conspiracy theorists. By and large, they are marginal people—on the left, intelligentsia without any grounding in reality, and on the right, misfits and ne'er-do-wells.

I believe that the above factors cause the blind rage and violence that we see so often in so many venues. There are other conditions that are not causes of rage but results of it. The first is crowding. The theory holds that crowding produces rage and violence. However, all of the shootings by teens in schools occured in rural or suburban districts. The repeated shootings in the post office had nothing to do with crowding, and the violence committed by the right-wing militias had nothing to do with crowding since these organizations are largely rural-based, even isolated.

Guns are claimed to be a cause of violence. There can be no question that our lax gun laws make it easier for people with rage and violence in their heart to obtain guns and harm a much larger number of people, but I believe that is effect, not cause. After all, guns were not unknown and unobtainable during the first three quarters of the twentieth century, and yet there were relatively (compared to now) few acts of random violence. Those who propose abolition of guns for teenagers (a worthy objective) need to explain how it will be any easier to keep kids away from guns than it is to keep them away from alcohol, tobacco, and illegal drugs.

Violence in entertainment (movies, TV, music, video games) is also blamed as a cause of violence. I don't see how the constant repetition of violence helps society, but is it a cause? First, ninety-nine point nine percent of the popular culture sees it and recognizes it as fantasy, not affecting their behavior. There are a few others, unstable people, who are fueled by unreality and who internalize the fictions portrayed in the above-noted media. Here, too, I believe we are probably dealing as much with effect as with cause.

Finally, drugs are to some extent a cause of violence, with people doing what they have to do to feed their habit. Most drug-related killings are business related, with nobody overly concerned if innocent bystanders are killed as well. It can also be said that drugs are a cause of violence, since feeding the need is what makes it worthwhile to deal in drugs, and the need is based totally on the pleasure principle—gratification of the here and now, no matter what the cost.

There has always been a balance between the rights of the individual and needs of the community. Sometimes it swings one way, sometimes the other. In wartime, it swings markedly, with people giving up individual rights for the good of the community. At other times, the pendulum seems to swing to the individual. I cannot remember, however, when it has swung so profoundly to the needs of the individual with so very little concern for the larger needs of the community. Illicit drugs, for example, are often thought of as a cause of the loss of civility and responsible behavior. I believe they are effect, not cause. The underlying principle of drug use is self-gratification. When this is not counterbalanced by appropriate control from the community, self-indulgence and the pleasure principle take over.

There is also a loss of authority and a lack of respect for authority. Parents, teachers, minsters, police, physicians all had some authority and influence in the community. Perhaps their authority was too complete, but we have swung to another, and dangerous, extreme, where everything is questioned and nobody is able to speak with an authority that is obeyed. If, for example, a teacher reprimanded a child, the child would have been punished three times—once by the teachers, once by the principal, and once by the parents ("What, you spoke back to the teacher?" *smack*). The scenario nowadays is that the teacher is threatened by the student, the principal and the school system is threatened by a law suit, and the parents not only do not punish their child, they claim that they and their child are victims and demand the green poultice to assuage their trauma.

Rage and resultant violence have infected us like a plague. It is not one group or a scattering of individuals, but extends across a wide spectrum of the population, as well as in different settings, including the roads, schools, work place, and home. The causes are clearly multifactorial, but I believe the most important factors are the obsession with self and the loss of moral authority from what should be exemplars of the community.

Recreational Drug Usage

A recent television documentary pointed out the incredible violence, cruelty, corruption, and lawlessness that exists around drug trafficking. Also the enormous profits associated with it—profits almost beyond comprehension—in the billions and billions of dollars. It surely brings out the worst in people. This particular documentary was about Mexico, but it could well have been about Colombia or any of the other neighboring states. It was unnerving to see the casual cruelty and violence, without a second thought being given to it. Even more unnerving was the corruption of an entire society. Government officials, party officials, the state police, the security forces, the local police, and the army.

Even the individual leading the antidrug policy was himself on the take. It used to be said that we, the Yankee imperialists, were responsible for all of Latin America's woes. The current woes regarding corruption are home grown, however. There is certainly no law that says that they are compelled to distribute drugs to the US.

We do bear a responsibility, however, since our apparent insatiable appetite for illicit recreational drugs has helped to unleash a tidal wave of lawlessness in Latin America. The first point to be made is that current recreational drug usage is not normal and was not always with us. When I was young, I knew of no one who was taking drugs. I knew of no one who knew someone who was taking drugs. Of course, I had heard that there were opium dens in Chinatown and that the ladies in the South enjoyed sipping Coca-Cola because it had a small amount of cocaine in it. There were undoubtedly others as well but it was not a national problem. Now it is.

What has gone wrong? Too much money may be part of the problem. More important, I believe, is the glorification of the self and the need for instant gratification. If it feels good, do it. No matter what the consequences. This idea started in the sixties, and the implicit narcissism found a fertile field. Who doesn't want to feel good? The other side of the coin is the lack of societal disapproval. How can we let people know that we are not sympathetic to their actions if we have to be nonjudgmental? How can the adult baby boomers decry the actions of their children when they did exactly the same thing? What kind of leadership can come from them?

I do not believe we have the same level of overwhelming corruption that was documented in Mexico, but how can an illegal operation in excess of fifty billion dollars fail to corrupt people along the way? Law enforcement agencies, the judicial system, the banks, and others profiting from the trade are open to corruption and undoubtedly are corrupted. Fights over turf by various drug lords in the U.S. has led to countless murders in our cities, including innocent bystanders.

It is difficult to understand the terrible consequences of the type of behavior we see as a result of illicit drug usage. The consequences of self-indulgence, of easy local availability of drugs, and the lack of societal outrage makes drug trafficking reasonably safe and enormously lucrative. A debate is underway with one side emphasizing interdiction, and the other, treatment. There is no reason why we should not use a combination of the two techniques, but at the same time, nobody seems to say much about stopping usage. Just say no—perhaps not the end but certainly not a terrible beginning to rid ourselves of the scourge. Ultimately, however, it will be societal values that will prevail. If society unequivocally rejects drug usage, isolating people who violate societal strictures, and individuals themselves are willing to take the necessary steps within their own families to show their disapproval, drug usage, at the very least, will be a more manageable problem.

Save the Bambis

Let it be clearly understood that it is man who is encroaching upon animals' spaces in nature, leading to the disruption of patterns of animals' behavior. It is a global phenomenon and far worse in many other parts of the world. Nevertheless, it is clearly a problem here as well. There are many measures that can be taken to lessen the contact between man and wild animal, but it cannot be eliminated. This is because of our growing population and the need for many individuals to have some sense of privacy, to have their own open space.

It is quite remarkable to see nature in the wild. In our close-by suburb, where every plot of land has been developed, we can still see foxes, deer, raccoons, muskrats, rabbits, squirrels, and chipmunks, as well as many types of birds. For the most part, there is little contact between man and animals, most of the animals being nocturnal, but it seems to me that the two are getting closer and closer, and not just the sick animals. The deer in particular are feeding more and more in plain sight, with no running away at the first sign of humans. I believe that some of the more rigid positions on the relationship between man and wild animals are a form of expiation for man's taking of the land. It is also true that if enough people wish to be closer to unspoiled nature, then most will be closer to a subdivision than to unspoiled nature.

There are downsides to living close to wild animals as well. Deer can transmit ticks and fleas, some of which are extremely toxic to man. Auto accidents caused by deer can be serious, even fatal to humans, let alone the deer. It is disheartening to see the carcasses of deer along the highways as they desperately cross highways to get to feeding grounds. Their browsing on expensive foliage is not something pleasing to homeowners, and, as their numbers increase because of natural predators, the sight of deer dying of malnutrition will not be a pretty sight either.

Many geese have stopped migrating: instead, making their homes near bodies of water, many of these artificial. A few geese are attractive, but swarms of geese are not, being incredibly noisy and making the land unusable because of the extensive animal wastes.

Small prey animals, like rodents and rabbits, are kept in check by the foxes and feral cats. The large prey animals—in this case, deer and geese—have no natural enemies and thus multiply until the land will no longer support them, and they will then die of malnutrition. The natural solution would be to introduce large prey predators such as wolves and mountain lions. That of course is not possible, and so, the sole solution I can see is that man must be the predator. Controlled animal hunts would maintain the balance of nature. Food from the hunts could go to the poor. License fees would provide money to buy more habitats. Perhaps not a perfect solution but more civil and humane than what is currently taking place. Saving the Bambis, at any price, is not the way to do it.

The Proper Role of Women in the Workforce

It was a dinner party. Two middle-aged women were reminiscing about their lives and careers. They were quite upset about the lack of opportunities that they faced when they were younger and how much better things are now. They pointed with much disdain how women could have careers only in education and health care, to them (and also to me) a markedly inhibiting list.

From the standpoint of the individual, there seems to be greater opportunity than ever existed before. Looked at from another standpoint; namely, the needs of the community, the picture doesn't appear that rosy. Aside from health, what is more important to our country's future than educating the next generation. Whereas before the best and brightest devoted their efforts to educating our children, now they want careers with presumably more prestige and money, leaving education to those less qualified. They seem to forget that it is their children and grandchildren who will suffer from the lack of the best teachers educating their young. The recent spectacle of over fifty percent of prospective teachers flunking an exam designed for seventh graders is frightening. In a way, the above mentioned individuals are shielded from the reality of poor teaching; they live in affluent suburbs, which attract the best teachers, and in one way or another, their children will get the education they need. The same is not true in rural and inner city school districts.

Of course, it is not my business or yours to tell each individual and each family unit how to behave. That is entirely up to them. From the point of view of the larger society, however, the woman's role is the most important one in the preservation of the species. Think what they do. They domesticate men, who by nature wish to roam far and wide, spreading their seed along the way. Women do this by providing a hearth and home, providing companionship, and providing or withholding sexual favors. They get the men to share in the raising of the children—no small feat. The women civilize children who are born in a state of nature, as we can see from some of the inner city youth, where without proper parenting, particularly female parenting, young males revert to predators and young females to breeders. Civilizing them is a job for both parents and the community at large and is no easy task. With exceptions, it cannot be done without the female. They maintain the family unit, pass on the values of the family, tribe, or community, and support the community in its myriad social functions. The net result of all that is that the larger society thrives and continues. Not so terrible.

The choice of work is also, surprisingly, a matter of contention. Teaching and health care, for example, are looked down upon as "women's work." That may be so, but looked upon from the point of view of society, not from the rights of individual, what is more important to society than teaching the young and healing the sick? Whatever individuals wish to do, they should be allowed to do within their competence, but again, from the point of view of society, shouldn't the very best go into teaching and health care?

That the role of women in health care is another area of contempt on the part of some women is both surprising and foolish. While it is true that there is a temporary surplus of nurses, therapists, technicians, etcetera because of the downsizing of hospital in-patient wards and the early discharge of patients; this imbalance in staffing will come to a new equilibrium, with a fall in quality as the profession fails as a desirable vocation for women. Although it is true that the physician is in charge of the investigation and overall management of the hospital stay, it is the day-to-day care and observation by the nurses that is so critically important to the well being of the patient and to a favorable outcome.

Of course, it is true that many tasks previously performed by registered nurses can be performed by lesser trained individuals, but a knowledge of both what is wrong and what is right in the individual patient, comes only with adequate training and experience, something that lesser trained individuals lack. A disturbing statistic is the number of errors made in a hospital, some leading to serious problems, including death. It is unfair to blame nurses for these problems, since physicians who write wrong orders (usually wrong amounts of a drug) and pharmacists who fill these wrong orders are also responsible for some of the mistakes. Nevertheless, nurses participate in the process and make their share of errors, usually when they are rushed.

All of this is, I believe, part and parcel of a struggle between the needs of the individual and the needs of the community. This has been present for a long time with a reasonable balance between the two needs. But recently, it has become particularly skewed, and the needs of the individual have become paramount, with little thought about the consequences for the community. And indeed there are consequences. Various organizations decry the lack of volunteers they need to continue to function. Keeping the community intact requires people available to do the necessary work to make such an effort. If it takes a village (community) to raise a child, the community must be a functioning, vibrant effort, which all too often it is not. It is not and should not be a gender-specific job, but if both parents work and come home exhausted at night, where is the will to do the necessary communal work?

Some women are superwomen and can do everything: work full time, run a household, spend time on community matters, and instill in their spouses a need for domestic bliss and in their children the values that they have within themselves. Most women cannot do all of that, and much stress ensues.

Of course, a great deal of good has arisen from the increased opportunities for women. It is incredibly foolish to exclude from many types of productive work fully one-half of our society. On the other hand, a trade-off is necessary, and a price must be paid. Again, it is absolutely not my business what any individual or family does, but speaking from the point of view of the needs of the community, a heavy price has been paid for looking at things strictly from the point of view of the individual and ignoring the needs of the community. Two things are necessary for our best females to accept the functions of child rearing, education, and health care. The first is greater financial rewards, and the second, even more important, is community approval of the performance of those tasks. If society looks down its nose at those endeavors, the best and the brightest will not do them.

Tragedy at Littleton

There have been more than a half-dozen episodes of school children massacring their fellow students (and teachers) in the past few years. This does not include one-on-one attacks or several-on-one, with guns or, more often, with knives. It also does not include executions of children by children, seemingly younger and younger each time. Statistically all of these events together represent an infinistesimal number of children. Nonetheless, we have never before had so many of such episodes; Compared to the past, it is overwhelming. It has certainly gotten the attention of everyone, with blather replacing thought.

The usual suspects are rounded up to account for the phenomenon. Crowding is often mentioned as a cause, but most mass shootings occurred in suburban or rural communities. Guns of course are mentioned prominently and repeatedly, since it is obvious that almost all of the school killings have been done with guns. The NRA reacts each time with incredible stupidity. They know perfectly well that no honest gun owner would have use for a Saturday night special, only those who wish to do bad things. There is no reason for anyone to own submachine guns or semiautomatic rifles. If it impinges on someone's Second Amendment rights, then so be it. We cannot have a coherent community (in the large and small sense) if everyone had absolute rights. For the larger good, sacrifices have to be made by all.

Instead of leading the campaign for a more rational selling of guns with appropriate precautions, as well as other measures, such as gun safety, they stridently insist on the absolute right to own guns of any kind. The best thing that can be said in their defense is that they cannot help themselves. As true believers (Second Amendment worshipers), they cannot respond in any way other than the way they do (see "High Priests"). There is an argument, not against the various methodologies proposed, but against the results. After all, if we cannot keep kids away from tobacco, cannot keep them away from illicit drugs, and cannot keep them away from alcohol, what likelihood is there that we can keep them away from guns? It is one thing to philosophize and pass laws, it is another to alter behavior.

What is often neglected is the overwhelming amount of violence that surrounds us. Movies, TV, video games, rap music, and the Internet show incredible violence and urges to violence. I don't believe they play a predominant role except in the cases of unstable children who live in a fantasyland. The sheer amount of violence surrounding us would make such an individual feel that it is the normal condition, not an aberration. Although they freely attack the right for some sensible limits to the Second Amendment, those on the left remain adamant about absolute freedom for the First Amendment. This is, of course, not possible, since unfettered liberty inevitably leads to license. This position is spearheaded by the American Civil Liberties Union (ACLU). They also cannot help themselves, since they also are true believers, worshiping the First Amendment, and their responses are always predictable. Whenever anyone proposes any attempt to modify the violence, it is claimed that this step would have a "chilling effect" on free speech (see "High Priests").

We live in a dynamic tension between the rights of the individual and the needs of society. This is constantly changing as needs change. Both groups (ACLU and NRA) apparently feel that we the public are ignoramuses who are unable to balance the two. Hence we must deal in absolutes or the whole country will come tumbling down.

The violence in the schools is matched by violence on the roads, in the workplace, and at home. Why? This is a new phenomenon, since previously, even in bad or, even, terrible times, this amount of rage and violence did not exist. The beginning of wisdom is to understand that something is wrong, terribly wrong, in our society today. What that wrong is can be a source of disagreement between reasonable people, but if you cannot understand that most of the remedies proposed treat effects and not causes, then you are unlikely to solve the problem.

Recently there has been much praise for the WWII generation. They are seen today as having been hard workers, embarrassed to be forced to take a government handout, willing to sacrifice themselves for their children's future, and willing to make the ultimate sacrifice in war for the benefit of their country. Why is it so different now? One reason is that individuals and group rights have become predominant, with no counterbalancing of individual responsibilities and community needs. For a variety of reasons, including legal ones, strong communities are less available now to serve as examples to the adolescents, to counsel families with disruptive children, and to look out for problems before they become serious.

There has been a loss in the community of those figures who are potential authority figures—police, teachers, principals, physicians, and, of course, parents and adult relatives. There is certainly a normal adolescent revolt against authority. But the response of authority to being constantly tested by the adolescent is to become passive, here, too, in accord with the prevailing permissive attitude and the underlying fear of lawsuits. The increase in the violence that now surrounds us all has to be a factor in some children internalizing and legitimizing it. Finally, no matter how good the substitute arrangements and how much "quality time" busy parents spend with their children, it is not the same as being there for them all the time.

Two Black Societies

It seems to me that when talking about black society, we are really talking about two separate and very different societies. The first is the black middle and upper class. They fully recognize the value of education and strive for it. They are as frightened of crimes involving personal safety as are whites. They have migrated to the suburbs in large number, although, of course, many still live within cities. Like the rest of America, they have two cultures—the outer one shown to the rest of the world in schools and the workplace and their own inner culture when alone among other blacks: their own language, humor, music, foods, etcetera. In short, this society, other than the color of their skin, is similar to whites of the same socioeconomic group. As time goes by, in my opinion, skin color will be less and less of an issue. Knowledge and ability will be what counts.

This group stands in marked contrast with the second black society—lower class, inner-city blacks. Obviously there are exceptions in all human behaviors and some few manage to rise above their surroundings; but these are exceptions. All too many lack a stable family relationship, are raised by a single parent (often herself a child), lack the transmission of values from one generation to the next, disdain education (those who do strive are told that they are "acting white"), are not disciplined in personal habits, unwilling to sacrifice the present for the future, and in general, lack a vision for producing upward mobility. Many join gangs to get the kind of support they do not get at home. An inadvertent social experiment has been undertaken during the past three to four decades. Children have begat children, with the result that all too many of these offspring have reverted to a state of nature: females as breeders, males as predator. On top of all of this, for a variety of reasons, there has been a lack of societal controls, to lead by example or to punish if necessary.

Given the problems outlined above, the first black society, the large and growing middle and upper class, has, in my opinion, adopted exactly the wrong strategy. They blame everything on racism, and they propose endless preferences and endless government programs. They are constantly looking backward, not forward, and they are constantly comparing themselves to and jealous of others. It is, of course, true that racism exists, but not legally. Hearts and minds of some people are beyond the law. They will modify, if not completely disappear, when the second black society is brought under control. Every immigrant group to come to America has felt the sting of prejudice, and most have moved well past it. Well, you say, the blacks were not immigrants at all or, at least, not voluntary immigrants. But they were. I am not talking about slavery but the huge migration of rural, share-cropping, poorly educated blacks from the Deep South to the North.

This started in the thirties with the Great Depression and accelerated in the forties with WWII, when jobs in the North were easy to obtain. Before that, the black communities in the North had a well-structured society, centered on the church, social organizations, and lodges and the steady presence of males in the home. They were entirely segregated from, but parallel to, white society. It is my belief that this migration of the huge number from the South to the North overwhelmed the existing black society. That and the civil rights struggle, which, however beneficial and necessary, helped produce a destruction of the far more orderly existing society. Perhaps most damning of all has been the black flight from the cities, without any sense of responsibility for those left behind.

If what the black community is doing is wrong, blaming every failure as racism, having a collection of unbelievably bad leaders and endless calls for preferences and ever larger government programs, then what could be done that would be right? First and above all, they must feel a sense of shame at the second black society, which is not only physically dangerous to them but also reflects so adversely on them and their image of themselves. A corollary of this is that they feel a personal and community sense of responsibility for the second black society and a determination to do what is necessary to improve that society. The only effective leadership possible in this venture would be black leadership. I'm convinced that if they show leadership, there will be an outpouring of aid from the larger white society, and done without any resentment. After all, it is no one's interest (except possibly the drug dealers) to have unsafe cities and a largely unemployable and uneducated mass of people when we have a critical need for workers, skilled and educated workers, in this country.

The things that the first black community can do are to build infrastructure. This would include neighborhood banks, which would give small loans for start-up neighborhood businesses and for home improvement, day care centers, preschool programs, enrichment programs in the schools, including the greater use of computers, improved community recreational facilities, charities directed to the inner cities, more and specialized teachers and school aides, self-help organizations like AA, Big Brother, direct investment, and many more.

Some years ago, there would have been an outcry against the above, arguing instead for more preferences and more government handouts. Things are changing, and the first black community is recognizing its responsibility to the second. The results can only be positive for everyone—less crime, more self-respect, and confidence on the part of the first black society (based on their achievements with the second society), less dependency on the various governments, less blaming everything on racism, and with hope, an improvement in the quality of black leadership. Go for it.

Victimhood

We have a strange phenomenon going on in our society, namely a proliferation of victims and the status of victimhood. Initially, it was race, but it has spread to gender, spousal abuse, health problems, physical handicaps, physical characteristics (height, weight, facial features, etcetera), mental characteristics (not only retardation but various stress syndromes), and, indeed, many others. One would believe that the last thing an individual would want would be to be considered a victim, but the behavior of some would lead one to believe that they revel in it. Certainly no group has claimed that they are no longer victims, thank you very much.

Recently I saw a segment on a TV news magazine about the Hollywood movie actor, Denzel Washington. It was reported, in the course of the segment, that he earns approximately eleven million dollars for appearing in a movie. That takes approximately six weeks of work. He has fame, fortune, lives *la dolce vita,* and is the heartthrob for millions of women, but is he happy? No. He is angry and upset because he apparently does not get all of the roles that he thinks he should get because of his race. In short, he is a victim. Apparently anyone can be a victim, even a multimillionaire. Now, there is no reason why he can't set up his own production company with his own money and do whatever roles he wishes, but it is apparently easier to claim to be a victim. If he were to say that life is not completely fair, but that he has gotten more than most, I could understand it, but a victim?

This is not of course to say that we are a perfect society, and there are indeed genuine victims who require redress. But why are we constantly adding new groups to our list of victims and why are no groups clamoring to be removed from the list? Why is there no sense of shame at being a victim as there was in the past? I believe the answer is that there are definite benefits to being a victim, as shocking as that may sound. The first benefit is that it puts the victim at the head of the queue. We so often hear that because of past discrimination, real or perceived, that preferential treatment must be given to this or that group. Once in (school, job, etcetera) it is virtually impossible to remove a victim, because it would validate the claim of victimhood. If actually removed, a ready explanation is at hand to explain failure—not personal shortcomings but victimhood.

There is tremendous psychological benefit to being a member of a group: in this case, a group of victims. One is not alone in facing the world, but there are others in a similar predicament. A related factor is not only to be part of a group but part of a cause. This is something larger than an individual, and it provides tremendous psychological dividends. The preparation and organization. The excitement of a protest, be it a march, rally, sit-in, picket, or other. The faint whiff of danger. All lead to tremendous psychological benefits. The same is true of course for nonvictim groups who find the need to organize, rally, etcetera.

Not for a nanosecond do I suggest that there are not genuine victims, that our society cannot be improved, or that there is no reason for groups of victims to organize. But I do see a proliferation of such groups, and I have suggested some of the reasons why that has happened.

VIII

Sports

A Quiet Sabbatical Year

It takes no great insight, even for diehard sports fans, to realize that there is something radically wrong with professional and big time college sports. Even the most casual perusing of the papers or listening to sports shows brings nearly daily stories so terrible that each one have been the topic of endless discussion in years past. Now they are so frequent that they barely make a ripple for a few days.

In the major leagues of professional sports, particularly the big three of baseball, basketball, and football, the attitudes of players and owners are difficult to fathom. The owners shamelessly blackmail the cities in which the teams are located into building them ever newer, ever grander, and ever more profitable facilities. At the same time, they raise the costs of attendance at these palaces to astronomical levels. I am surprised that they do not charge for the use of the restroom facilities (I am hesitant to mention this, since they may see this as an additional revenue stream). One may say, so what, these are private entrepreneurs who are entitled to whatever profit they can make. That would be so if they risked their own money to build their facilities (with the usual help for them from government as extended to other businesses in the area) but precious few do so. If their product (team) is consistently inferior and fans do not come, they berate the fans and threaten to move the team elsewhere.

If the attitude of the owners is bad, the attitude of the players is incomprehensible. The owners at least do function as employers, hiring hundreds of people to work for them. The player is responsible only for himself. It is true that there are a few superstars who by themselves are capable of bringing fans to the facility to watch them perform and, therefore, provide added benefit. For most, they are talented but eminently interchangeable, as manifested by the frequency of switches of players from one team to the next, often with no noticeable difference in the quality of the team. Of course, there were trades in the past, but nothing like we see today, particularly with the advent of free agency. It is difficult for the player to be loyal to the team and city, and, conversely, for the fan to be loyal to the player when he is here today and gone tomorrow.

It is the behavior and attitude of the players that is astonishing. I should mention, and emphasize, that there are many decent players who realize the situation and act accordingly, but they are the exception, not the rule. First, behavior. Thuggishness and criminal behavior are all too common. Drug abuse, carrying of illegal guns, rape, driving while intoxicated, attempted murder, and assault on coaches and other players are just some of the behavior that we read about daily. Well, apologists say, they are just a mirror of society. But they are not paid like the rest of society. They do not live like the rest of society. They are not treated like the rest of society. It therefore seems reasonable that their behavior should not simply reflect the lowest mores of our society but should be something more—role models, if you will. It doesn't seem to be an unusually onerous condition for the money, fame, and adulation showered upon them. It is quite true that professional athletes in the past were not choirboys, but, for the most part, their misbehavior was pretty innocent compared to what we see today.

Next, attitude. This is most astonishing since it is only a quirk of nature that gave them the talent to perform well in their chosen sport and has rewarded them beyond anyone's wildest dreams. One would think there would be some sense of gratitude for the astonishing rewards given for the playing of children's games. But one would be completely wrong. Childishness and churlishness are so common as to be almost unremarkable.

On top of their ingratitude is an astonishing arrogance. They constantly demand perks that they could readily pay for themselves, but they demand, and they receive. Limousines, helicopters, private airplanes, elaborate meals, etcetera are all considered their right. There was a recent article in the *Wall Street Journal* about players being traded from one team to another. The old team was responsible for their salary, so the new team paid only minimum wage. One player commented that the minimum wage was so little that he picked it up in cash and used it for poker money. And what was that insignificant sum? Two hundred thousand dollars. More money than ninety-eight percent of Americans earn per year. What can one say about such an attitude? It is true that a few players recognize their responsibilities to the larger society and behave accordingly, but unfortunately most do not.

What we see in the owners and players in the major leagues is mirrored in big time college sports, which is in fact simply the high minor leagues. The schools are maximizing their incomes with stadium enlargements (with fewer and fewer seats for the students), commercial naming rights for arenas and stadia, private boxes, and so on. The players are simply sharpening their skills until they can make it in the majors. They are professionals in every sense except their pay. The schools employ skullduggery, such as forged transcripts, having others take tests for the athletes, gut courses, whatever will bring a star athlete to the campus and keep him there for a while as they fill the venue. The athletes all too often engage in criminal behavior, such as rape and robbery, with the school doing anything it can to keep the athlete in school and eligible. And everyone pretends that this is all part of the educational experience one gets in college. On top of this, commercial enterprise (TV) networks pay hundreds of millions, in some few cases, billions, of dollars to be allowed to broadcast the various football and basketball tournaments. No wonder the heads of college administrators and the NCAA are turned by this siren song.

How can we bring sanity back to professional sports (major and minor leagues)? Not easily, but there is one solution that comes to mind. Have all fans take at a prearranged time, a one-year sabbatical from big-time sports. That includes attendance at games and watching on TV. What would one do with the time? Well, sports participation by all should dramatically increase. Increased time with family and friends in this stressed-out world we live in would be beneficial. Other hobbies, care of house, yard, car would be taken care of, at long last.

There is no reason to give up completely on sports viewing, for those like myself who enjoy them immensely. High school and small time (amateur) college sports could be watched and appreciated for the tremendous and legitimate enthusiasm they bring. Neither is there any reason not to watch minor league sports. A rule of thumb would be not to pay more than fifteen to twenty dollars per ticket or one hundred dollars for a family of four (that would include refreshments). Not an unreasonable sum of money for an evening's amusement and quite different from the three to five hundred dollars or more for attending and watching big time sports.

It is at least possible that sanity can be brought back to high profile sporting events if nobody comes to watch them. Perhaps some humility will overtake the players and owners. Perhaps some better judgment will enter the minds of the owners and players of high minors (the colleges). Perhaps not, but I believe it is worth a trial.

College Pros

In view of the ongoing problems of criminal and thuggish behavior exhibited by college athletes, particularly in basketball and football, as well as the corruption of coaches (for example, forging of transcripts to keep a player eligible), as well as the bind colleges are in to fund all athletic programs by means of revenue sports rather than as a line budget item, which, in turn, induces the schools to turn a blind eye to violations—as long as they are winning and they fill the venue, everything else is okay. To this end, I offer a modest proposal that should go a long way towards resolving this problem. Colleges need make only one decision: remain amateur or turn professional.

The former schools would treat its athletes exactly like all other students: their scholarships, if any, would be based strictly on need, and maintenance of athletic teams would be based on a budget and not on revenues generated from gate receipts, advertising, and television receipts. It is likely that all such teams would disappear immediately from all the various polls and ratings.

The latter schools would establish professional teams to represent them, primarily in football and basketball, but in any other sport if they so desire. These teams would be run either directly by the college or, more likely, on a franchise basis by a professional team. It would, in effect, create instant minor leagues for football, basketball, and other sports so selected. Different schools could be selected by a professional team to represent AAA, AA, or A levels of skills. Naturally all of the paraphernalia associated with the team's school colors, songs, mascots, bands, cheerleader, and so forth would remain exactly as before. It would not take long for old grads, students, and others to adjust to having bona fide professionals representing them rather than sub rosa professionals.

Such an arrangement would be a distinct advantage to the player, who could spend as much time as desired sharpening his skills and be adequately and openly compensated for it while doing so rather than having to wait for such impediments as classes and labs to be over before beginning practice. Advancement to a higher league category with improvement of skills would not have to depend on being a "hardship case" or some other subterfuge. There would be no debates about academic criteria for admission or for staying academically eligible so that he could continue being on the team. In the unlikely event that a player should want an education, he could take the novel route of doing it on his own time and paying for it, just as do all other students.

For the school, there should be little financial loss. Lack of income from gate receipts and TV (assuming it is run as a franchise) would be balanced by a lack of expenses, while significant income would be earned from rental of facilities and from concessions. The band, mascot, cheerleaders, etcetera could all be rented out. Further, schedules could be markedly expanded to match the level of the major leagues. In football, for example, instead of playing eleven games they could play sixteen games as do the majors. There could be three or four exhibition games and an elaborate playoff schedule that could last for months. Indeed, the only thing that could limit the number of games played is the willingness of the fans to pay for them. No concern about time off for exams.

The majors would accelerate, in their minor league, franchises, the use of skyboxes, naming rights, etcetera to enhance revenues, in which the schools would share. In basketball, they could also play the number of games played by the majors, and March Madness could extend to June, as do the majors. Should there be some loss of revenue, which would place nonrevenue sports in jeopardy, the schools could request funding by an online item in the budget, just as they do for all other student activities. For the coaches, their only concern would be to build winning teams and develop talent for the majors. They need not be bothered by such concerns as low grades or "building character." Coaches with such concerns would have long since gravitated to the amateur ranks.

For the student, the disappearance of a separate class of students amongst them, with all sharing the hidden knowledge that these "students" are really hired hands, could only be of benefit to their morale. For the faculty, the perpetual embarrassment of telling others how to solve the world's problems while being unable themselves to solve a problem much closer to home would at last disappear.

There would be some losers. The athletic directors would no longer be entrepreneurs but revert to their original role of directing athletics at all levels: varsity, intramural, etcetera. The NCAA would largely become superfluous or, at least, shrink to a more normal size. They would no longer be involved in policing and would not be handling hundreds of millions, even billions of dollars from commercial sources for various events, such as play-offs, etcetera. To my mind, that would not be a terrible loss. Bring on the changes. I can hardly wait.

Health Clubs—Then and Now

I have belonged to various health clubs over many, many years, and I have observed the remarkable changes that have taken place. In former days, virtually all were all male. Some were mixed gender but completely separate, each with its own hours. I cannot speak for the women, but for the men, it was a point of pride to have dirty clothing. To have torn clothing. To be loud and boisterous. To tell off-color jokes and brag about sexual exploits and prospects to come. The standard dress in the club after the exercise program was . . . a towel.

Now the clubs are completely integrated, except for the locker rooms. Who knows when that barrier will fall? The mixed gender exercise room is most decorous, as befitting a temple to fitness. Even the ogling is decorous. Clothing is always neat and usually fashionable. I recall seeing a woman working out in a two-tone grey and crimson speedo exercise suit. There were color-matched headband and socks. Makeup was perfect. Jewelry at the neck and wrist gently clinked. She employed proper breathing techniques while performing biceps curls . . . with a one pound weight.

No loud noises intrude. No off-color stories. I did spy some men in a corner once. They all laughed, so I knew an off-color joke had been told. I have never heard foul language. The facility is overrun with personal trainers. Many are used continuously by the members, who apparently must have difficulty remembering the original instructions from the trainers. The question is: have we made progress?

High School Football

The other day, I attended a high school football game for the first time in many years. It was quite an experience, particularly because for the first time in many years, the home team was a decent team, with a chance for postseason playoffs. The first thing that struck me was the garish uniforms the players wore, single-colored bright blue uniforms matched against single-colord bright red uniforms. Whatever happened to school-color jerseys and white or gray pants?

The cheerleaders were bright, well-uniformed, perky little things and totally clueless. They were busy doing their "routines," totally oblivious to the play on the field. They didn't lead any cheers or exhort fans to chant for the team to score, hold the line, etcetera. Even at critical moments, when fan attention was directed to the action on the field, they were busy doing their thing, still oblivious to what was going on.

The band was not much better. Their sole role in the stands was to play the one song that related to football, over and over again. During halftime they did their thing, routines totally unrelated to any theme that had to do with football, but obviously in preparation for marching band concerts to come. The announcer appeared far more interested in selling raffle tickets than in announcing the game, and the little kids were obsessively interested in only one thing—food. I mean lots of food—hot dogs, sodas, nachos, popcorn, candy, snow cones and much more, purchased in multiple trips to the concession stands. Dentist's delight.

Then there were the cruisers, boys and girls. Back and forth with necks craned to the stands. Isn't that the fifth time I saw that kid? In the same half? Will he/she find true romance on the next pass? Let's wait and see. Then there were the adults who never once glanced at the action on the field but were totally engrossed in conversation. Oh, well, there will be another game next week.

Would you believe, I had a great time.

Jock Talk

With the growth of professional and college sports has come the growth in number of sports reporters, sportcasters, media analysts, and interpreters. Although each public field, such as, for example, politics, has its share of banalities offered up by media types, in my opinion none come even close to the banalities of jock talk. No matter what the sport, they all seem to say the same thing. Here are some examples of what I mean.

Before the contest: "If the team is to win, it must fight hard. It must make no mental mistakes. It must be determined.

It must be focused. It must take advantage of the other team's mistakes. It must play as a team."

After the contest—a win: "The team showed heart. It played hard. It took advantage of the other team's mistakes."

After the contest—a loss: "The team played its heart out. They gave it everything they could. They showed great spirit. They have nothing to be ashamed of."

If possible, jock interviews are even worse. "How does it feel to score the winning touchdown (the winning basket, the winning goal)?" How do you think it feels? A usual form of interview is to make an eternally long statement and then shove the microphone into the face of the athlete being interviewed. What is he supposed to say? "You didn't ask a question?" "I disagree with your premise?" That never happens.

Jock sports shows are so full of banalities, on the part of the callers-in as well as the hosts, that it is difficult to stay tuned for anything more than the briefest of moments.

Perhaps all of the above is as it should be. After all, what we have is adults playing children's games for ridiculous amounts of money, for fame, and for glory. Why should the commentary be any better?

Lockout at the NBA Corral

As this is being written (12/98), the NBA has given the players two weeks to come to terms, or the entire season will be lost. That loss (of the entire season) does seem to be the most likely scenario. It seems remarkable as to how little I, and others I have spoken to, miss the NBA. This is in part because the real season starts with the playoffs, because the fans know that whatever the settlement eventually negotiated, they will pay in the form of higher admission fees and higher concession fees, and that, in a felicitous phrase that is not my own, "the dispute is between tall millionaires and short millionaires." It should also be noted that the people who are really hurting are the little guys—workers in the concession stands, ushers, and the like. I'm willing to place a small wager that making good their hardship will not be included in any settlement agreement.

I think it fair to say that both sides bear some blame. The owners have used creative accounting to mask their profits and have, in essence, blackmailed their communities to put up for them enormously profitable new arenas with the subtle or not-so-subtle threat to relocate to another community. There are a few owners, who as businessmen, invested their own funds in the franchise and in the arena, and they deserve the profits that accrue from it. Whatever the owner's shortcomings, profits not only go into their pockets, but also into the pockets of hundreds and hundreds of their employees.

What about the players? Their attitude continues to astound me. If one were observing the professional basketball scene from a quarter century or more ago, the current compensation and prestige would simply not be believed. The same of course is true for other professional sports as well, but the money earned in NBA ball is simply beyond comprehension for most Americans. This of course does not include extra money from endorsements, lectures, etcetera. One would think that being financially secure by the time you are in your early twenties would invoke a feeling of gratitude on the part of the recipients, but obviously that is not the case.

Were it not for the NBA, many of the players would simply be tall assembly line workers, tall bureaucrats, and tall trash collectors. The comment of one player that it would be difficult to live on $100,000 a year shows how far from reality they have drifted. Has their behavior been consistent with the enormous veneration in which they have been held (and which translates into dollars)? Hardly. Their need for perks (a hotel suite, limousine to take them to the game, private airplane rides, and the like), when they can easily afford these things on their own suggests that their appetite for more (and more) is insatiable.

As if all of the above is not enough, racism has been injected into the negotiations. The precipitate cause was the assault of a Carolina Panther football player (white) who in the heat of the game, with the team playing poorly, struck his coach (white). He apologized immediately and was fined with a one-game suspension and loss of pay for the game. This was compared to the punishment meted out to basketball player Latrell Sprewell (black), who, during a practice, assaulted his coach (white), returned to the court after going to the locker room, and started choking the coach. His attitude afterward was anything but conciliatory. He lost his job for a year.

The contention is that the harsher penalty on Sprewell was strictly the result of racism. It is difficult to give credence to such arguments, and it is to no one's credit to make such an argument when it is palpably not true. This makes black players in the NBA into victims. Imagine that. If they feel that way, they should resign; after all, there are players out there who would give their eyeteeth to be employed by the racist league and owners.

The NBA is a cash cow that is capable of making everybody wealthy beyond belief, but it will not happen unless players and owners work together, for their mutual benefit. Rather than always asking for a higher and higher percentage of revenues, why not settle for fifty percent but make every effort to enlarge the pie. They would surely come out ahead. While they are about it, why not press for a stricter code of behavior, offer support for those players who came before (e.g., cover nursing home costs) and who paved the way for the present, and establish a player's union foundation for current charitable purposes. It is surprising how little is demanded from the tall millionaires.

Olympian Headaches

I suppose it was inevitable that the Olympics would explode, giving everyone an Olympian-sized headache. The games have become so large (the world's largest athletic spectacle) and so profitable to the cities sponsoring them that, in desperation, chicanery, in the form of bribery, appeared to be an appropriate, even necessary, solution. Naturally it takes two to complete the bargain; there appeared to be many willing partners: namely, the members of the International Olympic Committee (IOC) selection committee.

There are many explanations why such a theoretically pure organization held in such high worldwide esteem would be so corrupt. Some say it is because of a cultural difference, where baksheesh (kickbacks) are accepted as part of the culture. Some say that members may come from such impoverished countries, where this is looked upon as a way of getting ahead. These explanations may be true, but I suspect that an overriding element is the arrogance of the Olympic Committee. This is best exemplified by the head of the Olympic Committee, Juan Antonio Sammaranch, who prefers to be called Excellency rather than by name or by title (president). In a sense, he and the other high officials are treated like royalty wherever they go. They are given the best of everything—best transportation, best hotels, best restaurants, extraordinary deference. After a period of time, it becomes expected, with the final stage being a sense of entitlement. They probably believe that all of the above is due to them personally, rather than to the office they hold.

So what to do about it. Obviously there will be a house-cleaning after the scandal, with a number of members sacked. Some rules will be rewritten, and behavior will become more discreet. The underlying problem, however, will not go away: namely, that the Olympics are so big and the financial rewards for the host city (and for many movers and shakers in the host city) so great that the problem is likely to be a recurrent one.

There are really three Olympic Games in one. The first (the Summer Olympics) is a true inheritor of the original Grecian Olympics: individual competition in which the only parameters that matter are how high, how far, how fast. Whether it was done gracefully or not, the above three qualities were the only criteria. All that was needed in the way of measurement was a tape measure and a stopwatch. For the Winter Olympics, faster described it all. The second Olympics are those where the athlete submits his or her performance to outside judgment. Factors other than athleticism, such as grace, comportment, and so on enter into the scoring. Subjectivity on the part of the judges became a factor. Unfortunately, particularly during the Cold War, politics also entered into the judging.

The third Olympics are team sports, which are becoming ever more numerous and ever larger. This is true for both the Summer and Winter Olympics. Some "teams," such as boxing and wrestling, were really made up of individuals, and medals were awarded on an individual basis. They were considered a team since they all came from the same country, had one training program, one head coach. Some teams, such as gymnastics, compete as individuals but also as a team. However, most teams are truly teams, with a medal awarded to the team and not to each individual (except by virtue of being on the team). The recent addition of sports such as baseball means the addition of hundreds, perhaps thousands, of new competitors.

I am not against any of the three components of the Olympics—individual performance as measured by the original Olympic standards, team performance, and judged events. Each has its own merits and its own afficionados. I am just suggesting that the current Olympics, both summer and winter are becoming too large to handle. As more wealth is accumulated around the world, more people want to see the spectacle in person, but there are only a limited number of seats at each venue. Of course, TV provides extended highlights, but it is not the same as witnessing in person what is going on, and one does not get the same feeling as when one is actually at the site. Then, of course, there is the entire matter of corruption, as mentioned earlier, with such enormous benefits accruing to cities awarded the Games that there is an enormous incentive to do whatever is necessary to secure the games for the city.

One solution for the Olympics might be to divide into three the current Olympics, each with its own sponsoring city. The three Olympics could all be held in the same Olympic Year (at same time or at different times?) or on a staggered year basis. By increasing the number of cities participating, the desperation of cities to land an Olympic event might be lessened. Also, it would permit a wider audience to see the Games. It is of course conceivable that each of the three separate Olympic Games would grow to the size of the current Olympics, that the corruption would be three times as large, and the entire situation would replicate itself, but I believe it is worth consideration.

Senior Softball

I have just completed my first year of senior softball. I had last played the game in any organized fashion some forty-five years ago. I wonder now why I didn't play a game I loved in any organized league, but there never seemed to be time. Now that I have retired, there was time, and I decided to try it again.

What an education my try-out was. Balls constantly scooted between my legs as I thought I was fully bent over, but I wasn't. I had difficulty throwing to first base, from second base. My lateral range was two feet at best, and I was totally unable to go back for a ball when I was in the outfield and helplessly watched the balls sail over my head. During the season, I had to relearn how to catch a fly ball, how to throw, pay attention to what was going on in the field, how to stroke and not hack at the ball while batting, and many other skills that an experienced Little Leaguer would know automatically. One additional skill I learned was how to catch a ball on the tip of my long finger. It was painful way to learn proper catching mechanics.

Now, I've been at team meetings before, but never one stranger than our first team meeting, when the very first question from the manager was "Does anyone know CPR?" This was followed by a series of questions about other illnesses and explanations of how to treat them with confidentiality. The players joined in with their own list of illnesses, done in the form of "Can You Top This?" "What do you mean you've had a triple coronary bypass. I've had that plus two small strokes," and so on. In coming weeks, other topics for discussion included grandchildren, investments, and repeated attempts at humor (extended discussions of stiffness and its location). I never heard any discussion of religion or politics, sure loser topics on a team.

I asked a teammate to help me with the scoring book, since I was not completely familiar with it. He told me he couldn't because everything was blurry. He had glaucoma. He was our first baseman. The pitcher would successfully field every ball hit to him, as long as it was within a five-foot radius, but no further. He was awaiting a total hip replacement for severe arthritis. The right fielder could not throw because he had a dialysis shunt in his subclavian artery in the neck, and it interfered with throwing. He was awaiting a kidney transplant. During the season, we had two players hospitalized for problems unrelated to softball. Frequently, players would leave the field in the middle of the game for a doctor's appointment, and we would have to realign everything. It reminded me of grade school, where one requested permission to leave the room. One player celebrated his eightieth birthday and two celebrated their fiftieth wedding anniversaries during the season.

There was never any rest in the dugout because somebody always needed a runner. Everyone had to bat, but there were three types of runners. A few batted and then ran the bases themselves. There were some who ran to first base by themselves, and if they got a hit, they were replaced at first base by a substitute runner. Finally there were some who batted but had a substitute runner starting from home plate. There was a constant call for substitutes.

Sliding was permitted but was seldom used: some because they were on some form of blood thinner and wished to avoid extensive bruising, others because they were afraid of fracturing their hip. Some both.

There were also several types of throwers. A few had reasonably good arms and could throw out a runner from shortstop or third base. These weren't great arms, but then again, they weren't up against great runners either. Some in the outfield would throw, but with so little range that there had to be an extra relay man to get the ball into the infield. Finally, there were those who could throw only underhand. This meant that the nearest outfielder had to run to the player, have him shovel the ball underhand, and then proceed with the rest of the play.

The various teams in the league are named by the color of their shirt, simple but trite. Here are some of the names I would pick: the Brooklyn Codgers, the Chicago Support Stockings, the Saint Louis Coots, the Florida Early Birds, the Cleveland Clinics, the San Francisco Joints, the Boston Varicosities, and so on.

The skills demonstrated (or lack thereof) reminded me of a progression: T-ball, Little League ball, Teenage ball, Adult ball, Senior ball (T-ball). In spite of the problem, everyone recognized that there were two main objectives in playing—having fun and avoiding getting hurt. My sentiments exactly.

Team Mascots (Games and Names)

There has been an ongoing hue and cry about the names of sports teams' mascots. Such mascots come in all forms but, for the most part, can be broken down into three groups. The most common by far are the animal mascots. They come in all sizes and varieties, but five species predominate—canine, ursine, feline, equine, and raptor. There are infinite varieties of names from these groups but also a lot of overlap—for example, a very large number of "Wildcats." The second group relates to forces of nature—tides, hurricanes, cyclones, etcetera. The third group relates to humans. It may be a small historical group (Knights, Crusaders, Cavaliers, Buccanneers) or it may be an entire ethnic group (Scandinavian, Scots, Irish, Cajuns). The largest of the ethnic groups by far are various interpretations of American Indians. It is here that a continuous battle has been fought for years.

The question arises as to why athletic teams choose mascots at all. The mascot represents those attributes that the school or professional team wishes to confer on its athletes—valor, courage, bravery, athletic ability, and so on. To prove that, look at the three categories of mascots. Those named for forces of nature are fierce, cataclysmic events, not swamps, mudflats, or tidal pools. Those named for animals represent a wide variety of species but to my knowledge, there are no skunks, hyenas, vultures, or jackals. After all, if all species are God's creatures, why not some of the above? Mascots named after humans evince the qualities mentioned above. Although they were capable of fighting, and fighting well, nobody in his right mind would name his team "Nazis" or "Fascists." The question to be asked is why anyone would not choose a mascot whose favorable qualities the team wishes to be compared to, and instead choose a mascot that brings dishonor to them as well as to the mascot. The answer of course is no one.

The only mascots that bring out passions pro and con are the various derivations of Indian. The fact that there are so many Indian derivations in both amateur and professional sports teams suggest that the attributes are greatly admired. If the mascots were named "Red Varmints" or something similar, it would of course demand reconsideration. But Braves? Warriors? Chiefs? Even the neutral Indians? Even just the name of a tribe (Florida State Seminoles, Central Michigan Chippewas)? How does one explain that several teams have Cowboys as mascots (Oklahoma State, Wyoming). It is okay to have cowboys as mascots but not Indians?

This has not stopped colleges from assuming the politically correct and dishonorable course of changing the mascots at the first whiff of grapeshot. I say dishonorable because some of these mascots have a long tradition with the school. Dartmouth was originally an Indian school. Isn't it perfectly natural for their teams to be called Indians? A little protest, and now they are the fighting Green. A half dozen or more schools have changed their Indian derived names to something more politically correct. It is my understanding that Saint John's University's Redmen were so named because of the color of their uniforms, not an Indian variant. This did not stop them from changing the name to Red Storm.

A second complaint is that they are mocking Indians with their gestures and costumes. These would include various war whoops and tomahawk chops, among others. That assumes that anyone in his right mind would believe that these activities have anything whatsoever to do with real Indians. Just because mascots get dressed in animal skins or feathers doesn't mean that they are mistaken for lions or tigers or hawks or eagles.

The next argument is that other ethnic groups would be upset if they were named by less flattering racial or religious epithets. Of course they would. And therefore no teams are given those names. But are the Irish upset by the nickname of

Gaels (Iona) or Fighting Irish (Notre Dame). The Scots by the nickname, Highlanders (Radford)? Would the Italians be upset by a mascot name of centurions or Garibaldis? Jews by the mascot name, Maccabees or Samsons? Latins by the name, Bolivars? Hardly likely. Rather, they would be highly honored.

Professional team owners appear to be made of sterner stuff. They have repeatedly rejected politically correct appeals to change their mascots, and rightly so. The only politically correct move by professional team owner was made by the owner of the NBA team in Washington, D.C., who changed the name of the Washington Bullets basketball team to the Washington Wizards. The only thoughts I ever had about the name Bullets, if I had any thoughts at all, was that it was alliterative (the team was originally the Baltimore Bullets), and that in some way it represented speed. It never even crossed my mind that the name Bullets had anything to do with the extraordinary number of murders taking place in Washington, D.C., largely by means of guns. To think that keeping the old name of Bullets or changing it to the new name of Wizards would have any effect whatsoever on the amount of crime and murders committed is simply beyond my comprehension. Perhaps it was nothing more than a smart marketing ploy to sell more merchandise. That at least would be far more comprehensible to me.

This campaign raises all sorts of associated questions. What does one do abut states (Illinois) and cities (Omaha) named after Indian tribes? Do they have to be changed? What do we do about various human mascots? For example the George Washington University Colonials have as a mascot a figure in a colonial costume with a head of George Washington. Now is that an insult to one of our Founding Fathers and our first president, or is it an honor? The larger question is whether it is an honor or a disgrace to have something named for you? Particularly when no insult is intended.

The ultimate in this type of thinking was demonstrated in an opinion piece in the *Washington Post* in 1996 by Senator Ben Nighthorse Campbell, in which he laid out the reasons why he thought the name of the Washington football team, the Washington Redskins, was an insult to his people. He went one step further and stated that if the Washington Redskins did not change their name, he would fight their attempt to obtain a new stadium on federal land. In the article, he listed a series of repugnant names for various ethnic groups and stated that these groups would be offended if such names were used, but he was clearly setting up a straw man, since no teams have such names. Is that surprising?

The owners of the team have never even considered, to my knowledge, changing the name of the team. That is because the name, "Redskins," is so far from a term of derision and disdain as to be ludicrous. It is difficult to think of a more universal symbol of love, respect, and veneration in Washington, D.C. and its environs than its football team and its mascot name, the Redskins. All the pols in Washington would love to have those very attributes for themselves. There are few people indeed who mistake the Indian logo and the name with the real thing any more than they mistake dinosaurs or the screen for the real thing. Go, Skins.

What we have here is political correctness at its stupidest, and an astonishing lack of courage on the part of college and university presidents. What was meant as a signal honor and tribute turned into an insult, and bad feelings were generated for no real reason. It appears to be a pattern of ever more minorities of every category to clamor—no, demand—that they be considered victims and therefore are entitled to redress. The rules to follow are that first, treat the feelings of the majority with as much sensitivity as you would expect to receive from them. Second, if no insult was intended, no insult should be taken.